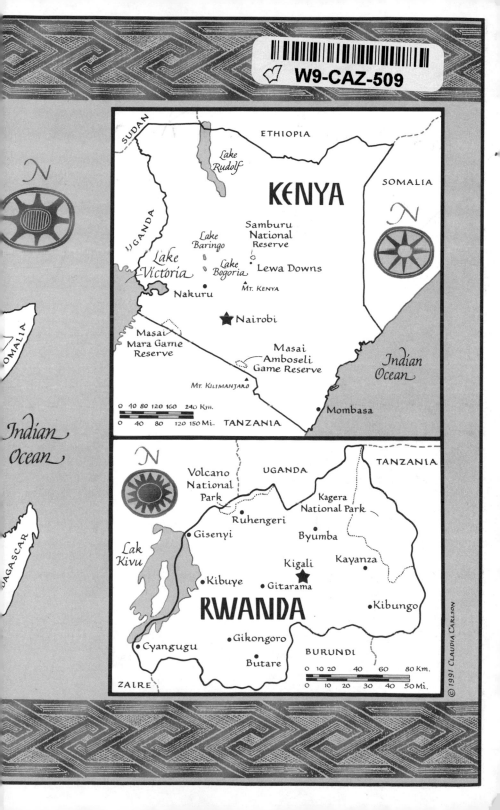

N

KENYA

SUDAN
ETHIOPIA
SOMALIA
UGANDA

Lake
Rudolf

N

Lake
Baringo
Samburu
National
Reserve

Lake
Victoria

Lake
Bogoria
Lewa Downs

Nakuru
Mt. Kenya

SOMALIA

Nairobi

Masai
Mara Game
Reserve

Masai
Amboseli
Game Reserve

Indian
Ocean

Mt. Kilimanjaro

0 10 80 120 160 240 Km.
0 40 80 120 150 Mi.
TANZANIA

Mombasa

Indian
Ocean

N

Volcano
National
Park
UGANDA
TANZANIA

Kagera
National Park

Ruhengeri

Gisenyi
Byumba

Kayanza

Lak
Kivu

Kigali

Kibuye
Gitarama

RWANDA

Kibungo

MADAGASCAR

Cyangugu
Gikongoro

Butare
BURUNDI

0 10 20 40 60 80 Km.
0 10 20 30 40 50 Mi.

ZAIRE

© 1991 CLAUDIA CARLSON

Sept/Oct 95

In anticipation of a great
trip to Kenya and thanks for
the most wonderful birthday
surprise I
ever had.

David

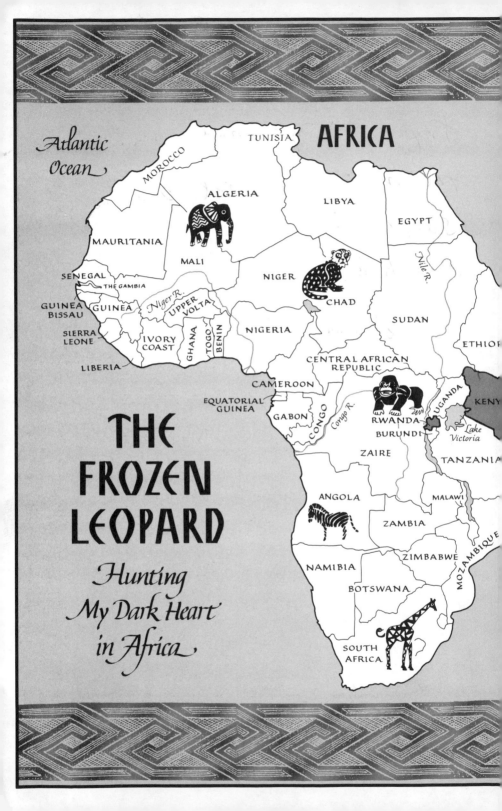

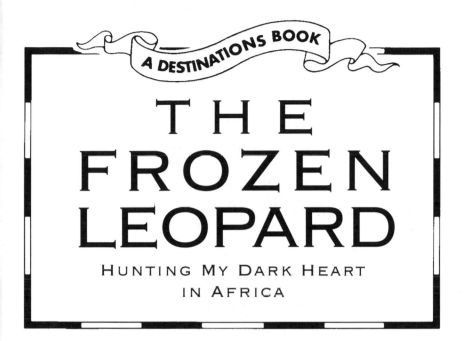

A DESTINATIONS BOOK

THE FROZEN LEOPARD

HUNTING MY DARK HEART
IN AFRICA

AARON LATHAM

INTRODUCTION BY JAN MORRIS

A TOUCHSTONE BOOK
Published by Simon & Schuster
New York London Toronto Sydney Tokyo Singapore

TOUCHSTONE
Simon & Schuster Building
Rockefeller Center
1230 Avenue of the Americas
New York, New York 10020

Library of Congress Cataloging-in-Publication Data
is available

ISBN 0-671-76760-7
ISBN 0-671-79278-4 (pbk)

For Taylor, Lesley *and* Von Sharon

CONTENTS

INTRODUCTION
BY JAN MORRIS

When Ernest Hemingway wrote his parable *The Snows of Kilimanjaro,* with its epigraph concerning a frozen leopard found near the House of God, the western summit of the mountain, he was making an admission. Mighty hunter that he was, the epitome of literary and physical *machismo,* he was conceding that there was more to Africa than killing animals and drinking whisky. It was a mystical story that he was writing, and inherent to its plot was the idea that the experience of the Dark Continent can take one nearer to things first, ultimate and finite.

Mr. Latham is a very different kind of writer, but in this book he is describing his own pilgrimage towards the same conclusion. Suffering at once from a personal tragedy and from that familiar writer's problem, a momentary collapse of confidence in his own powers, he sets out with a family party upon a protracted journey through East Africa. It is not really a dangerous journey—just a tourist safari in the modern kind, with guides, trucks, aeroplanes and cameras. It does, however, bring the travelers into intimate daily contact with the elemental Africa, its creatures, its peoples, its landscapes and its legends, and it gives true meaning to Mr Latham's subtitle: Hunting My Dark Heart in Africa.

This is not just that Search for Identity worn to death by the alternative cultures of the 1960s. Mr. Latham knows very well who he is—a sophisticated and successful North American writer, one of the stars of the New Journalism, Texas-bred and New York-cultured. He is a happy husband and father. He is no more alienated from our times than the rest of us. He suffers, though, from convictions of sadness and sensations of failure, and it is to Africa that he goes for diagnosis and prescription. The treatment is heady. At one time or another Mr Latham feels himself actually to have exchanged sensibilities with a giraffe, a rhinoceros, a lion, a cheetah, a wildebeest and a gorilla. Sometimes he feels himself the hunter, sometimes the hunted. In counterpoint however to these exotic experiences, always beside him are his wife, his daughter, his brother-in-law and his nephew, providing a therapeutic give-and-take between the familiar and the extraordinary, the real and the fantastic.

Hemingway's story ended sadly and without moral. Latham's is a parable of another kind. What this very worldly man discovered in Africa, what it did for him in the end, how he accounts for its peculiar effect upon its pilgrims—all this, set against marvellous panoramas of African life and infused with a curiously guileless sense of wonder and self-amusement, is the stuff of this gentle and consoling book.

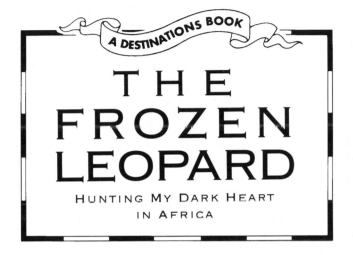

A DESTINATIONS BOOK

THE FROZEN LEOPARD

HUNTING MY DARK HEART IN AFRICA

Whenever I find myself growing grim about the mouth; whenever it is a damp, drizzly November in my soul; whenever I find myself involuntarily pausing before coffin warehouses, and bringing up the rear of every funeral I meet; and especially whenever my hypos get such an upper hand of me, that it requires a strong moral principle to prevent me from deliberately stepping into the street, and methodically knocking people's hats off—then, I account it high time to get to sea as soon as I can. This is my substitute for pistol and ball.

—Herman Melville, Moby Dick

CHAPTER
ONE

DRIZZLY
NOVEMBER
SOUL

ANDSCAPES. INTERIOR landscapes. Exterior landscapes. It was the rainy season in my soul, but dry season outside. I kept trying to open windows to let in the sun, but they were sealed shut by the dampness. I hoped this trip might change my forecast although I already knew that climate could be quite intractable. Lots of others before me had tried to change the weather with negligible results.

The soul drizzle had started when one of my scripts failed to move from paper to celluloid. The story was built around a ballroom-dancing contest; I called it *Cheek to Cheek*. The drizzle became a rain when another screenplay showed promise but was never shown in the theaters. It was about illegal, after-hours clubs that served alcohol all night; I called it *The New Speakeasies*. The rain turned to torrents when a third and most beloved movie project started well—it was to be produced by one of my best friends and directed by another—but it failed because of me. It was called *Rio*.

The story was about a young songwriter who found that he couldn't write songs anymore. But I found that I couldn't write the tale. I had somehow caught my hero's disease. In the story, which I couldn't write, the songwriter was supposed to be healed by traveling to Brazil where he discovers a form of magic known as *macumba*. I went to Brazil following in the footsteps of my fictional hero. I followed him to *macumba* ceremonies where I saw dancers who were possessed by spirits and who spoke in tongues. The believers called it being "ridden" by a god. I joined in the dancing, but I never felt a god on my back.

Several believers conducted me to the *macumba* priestess and told me to ask her a question, any question. She would know the answer. So I asked the first question that came to my mind: *Will I ever get her back again?* She said: *Sim, sim.* I paid little attention to the answer because I had supposed she would say "yes." That was her business. I might have forgotten the incident completely if a friend of mine hadn't kept bringing it up. My thoughtless question provoked a lot of questions from him: Who did I want to get back? Was she an actress? Was she the girl I had been in love with in college? I wouldn't say. He began to get on my nerves. Everything did.

The trip was a failure. I wasn't healed. I still couldn't write my story. The problem was simple: I didn't believe in magic.

I got so depressed that I gave myself a black eye. I hit myself in the face as a punishment for failure and my eye swelled up and turned the color of a storm cloud. Now my exterior looked the way my interior felt. I was in trouble.

I needed a cure for a failed trip and hard times generally. So eventually I began thinking of traveling again. Could one journey possibly heal the wounds of another? Did Odysseus ever pack his bags again?

I had long wanted to see Africa. I had read a lot of books about the continent by a lot of resonant names . . . Ernest Hemingway . . . Elspeth Huxley . . . Beryl Markham . . . Karen, Baroness Blixen, also known as Isak Dinesen . . . Joseph Conrad . . . Edgar Rice Burroughs. . . . I had swung through the lush jungles of their prose and now wanted to see those jungles for myself. Perhaps Africa could stop the rain. Well, it would pass the time anyway.

CHAPTER
TWO

ANOTHER
BLACK EYE

NO MATTER how bad you feel, you can always be made to feel worse by too many hours in an airplane seat. The flight from Washington, D.C., to London took eight hours. After a long layover at Heathrow Airport, we boarded another plane for the eight-hour ride that would bring us to our destination. My twelve-year-old daughter tried to sleep with her head in her mother's lap. Across the aisle, my ten-year-old nephew had his head in the lap of my brother-in-law.

I tried to get comfortable by doubling up my legs like folding chairs in the cramped space allowed them. I had plenty of time to think about ballroom dancers and after-hours parties and writers who could no longer write. While my conscious mind wrestled with writer troubles, my subconscious wrestled with its own demons, exhausting me mentally as well as physically. I couldn't stand it any longer and desperately sought the escape of sleep. But I couldn't sleep, couldn't even doze, couldn't. . . .

. . . And then I found myself waking up. I woke with a start as if we had hit unstable air. Maybe we had. Or maybe the bump had been in my subconscious. For I had dreamed that dream again. I used to dream it all the time, but I had been spared it for several years. The dream itself wasn't bad. Quite the contrary. It was wonderful. The nightmare was waking up. The dream fixed what was broken, but waking broke it again in the same old place. The mending fracture cracked and splintered the hurt worse than ever.

"Is anything wrong?" asked my wife Lesley.

"I had that dream again," I said.

"What dream?"

"About my sister."

"I'm sorry." She touched my shoulder. "Do you want to talk about it?"

"No," I said too sternly.

Now I felt more tired than ever, but I no longer wanted to go to sleep. I couldn't stand the idea of another dream. I sat with my eyes open, consciousness an ache inside my head, all the way to Nairobi, Kenya, East Africa. Great beginning.

Landing at long last, I was disappointed by the Nairobi airport which looked like an inner-city bus station back home. It was a dirty brown box. Its flight-control tower resembled a guard tower at a prison. So my first impression of Kenya was disheartening. The sight of that ugly terminal made me feel even more tired than I was before. No magic here.

After the torture of passport control—we spent an hour and a half standing in line—we finally met our guide, Derek Dames. He looked like Tom Sawyer in his early thirties. A second-generation Kenyan, born and raised, he had left his native land long enough to study architecture at Yale University. Returning to Nairobi, he tried working in a large architectural firm but didn't like it. So he went to work doing something he loves: designing safaris.

Derek had designed a safari for us that would take us from Mount Kenya in the north to Mount Kilimanjaro in the south, from unavoidable layovers in Nairobi in the east to volcanoes rimmed with gorillas in the west. We would spend most of our time in the bush living out of traveling tents pitched among the animals. We would be in East Africa all the time, Kenya most of the time, and Rwanda for a few days. We would spend a month on this safari, a Swahili word meaning simply "journey," which the English language has adopted and enlarged upon so that it implies a quest.

In a hurry to get started, we all clambered aboard Derek's Toyota Land Cruiser which was the tallest car in Africa. He called it "Double Decker" because it was so lofty and because he liked sharing his initials with his handsome, olive-green car. Derek Dames had used his Yale architectural education to draw up the plans for this vehicle which was ten feet long, six and a half feet wide, and *seven* feet tall. If you stood up in it with your feet on the seats, your head and shoulders stuck up through an open roof hatch and your hair blew in the wind. Or your hat blew off. Double Decker's towering picture windows, measuring three feet from top to bottom, were to normal windows what movie screens are to television sets. But as we bounced off down a narrow highway, there wasn't much to see. It was the dry season and looked it. We drove past parched fields of straggly brown grass. Where were the jungles?

Derek drove us to the elegant, old, half-timbered Norfolk Hotel in downtown Nairobi. . . .

. . . I woke up the next morning with no memory of anything that had happened after our arrival at the Norfolk.

Lesley assured me that we had had dinner in the hotel restaurant. She told me that I had eaten fried chicken, but didn't much care for it. She even maintained that we had trouble getting back into our room because I couldn't remember where I put the key. But I don't remember that key or anything else. Not even the dreams I may or may not have had in the night, for which I was grateful. I could do without dreams for a while.

As we moved our bags down to the hotel lobby, I wasn't tired but I was groggy and disoriented. I found myself wondering if I might still be asleep. Maybe my memory wasn't working right because I was actually unconscious. Maybe I was dreaming at this moment. Maybe the whole African safari was a dream. I hoped this wasn't going to be one of those stories that ended: *Then he woke up.* I often have trouble keeping straight what is a dream and what isn't, remembering a dream as something that really happened, or dismissing a memory of something real because it seems too dreamlike.

I was still in a daze as we checked out of the Norfolk. We headed in the direction of the airport, but made a stop along the way at Giraffe Manor. We parked in a crowded grass parking lot and climbed a tower that was high enough to allow us to feed the tall animals. We were given olive-green pellets, which didn't look very appetizing, but the giraffes loved them. They ate them out of our hands with slimy two-foot tongues. These giant animals were Rothschild's giraffes which differ from others in that they have no spots below their knees: They wear white stockings.

While I was feeding one of the giraffes, he got excited and butted me in the face with one of his horns. The horn had a ball on the end the size of a fist. He punched me in the left eye, the same eye that I myself had punched weeks earlier, the same poor, mistreated eye which had only recently shed its stormy discoloration. And now it was swelling up and clouding over all over again.

Africa wasn't healing old hurts. Africa was reopening old wounds.

CHAPTER THREE

CAMP

E CRAMMED our luggage and ourselves into a twin-engine Cessna and took off. I tried to pretend that I was Denys Finch-Hatton, the dashing pioneer pilot who won the heart of Karen Blixen, who immortalized him in *Out of Africa*. But actually I felt more like a down-and-out fighter who was thinking of looking for a new line of work. I was tired of planes and my eye hurt.

Looking down, I saw that we were flying over Nairobi National Park which was dotted with wildebeest ants and zebra ants and giraffe bugs. We were finally seeing wildlife, but they were too far away to be thrilling. Then the plane suddenly began to pitch wildly as if it had been butted by a giant, invisible giraffe monster.

"Gad is a very good pilot," Derek called reassuringly, raising his voice above the roar of the propellers.

Our handsome pilot in his dashing blue uniform and blue cap wrestled the air currents and brought the plane under control again. The bucking subsided into rolling.

"I brought some maps," Derek said, beginning to unfold them. "I don't know how much you know about Kenya . . ."

He used the plane ride north to enlarge our knowledge: Kenya is the size of France. It is even shaped a little like France. Both countries seem to have started out as squares that God crumpled, like pieces of paper, leaving all the lines ragged and uneven. France's western border is formed by the Atlantic Ocean; Kenya's eastern border is the Indian Ocean. In the south, the Mediterranean laps the shores of France; in the west, Kenya is washed by the waters of Lake Victoria. On the map, Kenya looks like France, but on the ground it still has the look and feel of a former British colony—although the marks left on it by some seventy years of English rule are beginning to fade.

Derek mentioned that Kenya also resembles Texas, for he knew I had been born and had grown up there. Like Texas, Kenya has a fairly dry climate, especially in the northwest. Its northern plains are covered with brush and shrubs, like Texas. In the south, it has mountains, valleys, and plateaus—and a little more rainfall—again like Texas. Looking down from the plane, we could see a jagged line where the green fields of coffee and tea gave way to dry, brown wilderness. The populations are also similar in size: Kenya has some 21.6 million people, Texas about 17 million. (By contrast, France, with much more arable land, has a population of some 56 million.) And both Texas and Kenya still remember their not-too-distant frontier pasts.

With the equator belted across its middle, Kenya is a country whose days and nights are always the same length and whose temperatures do not vary much either. Low-lying Mombasa and the rest of the coast are always hot, but mile-high Nairobi and the rest of the central highlands are almost always comfortable. The only seasonal changes have to do with precipitation, not temperature. The "long rains" last from March through May; the "short rains" fall in October and November. The nicest time of the year is usually July and August when the pale skies are clear and the nights cool and days in the upper sixties.

It was August now.

Kenya's population is 99 percent black. The largest minority is Asian. Next come the whites, mostly British. Only about fifty of the largest farms and ranches are still owned by white settlers or their descendants whereas some 1,400 were in white hands on independence day in 1963.

One of this dwindling fifty, named Lewa Downs, was our destination. It was owned by Delia and David Craig who would be our hosts. Back in Kenya's pioneer days, this old ranch raised cattle for market, but now it cares for wild animals mainly by leaving them alone. This private, semiarid sanctuary attracts beasts by offering them safety and rugged bush country and springs in a thirsty land. And it attracts guests by offering them animals. We descended onto a dirt strip which looked like a country road. Since Derek's self-designed Land Cruiser wouldn't arrive here until the next morning, we were met by one of the ranch's herd of Land Rovers. We were driven through a thorny landscape to our nearby camp.

We rolled into a grove of kelly-green acacia trees that sheltered our kelly-green tents. We didn't have any neighbors for miles and miles around, which is how my ancestors had lived when they first came to Texas. They started out under canvas, too.

Getting out, I stretched and took several deep breaths. The air was thin and dry. It didn't crowd you, didn't weigh you down, just left you alone. It was the kind of air I had always associated with cowboys, with self-reliance, with large visions and distant horizons. A red dust, like cayenne pepper ground very fine, rode the breeze and perfumed it. The smell was sharp, pungent, even peppery. The scent of Africa. Not only the African atmosphere but also the African smell seemed strangely familiar to me. My nose felt right at home.

Lesley and I shared a spacious tent which was big enough to stand up in. It had a somewhat lumpy canvas floor to keep out the rain, insects, and other assorted monsters. Our daughter, Taylor, had a tent of her own where she would sleep all alone listening to the night's wild sounds. My brother-in-law, Jeff, and my nephew, Matthew, shared a third tent. These comfortable bush wigwams had been designed by Ker & Downey in 1971 upon the occasion of their taking Prince Charles and Princess Anne on safari. The canvas smelled like clean shirts when you take them from the drawer and unfold them.

Behind the large tents were smaller tents that contained showers and other facilities. Derek explained to us that we shouldn't be shy about using this equipment because the prince and princess had done so. He added that even Queen Beatrix of the Netherlands had perched on such a seat. So we always called it Queen B's throne.

We would be looked after by a staff of nine, all dressed in kelly-green uniforms, who would follow us from campsite to campsite across the face of Africa. We shook hands with Mandiza, Kaptano, Francis, Mutie, Jean, Nzioka, Mutuku, Longozi, and Justice. Being cared for by so many might not have embarrassed royalty, but it did make us feel a little uncomfortable. Such luxury seemed to belong to a bygone bwana age.

We decided to clean up before dinner. Derek liked to joke that our camp had hot and cold running water because his staff was trained to run to and fro with buckets of both.

I asked a diminutive young man named Jean to bring me hot water for a shower.

Jean hurried off to the fire where water was perpetually heating. I followed along to see if I could help. I wasn't comfortable with being waited on. Taylor came, too. We found two containers—a huge fifty-gallon drum and a five-gallon bucket—simmering side by side on fragrant coals. Our camp always smelled of sweetly burning acacia.

Wanting to help, I walked over and picked up the five-gallon bucket by its bail. The metal, which was as hot as a branding iron, taught my hand what calves feel at roundup time. Smelling the burning flesh, I dropped the bucket so fast that I splashed hot water on my poor daughter. I didn't believe in magic, but I did believe in omens, and this one was bad. The hurt in my hand—also the soreness around my eye—seemed outward manifestations of the hurting within. I was further discouraged by the realization that I had traveled thousands of miles to get away from pain only to discover that it had gotten here before me in order to welcome me to camp.

Seeing what had happened, Kaptano, our cook, rushed over and examined my hand. He was a large man with graying hair and a voice like Louis Armstrong's.

"It's all right," I lied.

I shook my hand to try to make it feel better. Then I wondered if fanning it like that might encourage it to burst into flames. So I stopped.

"Be careful," he graveled. "That's hot."

"I know," I said.

"What do you need?"

"Hot water."

So Kaptano reached down with his bare hand, picked up the bucket by its almost red-hot bail, carried it over to a plastic bucket, and decanted several gallons of hot water.

"There," he said.

Jean appeared and picked up the plastic bucket and headed for our tent. In his other hand, he had a bucket of cold water. Giving up on helping, I followed meekly behind.

When Jean reached our shower tent, he set down his two buckets. Then he untied a rope that was attached to a pulley that was used to raise and lower a third bucket. He poured both hot and cold water into this new bucket, mixing them, getting them just the right bath temperature. When he was satisfied, he used the rope to raise this bucket, as if it were a flag, to the top of an eight-foot pole. Now our shower was loaded and ready to be fired.

Entering our shower tent, I pulled a chain that was attached to a nozzle. The nozzle was attached to a hose. And the hose was attached to the bottom of the elevated bucket. Splash. When I was wet all over, I turned off the water and reached for the soap. There wasn't enough hot water in the bucket to keep the shower going during the lathering. When my sore hand washed gingerly around my sore eye, both hurt. Still the hot water made me shiver with pleasure. I was surprised that this contraption worked so well.

When we were all clean and dressed again, we made our way to the mess tent for dinner. A bar had been set up at the entrance, stocked with every sort of hard liquor and soft drink. Ice waited in a large silver thermos. Derek played bartender. Since we all chose Cokes, the bar's supply was quickly depleted, but there was no cause to worry. Derek simply walked over to a full-sized refrigerator and fetched some more. Since darkness had fallen and the air was rapidly chilling, we gathered around a campfire built at the mouth of the mess tent. We chatted and munched on spicy french fries.

At about 8:30, Derek suggested that we all go in to

dinner, so we entered the large mess tent. A long table awaited us inside. Canvas camp chairs were arranged around it. A cloth tablecloth was held in place by clips. The china and silver were real. The napkins were rolled inside napkin rings carved in the shape of animals—an elephant, a lion, a warthog, even a rare rhino.

"I want the elephant," Taylor said.

Francis, who was Derek's headman, appeared at Lesley's left elbow with a platter of artichokes. Soon Jean began working his way around the table with a bowl of beef stew. Then came a plate of salami and ham and a dish of home-made mayonnaise. We were offered spring rolls and hard-boiled eggs and salad made from lettuce grown in Derek's own garden. The table even supported a large jar of peanut butter which made Matthew and Taylor happy. Best of all, Kaptano had baked a fresh loaf of bread in his coal-smothered Dutch oven. Dessert was fresh fruit and ice cream.

Around the dinner table, we talked about Queen Beatrix of the Netherlands who had unknowingly bequeathed her name to the throne in the small tent behind the larger tent. I admitted writing to the then-princess back when I was about Matthew's age. I told her how pretty she was and asked her to be my pen pal. She wrote back and said no thank you. I've still got the letter someplace among my treasured keepsakes.

Lesley told about meeting Queen Beatrix at the Bildeberg foreign affairs conference which had been held in Spain a few months back. At dinner one evening, my wife had revealed the secret of her husband's boyhood infatuation to the queen herself. Beatrix did not remember my letter in particular, but she did recall getting lots just like it. She laughed her raucous royal laugh.

"I always said no," she said.

At about 9:30, we all headed for our tents and our

camp beds. I carried a heavy Coleman lantern that burned with a roar to light our way. The tents unzipped down the front. We stepped inside and zipped up again to keep out weather and insects and predators. Derek kept reassuring us that not even the smartest cat had figured out how to unzip a Ker & Downey tent. By the light of the roaring Coleman lantern, we got ready for bed, which for me simply meant taking off my boots. Lesley helped. Our tent contained two beds of the sort one normally finds in army barracks.

"I wish we had a king-sized bed," Lesley said. "Maybe we could call the front desk and ask for another room."

"I don't think so," I said.

"Why not?" she asked.

"Well, as I understand it, they designed these tents for Prince Charles and Princess Anne, right? So I'll bet they put in twin beds because their royal highnesses didn't want to sleep together. So now we're struck with their beds."

"Don't you think they could afford two tents?"

"Is that how the royals do it?"

"Why don't you write and ask them?"

The blankets on the beds looked like army issue. The sheets were olive drab—but they had pictures of animals on them. I hadn't had critters on my sheets since I was ten years old. I lay down my bruised and burned body which was sore all over from so many hours of travel. The physical pain merged with the mental pain that had been with me for so long now. I longed for unconsciousness, which had become the only painkiller that gave me any real relief.

While we slept, a Masai watchman patrolled our camp carrying a flashlight and a bow and arrow.

CHAPTER
FOUR

RIDING WITH THE ANIMALS

14.95

6 2 4 - 6 6 0 0

Univ Book 6 3 4 - 3 4 0 0 Blue
Store

Portraits in the Wild

0 - 2 2 6 - 5 4 2 3 3 - 5

Univ. Chicago

Woodland Zoo shop

Us and Cassettes

H # 2814

r Exhibition Hall

TO THE SHOW, send or fax your order to
t 29th, and we will place the order for you!
ormation, please call 360-385-9663 or fax
 hear from you or see you at the show!

A GROUP, INC.
Lambert, Publishers Representative

T 6:15 in the morning, somebody rapped gently at the canvas door of our tent. It sounded as if he were using a feather duster as a door knocker. Then our tent door was unzipped and two cups of coffee—accompanied by four ginger snaps—were placed just inside. Our canvas home filled with smells intended to tempt us from our beds. We thought about procrastinating, but didn't because we remembered what was in store for us this morning: horseback riding. We had been warned that if we were late, all the horses might be gone. So we reluctantly pulled ourselves from under the covers to face a wintry morning.

I put on the top half of my long johns which are normally reserved for skiing. It was freezing here on the equator in August. The temperature was a function of the altitude, and we were quite high up. I was still shivering when I pulled on a sweater over the long johns.

We didn't even pause to eat breakfast this morning. Walking from the tent to the Land Cruiser, I still felt stiff from our sixteen-hour plane ride. So I walked a little funny this cold, dry, crisp morning. We all piled into Double Decker and set off in the pale light.

We were just leaving our camp when I saw what appeared to be a dead zebra lying to the left of the road. Another bad omen. I called out and Derek stopped.

Our spotter, Mandiza, jumped down from his perch on the roof of the Land Cruiser and went to investigate. His short but powerful body was dressed in a kelly-green uniform with "Ker & Downey" stitched over the heart. He spoke Wata, the language of his tribe, and Swahili, the lingua franca of Africa, but no English. He moved quietly as if stalking the dead animal.

Soon we all got out and followed Mandiza. I wanted to see what had happened to the zebra, but I didn't want to be late for horseback riding with the animals. I hoped this reconnoiter wouldn't take too long. I sometimes worry.

The zebra was lying on its side with its feet sticking straight out and a glassy eye wide and staring. She did not have a mark on her except for a little blood on her tail. Derek and Mandiza turned the stiff animal over to see if there might be a wound on the other side, but none was found. So this was not the work of some predator with claws and fangs. Whatever killed this zebra was about a millionth the size of a lion—something really dangerous, a bacteria or a virus. Soon we started back to the Land Cruiser. Our stop had been fairly brief.

We hurried on toward the horses, but soon we stopped again. Once more it was for a good cause, but I was still nervous. Derek saw a car coming down the hill from Ian Craig's house. The driver was Delia and David Craig's son and the heir to Lewa Downs. He was also an old friend of Derek's. We braked and so did the other car. The greetings were elaborate and unhurried as they always seem to be in

Africa. Finally Derek asked Ian to come to our camp for dinner that evening and bring his family.

"We can't because we have our son's headmaster coming to stay with us," Ian said, "but could we come and pinch a drink from you?"

"Please do," Derek said. "I've got all these teetotalers on this safari—and I've got a full bar."

So it was agreed that they would come for drinks about the time it got dark. At last we went our separate ways.

When we finally reached the main house, Derek said, "I don't see any horses. Where are the horses? I hope we're not too late."

So it had happened. We were too late and the horses were gone. We stopped and got out of the car, all of us bewildered.

Then we saw the horses. We had been searching in the wrong direction. We had been looking toward the corrals. But here came the horses from the other side of the house. They were saddled and ready to go.

Delia Craig, the mistress of Lewa Downs, came out to greet us. She was a tall, energetic, engaging grandmother. She introduced Kaliel, the wrangler who would accompany us on our ride, who seemed half her size. Assigning us horses, she commanded easily but charmingly. And she did so in a distinctive voice that sang the English language rather than speaking it. (Of course, the French always sing.)

Soon we all mounted up. I climbed aboard Tweedle Dum. Lesley rode Tweedle Dee. Jeff was on Joe, Matthew on Banini, and Taylor on Shabah. To the omnipresent scent of Africa—sharp, dry, and peppery—was added the heavier smell of horse which reminded me of my boyhood and a sorrel mare named Judy.

As we galloped off at a walk, my mood shifted from anticipation to apprehension. First of all, I had been expecting a western saddle but found myself perched atop the English variety which seemed insubstantial. Moreover, I had to hold the reins in my clumsy left hand because my right was still sore from the hand brand. Lastly, although I had been a rider as a boy, I hadn't ridden anything lately— except mechanical bulls in ersatz cowboy honky-tonk saloons. And every single time I had ridden one of those bucking machines, it had hurt me. I had lost whole patches of skin and almost lost my manhood. Wasn't a living animal an even greater threat?

We were soon stretched out single file. Kaliel led the way, followed by Taylor. My twelve-year-old daughter was blue-eyed and tall for her age. Her long, straight hair was light brown indoors but dark blonde in the sunshine which was where she preferred to be. She looked the way I imagined Becky Thatcher looked, but she was Tom Sawyer in spirit.

Next came Matthew. My ten-year-old nephew was brown-eyed, round-faced, and short for his age. He could play Charlie Brown in *Peanuts* or Garfield in *Garfield,* which suggests the breadth of his range.

Next came Lesley. My wife was a blonde, green-eyed Washington journalist who normally hated being outdoors. She was always better dressed than her husband, perhaps in the tradition of television people being better groomed than print people, but I suspect the difference would hold if she were a plumber and I were a bank president. In the bush, she wore khaki pants with creases and a khaki shirt with epaulets. Nothing wrinkled.

Then came Jeff. My brother-in-law, a likable round-faced Boston real-estate developer, seemed more like a low-keyed high school social studies teacher than the hard-driven businessman he really was.

I brought up the rear. At almost six feet four inches,

a big man with a small voice, I wore blue jeans and cowboy boots, as I almost always do. When I was a kid, I won a Huck Finn look-alike contest.

Cresting a small hill, we suddenly had a panoramic view of a vast, undulating plain. The tableau was as brown as West Texas with the same dusty green splotches. It was broken land, not quite flat, not quite hill country. Occasional buttes raised craggy heads. The ground was littered with scrub brush—punctuated with widely spaced trees. All of which was very familiar to anyone who grew up where I grew up. Moreover, all the plant life was armed with thorns, just like back home. In Texas, the sharp prongs would have adorned mesquite trees and brushes. Here in Africa, nature's needles guarded acacia trees and brush. The mesquites at home were rounded whereas the acacias here were all flat on top. God might have put down His or Her giant hand and flattened everything. We saw a field of capital Ts stretching to the horizon.

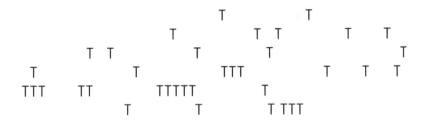

But the main feature here, as in West Texas, was the sky. It dominated everything else. It was a pale, thin blue with a few single-brush-stroke clouds. No dense forests blocked our view of its vast expanse. No weather front lowered it. This sky was a great, vaulting cathedral roof which lent a grandeur to all it sheltered.

At the horizon, a single mountain, magnificent Mount Kenya, the second tallest peak on the continent, gave us a giant optimistic thumb up. The first white man to report seeing this snowcapped mountain was a German missionary-explorer named Dr. Johann Ludwig Krapf who penetrated the highlands of East Africa in 1848. But his story of snow on the equator was widely disbelieved. Scientists actually wrote papers "proving" him wrong. Eventually in 1883 a Scotsman named Joseph Thomson—who would later give his name to a gazelle—rediscovered the snowcapped mountain. And people began to take equatorial snow more seriously.

Staring at this panorama, I began to relax. The tension simply seemed to sink away from me. Lately, I had usually been the one to do the sinking, not my troubles. But today I was a tall figure on horseback. And I was feeling more and more comfortable in the saddle.

I was beginning to feel at home on that hilltop.

Really at home.

It wasn't just that the landscape looked a lot like West Texas where I had grown up. It wasn't just that I was riding a horse which made me feel like one of my own Texas ancestors. It wasn't just that I tried to sit my mount the way my great-grandfather, the Texas Ranger, would have sat his. It was all that, but more. My sense of homecoming seemed to have to do with something that went back even before my great-granddad. I had actually lived in a lot of small Texas towns, sometimes in different houses in the same town, so my sense of home, my sense of belonging to a place, was normally tenuous. But not now. Now I felt at home, now I belonged, in this place where I was an alien. I was a stranger, but not in a strange land, not at all.

After pausing to admire the view, we rode on. In the hazy distance, we saw materialize a herd of shimmering stripes. A family of warthogs with their tails raised ran in the middle distance. And the weather was warming up.

Kaliel decided to play Kenyan Cowboy and round up a Kory bustard which is the largest bird capable of flight. He had us wait while he rode ahead to herd the big gray-and-white bird which was so solidly built that it resembled an anvil with wings. He drove it to the right. Then he drove it back to the left. It looked like a bustard trail drive, but Kaliel was actually trying to get the bird to fly. It didn't want to. It wanted to walk on the ground and keep its eyes on the dirt looking for seeds. It was a bird and yet it was of the earth rather than of the heavens. Kaliel finally succeeded in persuading the bustard to fly, but those vast, beautiful wings were clearly wasted on it. Which was how I had often felt lately, that my talents were wasted on me, because I stayed on the ground rather than soaring the way I should.

Riding on, we entered a dense thicket with thorns that clawed at us. I was so busy watching these needles that I didn't see what loomed in front of us until we were almost on top of it.

Then I looked up and saw a giraffe who was me. I was looking up at the towering animal, but simultaneously I was looking down at the insignificant man who was trying to increase his height by sitting on the back of the horse. I was both man and giraffe, subject and object, object and subject. Maybe my old difficulty with separating dream from undream was once again rearing its head, in this case, a stately head two stories tall. Or maybe I was experiencing what actors feel when they practice what is known as "the method," actually becoming the characters they play, or convincing themselves that they have become those characters. I had done enough work with actors to have some of their contagious dementias infect my psyche. Of course, a part of me must have known that I wasn't really a giraffe, but I certainly felt as if I were one.

I was "riding" the giraffe the way the *macumba* gods supposedly "rode" believers in Brazil. My spirit seemed to have entered the giraffe the way the gods entered the bodies of ecstatic dancers. Which made me feel like something of a small-time god myself. Perhaps in the great equation of the universe, humans were to giraffes as gods were to humans. Gods "rode" humans; humans "rode" giraffes. I remembered that Brazil's *macumba* was based on religions brought over by slaves from Africa. Maybe spirit travel was in this African air. Not that I believed any of this nonsense, but I *felt* it.

I loved being this tall, some eighteen feet from hooves to knobbed horns. I loved being able to see so far in all directions. I loved being a part of this vast sky. But I was, as William Wordsworth, nature's poet laureate, expressed it:

    . . . more like a man
    Flying from something that he dreads than one
    Who sought the thing he loved.

I loved being a giraffe *instead* of a writer. I loved being somebody else, loved being outside of myself, loved *not* being preoccupied with myself for the first time in a long time. I loved being a proud animal standing tall rather than a beaten-down human being cringing in a corner of my mind. I loved this vacation from myself, this escape from myself, this losing myself in nature.

I wasn't just any giraffe. I was a Lewa Downs reticulated giraffe. I appeared to be made out of rich, dark chocolate. My spots were separated from each other by lines of white frosting. The kind of icing pastry chefs use to write "Happy Birthday." I was proud to be a reticulated giraffe because I knew we were the most beautiful giraffes in the world. I preened.

But as "I" rode toward "me," something curious happened. I got bucked off. The giraffe wheeled and I lost eye contact as well as my grip. I wasn't "riding" it any more, but I had ridden it for an instant. My spirit had invaded it for a moment. I had been a giraffe.

I felt giddy and elated. Most of all, I was amazed to relearn an old lesson which I had all but forgotten: that there were still some great, new, unexpected experiences left in life. In my mid-forties, I had come to see life as repetition. Failure repeated failure. Even the repeated pleasures were growing shopworn from being handled over and over again. But here on an African plain, I had been surprised by a completely new experience: escaping not only my identity but my species. This newly discovered joy would take its place with others down through my life's stages . . . reading in grade school . . . rock 'n' roll in junior high . . . sex in high school . . . poetry in college . . . the novels of Anthony Trollope in my early thirties . . . a visit to the Van Gogh Museum in Amsterdam during the same period . . . marriage, fatherhood, and making my first movie in my mid-thirties . . . skiing a little later . . . and turning into a giraffe today. Life wasn't just repetition. I could still be surprised. I could still be amazed. Which was the most amazing discovery of all.

Kaliel wheeled our column and we pursued the giant living crane. Looking through my camera, I saw the giraffe looming in the background behind Taylor and Lesley the way the Eiffel Tower had loomed in other pictures on other vacations. But this was a living Eiffel Tower. We followed right in the giraffe's footsteps until we were so close I could only see the first few stories in my viewfinder. Then the giraffe got tired of pretending to be the Eiffel Tower . . . or Big Ben . . . or the Colosseum. The background took to its heels and ran out of the picture which none of the other monuments had ever done.

Riding on, we came upon more chocolate giraffes. As we drew closer, we saw two peanut-butter infants. Taylor rode so close to these babies that she could have tasted them if she had had a mind to. I couldn't believe how tolerant these wild animals were of human beings on horseback. They would run from people on foot or in vehicles, but they seemed to accept mounted men and women as members of their own four-footed fraternity. We were so close that we could see the dried umbilical cords still dangling from the baby giraffes' tummies.

Riding out of this forest of spotted long necks, we came upon a black-and-white herd. Some were common zebras, others Grévy's zebras. The Grévy's stripes are narrower and their ears larger than those of the common zebra. Some people say that a Grévy's zebra is a white animal with black stripes while a common zebra is a black animal with white stripes. The Grévy's zebra is closer to the horse while the common zebra is closer to the donkey. A Grévy's zebra can mate with a horse to produce an animal called a "zebroid" while a common zebra can mate with a donkey to create a "zedonk." But a Grévy's zebra cannot mate with a common zebra. I took a picture of a Grévy's colt nursing.

I tried to "ride" the zebras the way I had "ridden" the giraffe, but I couldn't. Perhaps it was because I saw them as a herd rather than as individuals. Perhaps I couldn't identify with plurals. Perhaps it was because I couldn't see myself as a lowly zebra whereas I could imagine myself as a lofty giraffe. Was species snobbery involved here? Perhaps it was simply that zebras couldn't be ridden, not spiritually, not literally. A lot of people had tried and a lot had been bruised by failure. Zebras looked so much like horses or donkeys that early settlers assumed they could be broken, but they couldn't. The exception that proved the rule was a pioneer who managed to train a zebra to pull a buggy and gained considerable fame. But he was the only one. When Hollywood wants to put an actor or actress on a zebra's back, they paint a horse.

Kaliel called a halt. In the middle of the bush, we got off our horses and sat down to an outdoor breakfast. A wilderness breakfast. *Petit déjeuner sur l'herbe.* It was all set up and waiting for us in the soft shade of thorny acacias. We had fruit and cereals and coffee cake and scrambled eggs and sausage and bacon. We sat in leather folding camp chairs and ate while we watched monkeys playing in distant trees.

"Something sort of strange happened to me this morning," I said.

"You got up early," said Lesley.

"So two strange things happened to me," I agreed. "I got up early and I turned into a giraffe."

"You're tall enough," said the diminutive Matthew.

"What do you mean?" asked Lesley.

"I'm not sure," I said. "It was like a dream, like I dreamed I was a giraffe, but I really thought I was one."

"I felt very close to those giraffes, too," said Lesley. "We moved and then they moved as if we were dancing. We were interacting. We were almost talking. Normally animals seem to be in their world and we're in our world. But this morning we're all in the same world."

"That's right," I agreed.

"So I'm willing to believe you were a giraffe," Lesley said.

"I'd rather be an elephant," said Taylor.

After breakfast, Taylor and I went for a walk and found the bones of a giraffe. It was so huge that it looked like the skeleton of a dinosaur. I raised its dead head by its dead horns and looked into giant empty sockets. I was feeling very close to giraffes.

While ranch hands were packing up the breakfast things, we got back on our horses and rode off again. Soon we came upon a beautiful black-and-white male ostrich who appeared to be injured. He was on his "knees," flapping what appeared to be a broken wing. Taylor and I dismounted to see if we could help. But as we drew near, he "recovered," struggled to his feet, stumbled a few more yards, and then collapsed again. We approached again. He recovered again and ran off again and fell again. I guessed what he was up to since I had seen smaller ground birds perform the same trick back home. Suspecting that he was luring us away from his nest and his offspring, I told Taylor to look for chicks. Eventually we discovered a dozen baby ostriches the size of chickens. They were gray and long-necked and almost invisible in the grass. Taylor pronounced them "cute." Children usually get these things right.

Getting back on our horses, we rode on right into another herd of reticulated giraffes. Males. Females. Teenagers. Babies. It was the largest herd yet and we joined it. We saw a six-foot infant sucking milk from its mother. We rode through this grove of giraffes as if they were so many moving trees.

We rode up to two males who were jousting, using their long necks as lances. One would slam its neck into the neck of the other, then the other would slam back. Their necks would intertwine like strands of a living rope. It was a ritualistic fight that looked like a dance. We sat below them, staring up at them, as if watching the two towers of the World Trade Center sparring with each other to see which one would be dominant.

Then Grévy's and common zebras joined the herd of long necks. Zebras often graze with giraffes, counting on the tall animals to act as watchtowers for predators. The spots don't mind the company of the stripes since they don't compete for food. Giraffes are above eating grass, and zebras do not covet treetops.

Taylor and Lesley rode ahead so I could take their picture against a background of compatible spots and stripes. Taylor was smiling at the camera when her horse suddenly bolted. My daughter was thrown and landed hard on her back. She got up crying. It was a terrible moment right in the middle of a wonderful morning. Perhaps all Edens must have their serpents. Lesley got down and hugged Taylor until the tears stopped. Then looking as if she was about to start sobbing again, the little girl climbed back up onto her horse's back. She even cantered.

Reluctantly, we left the giraffes and zebras behind and moved on. We saw a giant troop of baboons on top of a rocky hill. They were playing and eating and grooming. Babies rode on their mothers' backs.

As our ride was nearing its end, Kaliel suggested that I photograph our little band as it rode in a circle around a giraffe. It did make a pretty picture. In all my others, the family had been in the foreground and the animals in the background, but now the giraffe was in the foreground and my family in the background. It was sort of like suggesting to somebody: Why don't you go over and stand behind the Chrysler Building and I'll snap your picture.

The giraffe remained as calm as the Chrysler Building until it was almost completely surrounded. But when it finally noticed that it was in a human corral, it got nervous.

I could feel its nerves. I "was" once again a giraffe. I ran in one direction to get away from the humans, then changed my mind and ran in the other. Turning myself in midflight was about as easy as making a U-turn in a twenty-story crane. I swayed one way, then I swayed the other. I thought I might topple over. But then I regained my balance and made up my mind and ran like hell—that is, if hell moves both feet on the same side at the same time. As I took flight, I hung on longer this time, but I eventually lost my grip and fell back to earth.

As we turned toward "home," I was beginning to believe in magic.

CHAPTER
FIVE

VOICES

ELIA CRAIG had invited us to "luncheon" which was served in a stone arbor with a grass roof: an outdoor dining room with a formal table. Our hostess commanded as easily at a meal as around her ranch. She asked me to "play Papa," and I took a seat at the head of the table. Her husband David was away on an errand.

"How did you enjoy your ride?" Delia sang.

"It was wonderful," Lesley said.

"It was great," I echoed. "I'm not sure why, but I feel very much at home here."

"A lot of our guests say that," Delia sang.

"I've just been here one day," I said, "and already Africa seems to be having an extraordinary effect on me."

"A lot of our guests say that, too," Delia sang.

"Why is that?" I asked.

"I really couldn't tell you," she sang. "I've lived in Africa all my life. I don't know what it would be like to visit. You'd better ask a visitor."

Delia Craig had not only grown up in Kenya—she pronounced it "Keenya"—but had actually been born right here on this ranch. Her English mother had driven ambulances in Europe during World War I, like Ernest Hemingway. Returning home after the war, she entered a lottery and won a tract of land in far-off Kenya. Her father gave her a rifle and a shotgun and saw her off on the *Garth Castle* which sailed from England on Christmas Eve, 1919. Her land turned out to be in the Ithanga hills which was not far from Thika. One of her neighbors, a few miles distant, was a twelve-year-old girl named Elspeth Huxley who would grow up to be an author.

When Delia Craig's mother first saw her little piece of Africa, perhaps she felt the same way Elspeth Huxley felt when she first beheld her new African home. Her mother and father—Tilly and Robin Huxley—had purchased a farm that was a two-days' mule ride from a small tent village called Nairobi.

"This ride through sun and heat, jolted by the sluggish mules, prickling with sweat, seemed to go on forever," Elspeth Huxley later wrote in *The Flame Trees of Thika.* "We crossed a treeless *vlei* whose grass was short and wiry and where a duiker leapt away from under the mules' feet. Robin pulled up and said, 'Here we are.' We did not seem to be anywhere. Everything was just the same, biscuit-brown, quivering with heat and grasshoppers."

Listening to Delia Craig during lunch, I seemed to hear her voice blending with other women's voices, all talking about Africa. I heard echoes of Elspeth Huxley's voice. Echoes also of Beryl Markham's voice. Echoes of Karen Blixen's voice. All these voices were talking about Kenya back when the century was new and the country seemed new, too. Of course, the land wasn't new to the native peoples, but it was a blank slate to the Europeans who came to write their stories on it. And write several of the newcomers did. For Kenya was blessed with an extraordinary group of writing pioneers—mostly women. The voice of this wild country was feminine.

Nineteen nineteen was a year of good-byes. Delia Craig's mother said good-bye to her family in England and started out for Kenya. Meanwhile, in Kenya, Beryl Markham was saying her good-byes, too. Her father had brought her to Africa at the age of four while her mother remained behind in England. But her dad, a horse trainer, failed in Kenya and decided to move on to Peru. This time it was his seventeen-year-old daughter who chose to stay behind. On a horse named Pegasus with all her worldly goods packed in two saddlebags, Beryl set off for Nakuru where she became a horse trainer. The trade ran in the family. She later learned to ride the air even better than she sat a horse. She was one of the first woman pilots in Africa and the first human being to fly across the Atlantic Ocean from east to west—sort of a left-handed Lindy.

"So there are many Africas," Beryl Markham wrote in *West with the Wind.* "There are as many Africas as there are books about Africa . . . Doctor Livingstone's Africa was a pretty dark one. There have been a lot of Africas since that, some darker, some bright, most of them full of animals and pygmies, and a few mildly hysterical about the weather, the jungle, and the trials of safari . . . Being thus all things to all authors, it follows, I suppose, that Africa must be all things to all readers.

"Africa is mystic; it is wild; it is a sweltering inferno; it is a photographer's paradise, a hunter's Valhalla, an escapist's Utopia. It is what you will, and it withstands all interpretations. It is the last vestige of a dead world or the cradle of a shiny new one. To a lot of people, as to myself, it is just 'home.' It is all these things but one thing—it is never dull."

Delia's mother, the transplanted World War I ambulance driver, met and married a young man with a military bearing who had fought in the King's African Rifles during the war. They were both veterans and had that in common. They also had a daughter, Delia, in common. But the marriage only lasted three years. Then the young mother with the toddler daughter struck out once again on her own.

Africa seemed to be tough on marriages. As Delia's parents were breaking up, Karen and Bror Blixen's marriage was also in trouble. While Karen stayed home and tried to run the couple's coffee farm, Bror went off to become a big-game hunter and a famed philanderer. His biography is called *The Man Whom Women Loved.* One of those women turned out to be Beryl Markham. White Kenya was quite inbred. Everybody called Karen Blixen by her nickname which was "Tanne," but today the Nairobi suburb where she lived is called Karen in her honor.

In *Out of Africa,* Karen Blixen, the deserted wife, who chose as her pen name Isak Dinesen, wrote: "I had a farm in Africa . . . The geographical position, and the height of the land combined to create a landscape that had not its like in all the world. There was no fat on it and no luxuriance anywhere; it was Africa distilled up through six thousand feet, like the strong and refined essence of a continent. The colours were dry and burnt, like the colours in pottery. The trees had a light delicate foliage, the structure of which was different from that of the trees in Europe; it did not grow in bows or cupolas, but in horizontal layers, and the formation gave to the tall solitary trees a likeness to . . . full-rigged ships with their sails clewed up . . .

"In the highlands you woke up in the morning and thought: Here I am, where I ought to be."

Reading that last sentence back home before I had ever seen Africa, I had smiled to myself at the charming overstatement. I was sure that nobody woke up anywhere always thinking: This is just where I should be. But now I knew I was wrong. It was morning, and I was in the highlands, and I was where I ought to be, where I belonged, where I could simply relax and absorb a peace that was stored in the dry air. But would anybody believe me any more than I had believed Isak Dinesen?

One day while Delia's mother was out riding—enjoying the same landscape we had enjoyed this morning—she dropped her revolver. Perhaps she had been too intent on watching the giraffes or ostriches or zebras to notice it was gone. Fortunately a young farmer found the pistol, traced it to its owner, and married her. That marriage worked and lasted and bore fruit: two sons and another daughter.

"Do *you* carry a gun?" asked Matthew.

"No," sang Delia.

"But what if you're attacked by wild animals?" he demanded.

"The guns are more dangerous than the animals."

Delia didn't say any more, but I thought I knew what she was thinking. I had read about it in *Out in the Midday Sun,* another African reminiscence by Elspeth Huxley, who reported that Delia's half-brother Charles had "accidentally shot himself on Christmas Eve. He was twenty-five years of age . . ." A revolver had brought the parents together, but a revolver had killed the son.

When Delia's brother died, he was four years older than my sister was when she was killed. She was crushed by two drag racers who slammed into her car broadside. Neither of the murderers was hurt in the "accident," but one suffered a broken jaw when the police arrived. Delia's brother and my sister died with their lives unlived. Life isn't fair, death isn't fair either.

Sitting there with my jaw tightening and my eyes

unable to focus, I thought I knew something of what our hostess must be feeling. I had come a long way to find this secret sharer. I felt an urge to tell her that we had a tragedy in common. I wanted to know how she dealt with her loss. Did she have trouble thinking about her brother? Talking about her brother? Mentioning his name? But I didn't ask because I was shy anyway and a coward when it came to bringing up anything as painful as my sister's memory. I *never* talked about her. I tried not to think about her because it hurt too much. Death had taken her from earth, but I had banished her from my mind.

So I was surprised to find myself lingering over my memories of her now. Remembering the weight problem she had had growing up. Remembering how once I left home, to go east to college, she had emerged from her chubby chrysalis to become a thin, beautiful, popular young woman. Remembering how little time she had had as a beauty before she was killed. On the way here, I had dreamed that old dream that she was still alive, and now my conscious mind seemed to be resurrecting her in my memory. In Africa, the dead wouldn't stay dead.

Talking about her out loud would have been better, but silently talking her over with myself was progress of a sort. Progress that I owed in part to Delia although I would never be able to thank her.

Some people believe that many writers—not all but many—write as a form of mourning for a deeply felt loss. Beryl Markham lost her mother at the age of four; she lost her father when she was nineteen. Karen Blixen lost her husband to other women; she lost her lover Denys Finch-Hatton to a plane crash; she lost her African farm to creditors; and finally she lost Africa itself, going "home" to Denmark to write about the land she left behind. Elspeth Huxley lost Africa, too, retreating to England to write her books about flame trees and the midday sun and her parents dressing up in tuxedos and evening gowns for dinners in grass shacks.

And I had lost my sister. As we were leaving the cemetery all those years ago, I had promised her that I would write a book and dedicate it to her. And I did. But lately I had been letting her down. Which was one of the reasons I had come to the continent that Elspeth Huxley and Karen Blixen had left behind but had never gotten over.

CHAPTER
SIX

PREHISTORIC
MYSTERY

FTER LUNCH, we retreated to our green tents beneath our green acacia roof. We rested for a couple of hours in the middle of the day like all the other animals in Africa. I took a nap, but I kept being awakened by the Matthew bird who kept warbling outside my mesh window.

At four o'clock, we met in the mess tent for afternoon tea. As Beryl Markham observed, the Chinese gave the English the two tools they needed to forge an empire: gunpowder and tea. In the old days, hunting safaris were powered by the same two substances. But shooting had gone the way of the empire. And today safaris run on tea alone.

We sat down on canvas chairs, and Francis placed two silver thermoses in front of us on the table. One thermos was of course filled with tea, but the second contained coffee as a concession to the visiting Americans. There was also a small plate of ginger cookies—or rather "biscuits."

After tea, we set off on our afternoon game drive in

Double Decker. We picked up David Craig, our host who had returned from his errand, because he had something special he wanted to show us. David had a good-humored, weathered face that reminded me of an aging but still handsome camel. Delia Craig, like her mother before her, had married a soldier. David and Delia had fallen in love during World War II when he was thousands of miles from home, from England, serving in His Majesty's armed forces in Kenya, which was then still part of the British Empire. They married and he stayed on.

David gave directions which Derek followed. We drove past the occasional distant giraffe and scared some warthogs. When we finally stopped, we were in the middle of an empty field littered with rocks. Looking closer, we saw that the rocks stretched in a kind of river which was some ten yards wide and over fifty yards long. But we could see rocks back home. David selected a couple of likely specimens and came lumbering toward us as if looming up out of lines written by Robert Frost:

> Bringing a stone grasped firmly by the top
> In each hand, like an old-stone savage armed.
> He moves in darkness as it seems to me,
> Not of woods only and the shade of trees . . .

"Look at these stones," David said in his British accent which was still distinct from a Kenyan accent after all these years. "Notice that they look alike. They *all* look alike."

We studied the rocks, picking up one after the other, and discovered that David was right. They all could have been cut by the same Stone-Age cookie cutter. Nature would never have stamped out such uniform rocks. There had to be some other explanation.

"This is a prehistoric hand-ax factory," David explained.

He chose a particularly well-formed rock and presented it to us on his palm. This ancient hand ax looked like a flattened stone pear. Or it could have been a crude, prehistoric Ping-Pong paddle. All the edges had been chipped sharp by ancient hands that must have been almost human.

"Most people believe the hominids held this ax by the narrow end," David said, indicating what looked like the handle of the Ping-Pong paddle, "and used the big end to cut or pound." He paused for effect. "But I doubt this theory since the narrow end is just as sharp-edged as the large end."

We passed the ax around. We tried to grasp it by the handle, but it hurt our hands. The handle did indeed have sharp edges. It felt more like a knife blade than a handle.

"I believe the hominids probably threw these axs," David said. "I imagine that a lot of them would throw their stones at the same time. They probably discovered the broadside bombardment a half-million years before Lord Nelson at Trafalgar."

Which was how old this site was believed to be, but it could have been much older. Perhaps as old as 2 million years. We all sat down on our haunches and pretended to be missing links manufacturing the means of our survival and evolution. Did the shaped rock feel familiar in my hand, or did I just imagine it?

After dropping David off at the big house, we pressed on toward other ancient relics of the deep past: rhinoceroses. A uniformed guard with an old Enfield rifle and a walkie-talkie opened the gate of the Ngare Sergoi Rhino Sanctuary and we rolled through. An eight-foot fence was topped with barbed wire.

Once inside, Derek stopped Double Decker and got

out with a screwdriver in hand. He went to the wing mirrors, which stuck out on either side of the Land Cruiser like ears, and proceeded to remove them. Then he got back in the big car without explanation.

Another uniformed guard crawled up on the roof of Double Decker and we drove off, bouncing along the rough dirt roads. Delia and David Craig had given the 11,000 acres of land for this refuge. The money to build the fence and other structures—some 544,000 pounds sterling—was given by a fabulous character named Anna Merz. She not only founded the sanctuary but put up a house in the middle of it and moved in. We were on our way to pay her a visit.

We found ourselves driving through a fortress within a fortress where the rhino was making its last stand. Beyond the chain-link wall was a more massive wall of mountains surrounding us on all sides. The northwest was guarded by jagged peaks, the Mathews Range, which resembled the sharp pointed logs of cavalry forts in the Old West. The northeastern wall was dominated by a great, flat-topped mountain, Ololokwe. The southern wall was watched over by a magnificent guard tower, Mount Kenya. Within these walls were earthworks. Some giant African war god had dug deep, steep-sided trenches. These valleys were filled with the barbed wire of Africa, thorn trees and thornbushes.

When we reached Anna Merz's modest home with a tin roof, we drove into her front yard but didn't get out of the Land Cruiser because a large sign nailed to a shed warned: PLEASE STAY IN YOUR CARS. A handyman approached our vehicle and spoke to Derek in Swahili. It turned out that Anna was not at home because she was out looking for her "pet" rhino named Samia. The young rhino had not come "home" last night and had failed to appear once again this afternoon. So Anna had gone out to find

Samia and bring her in. The handyman advised us to take a tour of the sanctuary and come back later.

So we set off once more down a punishing road in search of the twelve black rhinos—the dangerous kind—who made their home in the sanctuary. We drove over hills and through canyons. We could have been in the breaks country back home in West Texas. But back home, the trees were rounded and the hills had flat tops, whereas here the hills were rounded and the trees had flat tops. We saw some giraffe heads and necks in the distance but no rhinos.

To get a better look, I climbed up through an open hatch onto the roof of the Land Cruiser. Taylor and Matthew joined me. There were three hatches in all, resembling removable skylights. Mandiza and the sanctuary guard sat on the roof with their feet dangling down through the rear hatch. Matthew and I sat with our feet hanging through the middle hatch. And Taylor sat in front, our figurehead. Riding the back of the bouncing truck was like trying to ride a bucking mechanical elephant.

Up on the roof, we were a part of the sky, the cloudless sky. This part of Africa got only about twenty inches of rain in good years. In bad years, it got almost none, the grass died and then the animals started dying, all except the rhino who had a friend. The only cloud in the heavens was one veiling Mount Kenya, a bride of earth in a lovely white gown.

"Watch out!" Derek called from down below.

We all ducked and the thorny branch of an acacia tree passed just overhead. It was a narrow escape. I had known horses to try to scrape the riders off their backs in such a fashion, but I had not expected a Land Cruiser to be so ill tempered.

"Look out!" Derek shouted.

We ducked again and disappointed thorns just missed

us once more. Now besides looking for rhinos, I started looking for predatory acacias. And I saw one . . .

"Stop!" I called out.

A huge spiked branch was heading our way. It was too low to duck and too big to push aside. The Land Cruiser skidded to a stop inches short of pain. We all climbed down off the roof—even Mandiza and the guard. Then we started off again.

"Rhinos," said Matthew calmly.

When we all looked at him, he pointed matter-of-factly. We couldn't see anything and thought he must have seen a rhino tree. But then we turned a rough corner and there they were. We were rolling along the crest of a ridge and they were in a valley down below. Derek stopped Double Decker.

"Be very quiet," he said. "They're nervous animals."

They had every right to be nervous since they had been hunted to the edge of extinction. Poachers shot them with machine guns and then cut off their horns with chain saws. The horns were ground up and sold as aphrodisiacs or miracle cures. Other horns were carved into handles for daggers that some Arabs loved to carry.

We gently reached for door handles, turned them slowly, and got out as silently as we could. Then Matthew slammed one of the car doors. The rhinos looked startled but didn't run.

We walked quietly to the edge of the cliff and looked down at a mother and baby. Raising binoculars to our eyes, we saw the mom toss her head from side to side. The calf seemed more relaxed. Of course, these black rhinos—the aggressive kind—weren't actually black. No more than white rhinos are white. Both black and white rhinos are gray. The white rhinos were originally called the "wide-mouthed rhinos," which got shortened to "wide rhinos";

then over the years "wide" got transmuted into "white."
So you can't tell the temperament of a rhino by its color,
but only by the color of its name.

The calf nuzzled up close to its mother and started to
nurse. It looked like a bumper car drinking from a Sherman
tank. Looking down into the deep valley, we seemed to be
looking back in time, almost as if we had dug this hole
and excavated these ancient animals. Teddy Roosevelt once
spoke of having "a Pleistocene day" in Africa. We were
having a Pleistocene afternoon. The clouds around Mount
Kenya rose up and away—as if the bride's veil had been lifted.

Derek talked softly in Swahili to the guard who had
large holes in his earlobes.

"He says the mother's name is Juno," Derek explained
in a low voice. "The calf's name is Jupiter."

When Jupiter had had enough to drink—a couple of
gallons—he lay down for a rest. But Juno stayed on her feet
keeping watch.

"What do you think rhino heaven would be like?" I
asked.

"No poachers," said Matthew.

"No daggers," said Taylor.

We decided to go back and see if Anna was home yet.
On the way, Derek noticed a huge pile of rhino droppings
beside the road, so we stopped. We all got out and gathered
around.

Derek explained that rhinos don't relieve themselves
wherever they happen to be when they get the urge. No,
they walk miles to a communal latrine. And when they have
finished, they scuff their droppings with their feet before
leaving. Derek, who was wearing sandals, demonstrated by
scuffing the pile of dung with his feet.

"This is how rhinos, who are solitary animals, keep
track of each other," Derek said. "It's like a community

bulletin board. They can tell a lot from the droppings. If a male finds the droppings of a female in estrus, he will follow her. Tracking her isn't too difficult because she has scuffed her feet in the muck."

Driving on, we saw three warthogs running beside the road in the yellow grass. They were so ugly that our hearts went out to them in spite of their deadly tusks. These wild pigs looked a little like Miss Piggy since they had mops of long blond hair on the tops of their heads and streaming down their backs. As they ran, they all held their tails straight up in the air like citizens-band radio aerials.

"Tail up, tail up, tail up, tail down," Derek said.

When the warthogs stopped, all the tails came down simultaneously. Then they started off again, running, the world's ugliest chorus line.

"Tail up, tail up, tail up, tail up, tail down."

It's hard not to love a warthog.

"Tail up, tail up, tail down."

WHEN WE pulled back into Anna Merz's front yard, we saw her sitting beside her beloved Samia. She was as gray and wrinkled as her favorite species. We stopped but stayed in the truck as instructed by the sign. Anna—small and hard and fragile—got up and came toward us. The young rhino followed.

"How old is she?" asked Lesley.

"She's four and a half," Anna Merz said. "She's only half grown. It'll be three and a half years until she's mature. I think she is a bit small for her age. I think probably being hand raised, she's not as big as the ones raised by their mothers. But she's healthy and that's all that matters."

The healthy Samia butted the Land Cruiser.

"Hey, be careful," Derek said.

"You should be highly honored if you carry Samia's signature on your lorry," Anna said.

"Now you know why I took the wing mirrors off," Derek said.

"Oh, you did, did you?" said Anna. "You know that habit of hers."

It seemed that Samia liked to scratch herself on wing mirrors and always ripped them off in the process.

Taylor reached out of the truck window and petted the gray nose and horn. Watching this scene, my heart went out to the two youngsters: one mine, one Anna's.

I wanted to "ride" the rhino, which reminded me a little of a brahma bull, but I couldn't. My spirit kept ricocheting off the baby's ancient armor plate. Perhaps the rhino was too far down the evolutionary tree, too closely related to the triceratops which it resembled, to be "ridden" by a modern mammal. Maybe it was just too dumb. My reveries were interrupted by the sound of Derek's distinctive voice.

"Anna, come to dinner tonight," he suggested.

Dinner invitations mean more in the African bush than they do in cities, for people are so isolated out there. This isolation reminded me of the way my grandparents lived in the American West. Whenever a stranger appeared on the horizon, that newcomer was always invited to dinner. And the invitation was always accepted. Such chances were too rare to be passed up.

Anna said she would come.

O N THE way home to our camp, Taylor insisted we stop again at the ancient ax factory. We indulged her.

Getting out of the Land Cruiser, we walked again in a garden of stones shaped by hands as old as Adam's. Taylor bent over, picked up an ax, and turned it this way and that—an age-old tool in brand-new hands.

"I think I've got it," Taylor said. "I think they held the ax by the big end and pounded with the point."

She was suggesting that the hominids held the ax by the "blade" and pounded with the "handle." She was turning the so-called ax upside down. But perhaps modern humans have simply imposed their idea of "ax" on a tool that was something else entirely. I tried gripping the stone by the big end and pounding with the point. It fit my hand perfectly. It worked. I felt sure that a hand not so unlike my own had shaped this stone to fit itself. It was as though we clasped hands. I was standing on hallowed ground holding a hallowed scepter.

"Taylor, I think you're right," I said.

She had seen the "ax" with no preconceptions—the way a child sees—and had solved its mystery.

Since it was really getting late and our guests would be waiting, we had to go. We raced the last few rough miles back to camp. As we were approaching our tents, we saw red and white lights blinking high overhead. They weren't moving, just hovering there, suspended. We all wondered what it could possibly be.

"It's E.T.," Taylor said.

And it did look a lot like the spaceship that had first abandoned and then returned to take the Extra Terrestrial home. The blinking red and white lights began slowly descending. The winking flashes came all the way down to the ground. The spaceship settled in the large meadow that spread in front of our tents. A hatch opened and a small creature emerged. Walking on stubby legs, it started coming toward us.

"It really is E.T.," Taylor said.

The blinking red and white lights lifted off the earth and rose again into the heavens. Had it brought E.T. back "home" to our planet again? As the creature drew closer and closer, and the light from our camp fire began to illuminate it, it started looking less like a friendly monster and more like a beaming boy. We reached our fire about the same time he did. There was already a crowd around the flames—Ian Craig and his wife Jane and their son's headmaster and the headmaster's wife and another couple who had drifted in from somewhere. The Craigs introduced us to everybody—even to E.T.

He turned out to be their ten-year-old son, Bation. He had been trout fishing high up in a stream that raced down Mount Kenya. A helicopter had taken him to the mountain and now had brought him home. We complimented him on his entrance, but he seemed unimpressed by his chopper ride. In a land of vast spaces and bad roads, he was as matter-of-fact about whirlybirds as Taylor was about taxis.

Drinks were poured around the camp fire.

Jane Craig told of yesterday's adventure. A native boy had been washing his hands in a river when a crocodile attacked him. He was brought to the Craigs who in turn drove him to the nearest hospital, which was miles away. When they got there, the hospital didn't have any anesthesia. The boy kept screaming while he was being stitched up.

"It was unbearable," Jane said. "I kept wondering how I'd react if it was one of my own children."

Fortunately the doctor was hopeful that the boy would be able to use his hands again.

Jane and Ian also told about the shooting of a lioness on the ranch. She had been killing the ranch's cattle, so the Craigs decided she had to be gotten rid of. Ian Craig—

who was a game warden and therefore allowed to deal with problem predators—took his rifle and shot the lioness.

Two nights after the shooting, Ian woke up in the middle of the night with an awful premonition. In his dreams, he had suddenly realized that the lioness had cubs, and they would be starving to death. He was distraught. The next morning, he went out with a spotter and found the cubs and brought them home. They were cute as kittens and were cuddled in laps for a month or so. When they began to turn into lions, the Craigs sent the growing cubs to George Adamson, the famous conservationist, who looked after a pride in a national park called Shabba. Years ago, George Adamson and his wife, Joy, had raised a lioness named Elsa, made famous by a book and movie entitled *Born Free.*

The Craigs were leaving as Anna Merz arrived. She came not in a spaceship with winking lights but in a beat-up, four-wheel-drive Suzuki with no wing mirrors. But she turned out to be as strange and wonderful as E.T.

CHAPTER
SEVEN

A LOVE STORY

Farewell, farewell, you old rhinoceros,
I'll stare at something less prepocerous.

NNA MERZ would have hated Ogden Nash. She was as fierce as a rhino mother in defending the reputation of "her" rhinoceroses. She believed that her adopted species was a victim of cruel and unfair stereotyping and prejudice. And she wasn't going to have it! Not anymore!

"Rhinos are very intelligent!" she proclaimed, sitting beside our camp fire with a drink in her rough hand.

I was glad she hadn't been able to hear my thoughts earlier. Nonetheless I felt rebuked for having considered rhinos to be dumb latter-day dinosaurs.

"Rhinos are as intelligent as elephants," she declared. "Rhinos communicate by breathing, by a breathing pattern."

An article in *National Geographic* had recently reported evidence that elephants communicate with rumblings too low for the human ear to hear. But Anna was sure that a rhino could do anything that an elephant could do, except use its nose to drink. And who would want to?

"There are eighteen breathing noises that I can understand," she said. "There is a breathing greeting that you can hear from a hundred yards away. It's a long outward breath. There is a breathing pattern that means, 'Who are you?' It's a medium breath, two short breaths, and a long breath. I persuaded a very aggressive male named Godot to come to me by calling, 'Who are you?' He came right up to me and said, 'Who are you?' Then the conversation broke down because I didn't know what to say next."

Even Taylor and Matthew were listening raptly to this small woman who loved such huge creatures.

"Samia can put whole sentences together," Anna went on. "She will make the sound for 'raining,' then the sound for, 'Come and play,' then the sound for, 'Where are you?' I have to go out and say, 'No, I can't play.' She goes crazy when it rains and would knock me across the yard. It is really exciting when you can understand what they are saying. They think I'm another rhino but with an accent."

Our American ears also thought she had an accent. She was born just outside London but was brought up just outside Cornwall. She had lived in Africa many years but still had England in her mouth.

"We had a very gentle rhino named Morani," Anna Merz continued. "He was beaten up by our dominant male, Godot. His backside was injured so that he couldn't pass water. So Morani had to be moved to another area to save his life. He was the first male rhino in the new Kashogi Rhino Sanctuary. I didn't see Morani for eighteen months. Then I paid him a visit in his new home. From a hundred yards away, I gave a greeting breathing. He came straight up to me. He put his horn right up to me. That was the most exciting thing that had ever happened to me in my life. It vindicated my idea that rhinos are intelligent."

Derek suggested that we all go in to dinner. We entered

the canvas mess tent and took seats in canvas chairs. We asked Anna to sit at the head of the table where a napkin ring carved in the shape of a rhinoceros awaited her.

"What made you decide to try to save rhinos?" I asked.

"I'd lived for twenty years in West Africa," Anna said. "I'd seen extinction. I saw how fast it could happen. I knew much more than the people out here. Nobody believed it could happen here. But I knew it could and I was worried about the rhino. In 1982, I came as a tourist to Lewa Downs and met the Craigs. I had some money and they had some land. We started the fence in January of 1983. I moved here in January 1984. We got our first rhino in March of 1984 which we named Godot because we had been waiting for him so long. We closed the fence and released the rhino in April of 1984."

Then Anna Merz told her great love story—a truly moving tale of motherly love.

It began during the hard winter of 1985. A cruel drought killed the plant life and soon the animal life was starving. The kudu died on the sides of the hills. The rhinos' ribs showed through their thick skins.

Into this hungry place came a young pregnant female rhino who had been moved from her home range to save her from poachers. Between three and four in the afternoon on February 15, this rhino, whose name was Solia, gave birth to a calf. Then she got up and marched away from her baby without looking back. She evidently didn't have any milk, perhaps because of the drought, perhaps because of the stress of the move. Knowing she couldn't feed her calf, she turned her large back on it. The baby lay in the grass crying. Anna watched from the other side of the valley. When darkness fell, the mother was farther away than ever.

The next morning, Anna rushed to the baby to see if

it was still alive. It was. She listened to it cry for hours. While keeping watch, Anna got on her radio and started organizing a plan to keep the calf alive if the mother did not return. She contacted a veterinarian who suggested that the big baby be fed a diet of half low-fat milk and half skimmed milk with a splash of syrup. When the mom didn't come back by late afternoon, Anna filled a five-gallon can with this cow's-milk recipe and improvised a nipple. The abandoned baby rhino whimpered in fear but eventually drank some milk.

It was getting dark again. Anna parked her Land Rover near the calf to try to guard against its being eaten by hyenas during the night. She stayed in her truck all night keeping the vigil.

The next morning, Anna fed the foundling again. The childless woman stayed with the baby rhino all day—the third day of its life—and continued to feed it every three hours. Still the mother did not return to the baby she had produced. Anna never left.

As darkness was falling once more, Anna gave up on the mother and took the baby home with her. She placed the baby in the stable, as if she were reliving a combination of Noah's Ark and the Christmas story. But at midnight, she gave in and brought the baby rhino into the house. She tucked the huge infant into her own bed and then got in beside it. She even attempted to comfort it with hot-water bottles.

The next day, Anna continued to feed the baby every three hours. It was a female. Her new "mother" named her Samia.

In the evening, Anna's husband returned from Nairobi and was introduced to the new member of his family who would not only be sharing his house but his bedroom. At least, he and his wife had twin beds. Her husband thought the separate beds were an even better idea when the diarrhea started.

After five weeks, Anna Merz got in touch with Daphne Sheldrick who operates an elephant orphange on the grounds of Nairobi National Park. Daphne had dedicated her life to saving the world's largest land mammal, but occasionally took in a few orphan rhinos when they had nowhere else to go. She told Anna that baby rhinos couldn't tolerate cow's milk, just as some human children couldn't. So the rhino calf should be fed what those human infants are fed: nondairy formula.

At first, the new diet made Samia even worse. Her diarrhea went from bad to epic. Her already low temperature dropped.

"Having a rhino in bed with you with diarrhea takes a lot of dedication," Anna recalled. "I was determined I wasn't going to let her die. I had raised a lot of chimps in West Africa. You can stick them in nappies and rubber diapers. But you can't do that with a rhino."

Anna's husband moved out of the bedroom and into his office, but after several months Samia started getting better. And she started putting on weight. At birth, the baby weighed about seventy pounds, but within a few months it had grown to two hundred pounds. Samia was so big that Anna could no longer lift her into bed at night. She would lift the baby rhino's front feet onto the mattress and then get behind her and push her on up. Then they would sleep together, the little "mother" and her "baby" who was twice her size.

When Samia was four months old, Anna finally moved her back into the stable. At night, she wrapped the baby rhino in a rug to keep her warm.

"She looked like a huge armadillo gone mad," Anna recalled.

JUST WHEN the baby rhino began to look and act as if it might actually survive, something happened that threatened to interrupt her convalescence. Anna received word that Pope John Paul II, who planned a papal visit to Kenya, wanted to bless baby Samia.

"I was furious at the Pope," Anna remembered.

Her little rhino wasn't well enough to travel. The Pope could just find himself another baby animal to sprinkle or kiss or lay hands on or whatever he was going to do. Let him bless an elephant!

Anna got in her Land Rover and headed for Nairobi. She was going to see the government and tell some people off. She got as far as the Lewa Downs airfield—a dirt landing strip cluttered with game animals—where David Craig intercepted her. When she stopped to talk, he handed her a big glass of vodka.

"This business with the Pope has got to stop!" Anna said angrily.

"Drink the vodka," David said.

She took a gulp.

"If you want to get kicked out of the country," David continued, "this is the way to go about it."

By the time she had finished her vodka, Anna had been persuaded to delay her trip.

A little while later, Anna Merz and David Craig met once again at the Lewa Downs airstrip, but this time it was to load Samia into a crate and then stuff the crate into a small plane with propellers. David said the plane wouldn't be able to get off the ground. And if by some papal miracle it did, the overloaded aircraft would never make it over the mountains. But the government officials were less afraid of crashing than of disappointing the Pope.

The heavy plane waddled down the dusty airstrip, straining, straining, straining. Anna could see trees rushing at them through the windshield. She was terrified that she had gone to all that trouble, lived through all those diarrhea nights, to save Samia's life, only to see her baby crushed in a moment of chauvinistic stupidity. The glory of Kenya wasn't worth her Samia's life. Meanwhile, the little rhino was going mad inside her crate. Anna was just plain *mad*.

At the last moment, the plane somehow hopped off the earth, barely clearing the tree line. But Samia still wouldn't calm down. Now everybody was afraid she would fall right through the bottom of the aircraft. They hadn't counted on a baby being quite so big or jumping up and down. Anna could imagine her Samia falling through all that empty air and then hitting the face of Africa the way a bug hits a windshield. Some bug.

When they reached the mountains, the pilot agreed that his airplane, pregnant with rhino, had no chance of clearing the peaks. So he decided to fly around them. Which was all right but he was afraid they might run out of fuel.

By the time they finally landed in the Masai Mara Game Reserve in far southwestern Kenya, Samia was frantic, sweating, and dehydrated. Anna wasn't in much better shape. She was angry with everybody including herself.

She was mad at herself because she had forgotten to pack something. She had remembered to pack Samia's formula. She had remembered to pack the baby's pajamas— the rug she wore at night. But she had forgotten to pack Samia's potty.

Since rhinos use a communal latrine when they relieve themselves, Anna realized that she should have brought along some rhino droppings to help put her baby in the mood. But she hadn't. Now the little rhino, who was about to be blessed by the Pope, was constipated. Who knew what might happen?

"We'll give her an enema," said an official.

"No, you'll hurt her!" cried Anna.

She was supposed to fly right back to Lewa Downs immediately. She hadn't even been invited to the ceremony at which her baby was to be blessed by the Pope. She was the wrong sex and the wrong color. Since she hadn't planned on staying, she hadn't brought any cash or credit cards. But she couldn't leave her Samia in that condition. So she borrowed some money from the head of the Masai Mara lodge so she could stay with her baby until it had a bowel movement.

"We'll have to get her some rhino droppings," Anna said.

"We hardly have any," said an official. "We have maybe six rhinos in a 10,000-square-mile park. Droppings may be hard to find."

"Then I'll have to make do with zebra droppings," she said. "Anyway I'll try it. They look similar."

"There are a lot of lions," he said. "Stay away from the trees."

At six o'clock in the morning, Anna led Samia forth into the wilderness in search of the illusive droppings of zebra. The "mother" kept looking all around for the lions who wanted to eat her "baby." She kept her charge as far away from the trees and even bushes as possible.

When she finally did find some zebra droppings, Anna got down on her hands and knees and sniffed them the way a rhino would. Then she stood up and scuffed the droppings. She gave them several good kicks. Samia watched her "mother" curiously but did not seem to be interested in or fooled by what the zebra had left behind. Maybe the little rhino was not only smart but *too* smart. Perhaps this ruse wasn't going to work after all.

Fearing the enema, Anna decided she had to keep trying. So she led the way and Samia followed. Fearing lions, she kept glancing at the trees. She might have been a suburbanite walking her dog in the park, but this was the biggest dog in the world. Hearing a noise, an alarmed Anna looked behind her and saw something really fright ening: a minibus.

The minibus was filled with tourists whose hands were filled with cameras. Anna, who lived in isolation with her husband in the middle of her own sanctuary, wasn't comfortable with strangers. She wished they would go away. They made her feel even sillier than she felt already. An unlikely parade marched across the Masai Mara . . . Anna . . . followed by her faithful Samia . . . followed by the van. Were the lions amused as they watched from the cover of the trees?

Finding another clump of zebra droppings, Anna hesitated. Could she really bend down and sniff this excrement with all those strangers watching and taking her picture? Well, what else could she do? So she got down on her knees as if to pray and leaned over and smelled the droppings. *Click. Whir. Click. Whir.* Then she stood and contemplated her next task. Could she kick these feces while she was posing for so many photographers? But she had no alternative. So she scuffed and kicked and listened to the cameras. What must they think of her? Making the situation even worse, Samia just looked at the disturbed droppings, not moved to do anything.

So the parade moved on. Anna would look at the ground for droppings, look at the trees for lions, and look behind her for tourists. The droppings were hard to find.

The lions were invisible. But the tourists were multiplying. Another minibus joined the first. The parade was growing longer. But Anna couldn't call off her quest. Samia needed relief.

Now Anna became a victim of a new law of the jungle. This law holds that safari minibus drivers don't look for animals—they look for other minibuses. Any time these drivers see a herd of vans, they know something interesting must be going on. So they head in that direction. The minibuses following Anna and Samia attracted other minibuses the way vultures on carrion draw other vultures. The parade kept getting longer and longer and longer.

"Soon all the minibuses in the Masai Mara were following us," remembered Anna. "I felt like an idiot. After three hours, Samia finally did her stuff."

Hallelujah!

Anna carefully gathered up the droppings and put them in a bag. Now she could make a proper latrine for Samia.

"Then I was kicked out of town. Out of the Mara."

So Anna wasn't there to see Pope John Paul II bless her beloved Samia. She still wasn't invited, even after she had performed such a Herculean task to insure the dignity of the ceremony. So she began to hope that something would go wrong after all.

"I had a vision of Samia getting her horn under the Pope's robes and tipping him over."

But the baby rhino's manners turned out to be impeccable—and her bowels were well behaved too—when she met the Holy Father.

But when Samia finally came home to Anna, the baby rhino was sick all over again. Once more, she had a depressed temperature and diarrhea. Once again, the bed was soiled in the night. Once more, Anna was afraid she might lose her "baby." The "mother" patiently nursed her "child" to health.

WHEN SAMIA got better, Anna started taking the little rhino for walks every day. Usually the family dog would accompany them.

"I told Samia what to eat," she remembered. "I told her what to do. I introduced her to other rhinos and other rhinos' droppings."

One day, Anna and Samia and the dog walked around a bush and found themselves face to face with Juno whose horns suddenly looked like Mount Kenya and Mount Kilimanjaro. Anna loved rhinos, but she was smart enough to be afraid of them. Samia was startled too, since Juno was the first other rhino she had ever seen in her life. Anna gave the alarm snort and started running down the hill as fast as she could.

In the wild, when a rhino calf is frightened, it runs underneath its mother for protection. That is instinct. In that respect, Samia wasn't any different from any other little rhino. She was frightened and did what came naturally. She ran under her "mother" who was half her size.

"Samia ran under my legs," Anna remembered. "I was riding her. Which startled her. So she ran under a thorn bush. I lost my spectacles and my teeth. Samia stepped on the dog's tail, and the dog bit Samia on the nose. It was bedlam."

ONE NIGHT, Anna was taking a bath when she heard her front door open. She was frightened because she was alone in the house. Her husband was out of town.

"Who's there?" she called.

Samia poked her head through the bathroom door. Anna was glad to see her "baby," but suspected she was in for trouble. Samia headed for the bathtub as if she were going to get in it with her "mom." So Anna jumped out of the tub. She didn't want to be crushed—or drowned in her own bath water.

Anna ran for the bedroom with Samia following right behind. Remembering the good old days, Samia started trying to get into Anna's bed. But the bed collapsed. Its legs went in all directions of the compass.

Roaming around the house, Samia got stuck in the doorway to the dining room. Anna had to grease her with cooking oil to get her out.

"IN THE past six months, there's been a subtle change in Samia," Anna said. "Before, if she sensed danger, she would run under me or get behind me. Now she runs in front of me. She protects me. I feel safe because if we meet a buffalo, she will protect me.

"She used to knock me around, but now she's gentle with me. I used to have to wear steel-toed boots because she was always stepping on my feet. Now she is careful not to.

"I used to teach her to climb steep places. She was clumsy. I would get behind her and push her up the hill. Now when we come to a steep place, she holds her tail out until I take hold of it. Then she pulls me up the hill."

Our camp fire had burned down to coals. Matthew was asleep. I walked Anna to her Suzuki.

She said, "Samia can open the car doors with her horn."

She started the engine and drove home to her rhinos—
to one in particular.

THE NEXT morning, we drove past the rhino reserve
to say good-bye to Anna and Samia. They were in the
front yard playing and came to greet us.

I was surprised to discover that my nose felt too long
and itched. I wanted to rub it on something. I was a rhino.
I was Samia. I gave a long greeting snort.

CHAPTER
EIGHT

BIGGER
GAME

WAS SAD to leave Lewa Downs where I felt so at home. As we drove away, I was already homesick for it and the peace I had found there. I had felt the same way when I finished reading T. H. White's *The Once and Future King.* I was unhappy because I couldn't live in that magic land anymore. I missed Merlin.

We drove north on red-dirt roads over what Derek called MMBA: miles and miles of bloody Africa. The land seemed to get drier and drier with every passing mile. If we kept going in this direction long enough, we would reach the Great Sahara Desert.

Our destination was a desolate corner of Kenya named for a tall, handsome tribe: Samburu National Park. This rough land had brought forth a people of porcelain delicacy. The women were as colorful as the landscape was drab. We passed them walking along the road wearing brightly colored robes and fabulous beaded necklaces that started just under their chins and reached halfway down their breasts.

They looked like brilliant vases with long slender spouts moving across the desert. My eye went again and again to the gorgeous chokers around their throats. This was a land of graceful necks.

I saw a blur and Derek slammed on the brakes. As the Land Cruiser skidded to a stop, the blur came into focus. A herd of camels—wild and living free—were crossing the dusty road. We really were in the desert. And yet once again, I was feeling right at home. I kept asking myself: *Why?*

We gave the dromedaries the right-of-way and then drove on beneath the dome of the cathedral sky. As the land got drier, the blue in that sky got thinner and thinner. The cathedral ceiling was fading to white. And the smells thinned out along with the colors. Odor hitchhikes on moisture and there were very few rides out here. You couldn't even smell a giant in this air, but that didn't mean there weren't any giants around.

Since we had already been in Africa for a few days and still hadn't seen an elephant, Derek was getting nervous because he was afraid we were getting impatient. In his experience, Americans never seemed to feel they were really in Africa until they had seen their first elephant. Derek knew that a large herd often wandered back and forth across the dry and dusty plains of Samburu. So he was carrying us across this wasteland to look for them. At about five o'clock in the afternoon, we came across one of the great, gray, almost mythical beasts standing in a clearing.

Derek drove the Land Cruiser off the road so we could get closer. All of us—including a hitch-hiking park ranger—climbed up on top of the car for a better view. As we drew nearer, the big bull elephant started to retreat. We followed. We were right on his tail as if we were circus elephants—the flesh-and-blood elephant leading, the metal elephant right behind. Then the fleshy elephant headed off through the brush toward the river where we couldn't follow.

Derek put the Land Cruiser in reverse and started backing up slowly. Those of us on the roof looked behind us just in time to see an even larger bull burst out of the brush and charge toward us. Down below behind the wheel, Derek couldn't see what was going on and was oblivious.

Watching the elephant's huge angry ears flapping, I grabbed for my camera to record the tragedy. Lesley felt elated by the danger. Taylor felt excited, too. Derek didn't feel anything because he didn't know what was going on. The elephant kept coming, seemingly intent on making a man-and-metal sandwich.

"Go forward!" shouted the park ranger.

"Reverse!" screamed Mandiza, proving he could speak some English.

Derek got excited and simply stepped down hard on the gas pedal, gunning the car. Since the car's gears happened to be engaged in reverse, the Land Cruiser raced backward. But the driver still had no idea what the emergency was. Nonetheless, the Land Cruiser was now charging the elephant that was charging the Land Cruiser. Ears flapping, wheels spinning, emotions surging . . .

The elephant charged right at us—all I could see was eyes and forehead—and at the last moment veered off to the left.

When we all calmed down, Derek said he had done just the right thing without knowing he was doing it. He explained that when an elephant charges you, you are supposed to charge him back. Which is what he had done. By accident. An accident had saved us from an accident.

We left our first elephants behind, but soon came upon others. A family of gray behemoths were all mixed up with a family of gray-brown baboons. Derek explained that baboons like to hang out with elephants because the giants shake the trees—sometimes even knock trees over—and bring down showers of delicious nuts. A mother elephant and her baby ate leaves and branches next to a mother baboon and her baby munching on nutmeats. A giraffe wandered about in the background.

Driving on, we came upon herds of animals gathered around Buffalo Springs, a welcome oasis in this desert. Before us lay a large, circular clearing covered with lush grass. Placed at regular intervals on this meadow were blobs of color . . . the mahogany of the impalas . . . the gray of the oryx . . . the reddish brown of the warthogs . . . the tan of the Thomson's gazelles . . . Africa's artist's pallet. The oryx were particularly beautiful with long, straight horns which, when seen from the side, looked like the horn of a unicorn and may have given rise to the myth.

Derek explained that the springs that had brought the animals had come to Kenya the same way we had just escaped from that elephant: by accident. It happened back during World War II. The Italians, who had already taken over Ethiopia, wanted to expand their territory. So they sent bombers into Kenya to pound Nanyuki, but the pilots miscalculated and dropped their bombs in the middle of the desert instead. These bombs blew holes in the concrete-hard desert floor, creating springs! Which explained how Buffalo Springs came to be there and suggested why the Italians hadn't taken over the world. We drank Cokes to toast the springs.

We didn't see any gerenuk near the springs because they don't drink water. The gerenuk and the elephants are the glories of Samburu. We had seen the one, so now we went looking for the other. We soon came across a half-dozen of these delicate antelopes, a buck and his harem, feeding on the tiny leaves of acacia bushes which provided them with not only food but drink. For they were somehow able to extract water from the gray, dusty vegetation.

Gerenuk are the Audrey Hepburns of the animal kingdom. They have long, thin, graceful necks. Their bodies are thin, too, and they have stiltlike, spindly legs. They also have huge round ears. So perhaps they look like the children Audrey Hepburn and Alfred E. Newman might have had. But fortunately they favor their mother more than their father. The gerenuk of Samburu reminded me of the Samburu women. What was it about this harsh country that caused it to be populated by such delicate creatures with such wonderful necks?

Leaving the buck and his wives to enjoy their acacia banquet in peace, we followed a road that climbed steadily to the top of high, dry plateau. As the sun was flirting with the horizon and the shadows lengthening, we discovered a large bachelor herd of perhaps thirty gerenuk. A couple of bachelors faced off and began dueling with their saber horns. If they learned to fence well enough, they might win a herd of females someday. The larger gerenuk soon drove off the smaller. Size seems to count for a lot in the animal world.

Then two gerenuk did what sets them apart from all other antelope. Actually, it sets them apart from all other *animals* except for man and the other primates. They stood up on their hind legs. They didn't rear up. They didn't stagger. They just stood up the way *we* do. Their balance was almost as good as our own. They stood up in order to eat from the otherwise out-of-reach branches of an acacia tree. The gerenuk hooked their forefeet over lower limbs to help them keep their balance. If evolution had dealt this animal a different "hand," they would have had thumbs and fingers instead of hooves. They are antelope who aspire to join *our* club. Or perhaps they want to join the giraffe club, for they are the only animals who give the long necks any competition at all.

Two more gerenuk stood up on their hind legs. I remembered my mother telling me not to eat standing up. Then another gerenuk stood up. Five in all. They were hungry customers in a cafeteria, standing up and hanging onto their trays. For some reason, they looked like little old men. As the sun sank beneath the horizon, the standing gerenuk's tall shadows got taller and taller and taller.

Since it was getting dark, we headed for our own dinners. On the way "home," we saw leopard tracks. Derek dropped us off at the park's lodge since we wouldn't be at Samburu long enough to justify making camp. He left us with instructions to meet him in the restaurant at eight o'clock for dinner. We were right on time, but he wasn't. We waited an eternity, but he never arrived. Had the leopard gotten him?

A little irritated, we left the restaurant and went looking for our AWOL safari guide. We found Derek attempting to repair the carburetor of his Land Cruiser. He had a helper whom he introduced as "Willy Gerenuk."

Willy turned out to be a German scientist who had been studying gerenuk since 1977—as long as Taylor has been alive. He started out, as he put it, "like Robinson Crusoe," alone on top of a big rock. He lived by himself in a tent and paid his own meager expenses. A large snake eventually took up residence under his canvas home. Of course, he did all he could to drive the snake away. When he finally succeeded, the rodents moved in. So when the snake showed up again, he welcomed it home with open arms. From then on he had a friend—his Serpent Friday— and no more rodents. A couple of years ago, he finally received a grant from the German government to continue his research.

Willy Gerenuk told us that one gerenuk family, a male and a couple dozen females, was in the process of expanding its territory. But whose land would they take? They seemed bent on expropriating the territory of the bachelor herd who were old friends of ours. A protracted battle was playing itself out. I was pulling for the bachelors since I knew them better.

On the one hand, Willy Gerenuk appeared to be as exotic and eccentric as his beloved, upstanding antelope. But on the other hand, this Gerenuk man seemed remarkably familiar, an old friend, a spiritual brother, what Joseph Conrad called a "secret sharer," what Charles Baudelaire called *"mon semblable—mon frère,"* what Jimmy Stewart called "Harvey" in a movie about a big-eared alter ego. For in Willy, I recognized another searcher trying to solve a riddle, a mystery. I was fairly sure that he had not spent over a decade in a tent on an African rock simply because he wanted to unravel the secrets of the gerenuk. He wanted that, of course, but he must also have been after bigger game. Surely his real goal was to unravel the mystery of Africa itself. We were on the same quest, but he had a dozen years' head start. I felt jealous and competitive and achingly sympathetic. I wished him good fortune on his long pilgrimage. And I felt that he wished me luck as well.

The next day on our early morning game drive, we came across a gerenuk fawn looking like Bambi without spots. Its big eyes were real rather than just the vision of a cartoonist. When the baby saw us, it ran underneath a bush and stayed there without moving. Willy had told us young gerenuk spend most of their time doing just that. They hide under bushes because the predator most likely to prey upon them is the eagle.

CHAPTER NINE

HEART OF DARKNESS

ID WE look like an eagle to gerenuk fawns cowering beneath their shrubs? The twin-prop Cessna carried us back to Nairobi where we transferred to a Kenya Airways 707. After a two-hour delay, we took off and flew for three hours almost due west. The air was turbulent which seemed appropriate since we were on our way to visit an often turbulent land. From the air, Rwanda resembled a tempestuous ocean with giant green waves, which closer inspection turned into mountains, but even after the illusion of violent water passed, that sense of storm remained.

Rwanda lies slightly to the east of Africa's midline, where the continent's heart would be. In some ways, it is—or at least has been—a heart of darkness. For in the past, this piece of Africa has been a murderous place.

Cut off from the rest of the continent by high mountain ranges to the west and Lake Victoria to the east, it is a very isolated place. Africa's original colonizers, the Arab slave traders, left it alone. So did the Europeans until comparatively recently. For eons, it was Eden before the fall, but the fall would come.

The original inhabitants of this Garden were pygmies. Then a slightly taller tribe known as the Hutus descended upon the land and displaced the little people. Then about four hundred years ago, another even taller tribe called the Tutsis—sometimes referred to as the Watusis—invaded the area. In terms of size, the Tutsis were to the Hutus as the Hutus had been to the pygmies. The Tutsis did not drive out the Hutus but rather enslaved them. These giants founded a Tutsi kingdom that included all the territory that is now Rwanda *and* Burundi.

A Tutsi *mwami* or king sat on the thrown and other Tutsis made up the aristocracy. The much more numerous Hutus were serflike peasants. And so matters stood for centuries—laying a firm foundation for racial hatred.

About the turn of the century, Germany laid titular claim to this part of Africa, but it was not a gifted colonizer and did little more than color the area German on its maps. They sent in a few missionaries and set up a few trading stations. But they left the Tutsi *mwami* on the throne and allowed him to rule.

After the Germans lost World War I, they were stripped of their colonies. When the victors divided up the world anew, the Tutsi kingdom was given to Belgium as a protectorate. The Belgians kept the Tutsi *mwami,* but they were more active than the Germans had been. They sent in bureaucrats and many more missionaries. For administrative purposes, the Belgians divided the kingdom into two sections—the northern called Rwanda, the southern called Burundi.

Moreover, they encouraged a much more important

and potentially deadly division: the one between the Tutsis and the Hutus. The Belgian bureaucrats favored the Tutsis, making sure they got the best educational opportunities and the best jobs. But the Belgian missionaries favored the Hutus since their religion told them to help the downtrodden. So ambitious Tutsis ended up going into the government and ambitious Hutus going into the church. And both tribes hated each other more than ever.

After World War II, this corner of Africa was made a United Nations trust territory. But the Tutsis still remained on the throne.

In Rwanda in 1959, the small but numerous Hutus— 85 percent of the population—rose up in bloody revolt against their tall, stately Tutsi masters. These Lilliputian peasants killed thousands of their larger masters and toppled the Brobdingnagian monarchy. Shortly thereafter, Rwanda and Burundi voted to become two separate, independent countries. Rwanda was ruled by the victorious Hutus. But the Tutsis clung to power in Burundi.

In 1972, fearing another bloody Hutu uprising, the Tutsi rulers of Burundi launched a preemptive strike . . . a preemptive mass murder . . . a preemptive genocide. Tutsi soldiers began slowly but systematically rounding up all Hutus with an education. They would visit a community, take away all Hutus with eyeglasses, and shoot them in the head. A few days later, they would come back and get all the Hutus who wore ties and kill them. Later still, they would return and abduct all the Hutus who wore white shirts and murder them. They did a thorough job of wiping out the entire class of Hutus who might possibly have had the potential to develop into leaders of their people. In all, the Tutsi soldiers massacred more than 150,000 members of the Hutu tribe—perhaps twice that number. But this vast bloodletting was a world away from the traditional news centers—and news bureaus—and so was largely overlooked by the world press and so the world.

WHEN RWANDA gained its independence, it was a democratic republic, but in 1973, a military officer named Juvenal Habyarimana took over the government. He established a relatively benevolent military dictatorship. Habyarimana is actually fairly popular in Rwanda in part because he is not nearly as corrupt as the leader of neighboring Zaire. Of course, Zaire is a country rich in natural resources with much to steal whereas Rwanda is a poor country with relatively little to plunder. Still Habyarimana is given considerable credit for being the more honest man.

"He drives his own jeep!" his supporters boast.

Juvenal Habyarimana rules over a land that is about the same size as Vermont, but which has ten times as many people. With a population approaching 7 million, Rwanda is the most densely peopled country in Africa.

IN 1988, the Hutus gained a measure of revenge for the 1973 massacre of their people in Burundi. That August thousands of Hutus poured across the border from Rwanda into Burundi armed with machetes. And they started hacking to death any Tutsis they could find—men, women, and children. Whole villages were wiped out. The short Hutus chopped off the legs of their tall Tutsi victims at the knees—literally cutting them down to size.

August in Burundi—as in many placcs—is school vacation. So many Tutsi parents had sent their children north to the mountains to visit grandparents who still lived in rural settings. The grandchildren were supposed to have a few weeks to enjoy nature, but instead many of them were exposed to the worst side of human nature.

The editor of the newspaper in Ntaga had sent his children to visit his parents in the countryside. Which was where the Hutus with the machetes found them. The editor lost his parents, several brothers and sisters, a few in-laws, and all nine of his children.

The Tutsi government retaliated by sending in the army to restore order and conduct a countermassacre. And their guns made them more efficient killers. The Hutus with their machetes left messier bodies, but the Tutsis with their rifles left more bodies. Some 10,000 died in all in this mutual massacre.

In Joseph Conrad's *Heart of Darkness,* his antihero Kurtz cries out, "The horror! The horror!" This could serve as an epitaph for these years of massacre.

Even now, only a few planes fly into this country each week, so relatively few outsiders visit this dark heart of Africa. Rwanda remains isolated.

Landing in Kigali, the capital of this star-crossed Shangri-la, we transferred to a white minibus for the long, bumpy drive to Gisenyi where we would be staying for the next couple of days. It was a difficult but gorgeous trip. Rwanda is sometimes called the Switzerland of Africa because of its beautiful mountains. The average altitude of the country is almost a mile high, which makes the average temperature only sixty-eight degrees. But this equatorial Switzerland differs from the one in Europe because patchwork fields climb right up to the tops of its mountains. Rwanda looks like the farms of Holland superimposed upon the peaks of Switzerland. So much land is cultivated because there are so many mouths to feed. The beautiful people in this beautiful land always face the real danger of starvation.

Rwanda, with all its natural wonders, is one of the poorest countries in Africa. And it keeps on getting poorer because its already too large population is increasing at an alarmingly fertile 3.7 percent a year. We drove past countless women carrying containers of water on their heads and babies on their backs. There were so many babies bound up in their colorful wraparounds—called *imikenyeros*—that the newborns seemed to be a part of the national costume. The efforts to control population have been a failure in large part because Rwandans think of children the way we think of Social Security: A large family increases your chances of being taken care of in your old age. And in Rwanda, old age begins at forty. The Rwandan people and the famous Rwandan gorillas have about the same life expectancy.

We drove for two hours on the narrow paved road that wound like a black serpent through Eden. Reaching the end of the asphalt snake at long last, we pulled up in front of Gisenyi's Meridien Hotel. Having left our tents behind, we would be sleeping under a wooden roof for the next three nights. We were shown to our quarters which looked like motel rooms. We ate room-service spaghetti with meat sauce and went to bed early because we would be getting up early.

"Do you think we can do this?" I asked in the night.

"No," Lesley explained.

CHAPTER
TEN

MOUNTAIN BROTHERS AND SISTERS

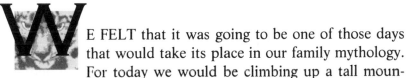E FELT that it was going to be one of those days that would take its place in our family mythology. For today we would be climbing up a tall mountain while we climbed back down evolution's family tree. We were going to be a family in the mist for we would be visiting the high, misty home of the gorillas who had been made famous by the martyred conservationist Dian Fossey. We would walk the same slopes she had walked. We would probably see some of the same gorillas she had seen and studied and described in her book *Gorillas in the Mist*. We would even be near the very place where murder had cut short her battle to save the mountain gorillas from extinction. We would be walking in her footsteps and in the footsteps of our own mighty "ancestors."

I hoped that we would learn more about gorillas, of course, and more about ourselves as the children of the gorillas, naturally, but also more about the Mother of Gorillas who had once been one of my heroines. I had read everything Dian Fossey had written. I had driven hundreds of miles to attend her occasional lectures back home in America. I had sat in audiences and listened to her "pant-hoot" like a gorilla. I had even heard her say that she liked gorillas better than people which was a little eccentric. But after her death, Dian Fossey had come to seem more than eccentric. There were reports of drinking binges on top of the mountain. There were stories of physical assaults on Africans whom she suspected of poaching. There were rumors that she had simply gone insane up there in those misty clouds. I was as interested in the mystery of who she really was as I was in the mystery of who killed her. But would climbing her mountain actually bring us any closer to her?

Actually my obsession with the Dian Fossey riddle went well beyond curiosity—beyond a search for truth or its reasonable facsimile—for she reminded me of my sister. They were both brunettes who wore their hair about the same length, down to their shoulders. They were both quite tall, which surely had not always been easy. They were both shy in their ways. And they had both been murdered, one by person or persons unknown, the other by drag racers. Shortly before her death, I had spoken to Dian Fossey after a lecture at Hunter College in New York City, and I had had the feeling that I was talking with my dead sister. I found the experience painful. Now I wanted to know more about this shadow of my sister. I hoped the painful climb up Dian Fossey's mountain would somehow ease the pain that my sister's memory always caused me, but I didn't tell anyone because I almost always avoided that subject. . . .

We had been repeatedly warned that it would be a most difficult climb. We could expect to fight our way up steep jungle slopes for from one to three hours depending upon where the gorillas happened to be today. If we could keep going long enough, we were virtually certain of seeing the giant apes, but not all climbers succeeded in their quest because some tired, gave up, and turned back. We were not particularly fit and so hoped for a short hike. Of course, we couldn't help worrying about what might happen if our gorilla hunt turned into an endurance contest. Each of us was wondering: Would I turn back? No, don't even think such thoughts. But would I?

I was afraid I might be growing accustomed to failure, might be coming to expect it, might even be going out to meet it more than halfway. Failure, my buddy, *"mon semblable—mon frère!"* Would I fail on this climb because I was used to failing? Would I bog down halfway up the mountain the way I had bogged down in the middle of my screenplay about magic? Would I leave the climb half done the way I had left the script half written?

This testing day began with a wake-up call at five o'clock in the morning. None of us had slept very well because we were excited and nervous. But we got up and dressed quickly in long pants and long sleeves because we had been warned of nettles. And we all made sure we had our gloves which were supposed to provide additional protection against the stinging plants. I had brought along some football gloves—the kind wide receivers wear—with Redskins logos on the back. All the others had purchased the type of gloves baseball players wear when they walk up to the plate to bat. But hitters normally wear only one glove. When they had gone into sporting good stores and asked for both left- *and* right-hand batting gloves, the sales clerks had looked at them as if they were crazy—or switch-hitters.

We put on thin pairs of propylene socks followed by thick pairs of wool socks. Then we laced up bulky Gore-Tex hiking boots which were as comfortable as bedroom slippers. We also stuffed brand new Gore-Tex rain gear into

Taylor's backpack which was normally used to carry books to school.

At breakfast in the large, almost-empty hotel dining room, Derek seemed unusually somber.

"I've got some bad news," he said. "Our driver tells me that children under fifteen aren't allowed to visit the gorillas. We'll just have to hope they don't look at Matthew too closely. I think Taylor can pass all right."

Taylor looked older than her twelve years, but Matthew appeared younger than his ten. The fruit cocktail with its exotic mix of tropical produce didn't taste quite as good any more.

At six in the morning, we all piled into a white minibus and headed for the gorillas. It was the beginning of a long journey. We drove along a two-lane, blacktop road that wound its way along the steep sides of volcanic mountains. I felt slightly ill at ease, not just because Matthew might not be allowed to see the gorillas, not only because the climb promised to be a test of character and strength, but also because I felt myself to be an alien in this landscape. I had been so comfortable, so at home, in the savannas of Kenya, but now I was an elephant up a tree.

On the ninety-minute ride to the first turning off place, a town named Ruhengeri, our guide tried to make our ten-year-old look like a fifteen-year-old. Derek took away Matthew's simple, wide-angle Kodak and hung his own Zeiss-Ikon with telescopic lens around the boy's neck because a fifteen-year-old would have a better camera. Derek also took away the orange Day-Glow string attached to Matthew's sunglasses because a fifteen-year-old wouldn't want to look silly. And Derek gave Matthew one of his own safari vests which was at least two times too big for him. We talked about painting pimples on his face with a ballpoint, but the road was too rough for such artwork. Having done about all we could, we stopped looking at Matthew and started observing Rwanda as it hurried past us.

"This can't be Africa," I said. "None of the trees have flat tops."

"All these trees are immigrants," explained Derek. "Rwanda cut down almost all its trees for firewood and to make charcoal. But then the soil erosion was so terrible that the government decided to try to bring the trees back. It needed a tree that wouldn't take a lifetime to grow. So it imported fast-growing eucalyptus trees from Australia."

Perhaps that was why I didn't feel at home here. The trees weren't the right trees. They were the wrong shape. But then why did flat-topped trees—so unlike the trees where I really lived—make me feel at home? And why did big, bushy trees—so like the trees at home—make me feel like such a stranger?

These leafy newcomers grew alongside the road. They also separated some fields—thin green lines—providing wind breaks. They all looked touchingly young, like Matthew and Taylor. Still we kept passing charcoal cookers, smoking metal cylinders, which went on turning tree wood into charcoal beside the road.

When we reached Ruhengeri, we stopped to buy Evian water for the trip up the mountain. It cost $5 a bottle.

"It would be cheaper to drink gin," Derek said.

Then we had a twenty-minute ride over a bumpy dirt road to the headquarters of the Mountain Gorilla Project. Leaving Matthew and Taylor in the minibus so no one would get a good look at them, we got out and headed for the main building. Soon we were chatting with Dean Anderson, the short assistant director of the project, and David Vekasy, a tall Peace Corps volunteer. We were getting along fine until Cali, our driver, walked up and joined the conversation.

"Nous avons un problème," he said in French, one of the two official languages of Rwanda. (The other is Kinyar-wanda.) He went on to say that our party included a boy who was under fifteen.

"You have to be fifteen to visit the gorillas," said Dean Anderson. "Do you have someone with you who is under age?"

"No," we lied badly.

"Could we take a look at the children?"

"Of course."

We walked back to the minibus and asked our ten-year-old and our twelve-year-old to step out. Matthew looked about seven. The Mountain Gorilla Project officials were so preoccupied with him that they didn't pay any attention to Taylor.

"We're sorry," Dean Anderson said, "but he can't go. We're afraid children under fifteen might spread childhood diseases to the gorillas."

We had supposed the age limit was to protect the chil-dren from the gorillas, but instead the rule was meant to protect the gorillas from the kids. So we stopped insisting that Matthew be allowed to go.

Jeff said he would remain behind with his son. Derek said he would stay too and take them on a hike.

Taylor, Lesley, and I said good-bye to the others and got back in our minibus for the drive to the foot of the mountain. We had been assigned to visit Group 11 today. Slightly over three-hundred gorillas—divided into thirty-two family groups—lived on this range of volcanic mountains. About half of them were regularly visited by tourists or researchers while the other half rarely met human beings at all. We would drive as close as we could to the place where our group had been seen the day before and then walk in from there. The van bounced over one of the worst roads

I have ever endured in my life. To call this track rough would be like calling Hitler not very nice. I held onto the seat in front of me and was in constant discomfort for forty-five minutes. The rough ride was softened by the smiles and waves and *bonjours* of black children along the way.

When we finally reached our destination, we piled out of the minibus, stretched our legs, and looked around. We didn't really know what was going to happen to us today—and were apprehensive—but we couldn't wait to get started.

Cali introduced us to our two guides, François and Jean, who wore olive-green military uniforms. One of them carried a machete. The other toted a rifle. What was he afraid of? The gorillas? Other wild animals? Poachers?

Lesley and I were also introduced to our porters. For some reason, Taylor didn't get one. Perhaps they figured she could take care of herself, and they knew her parents couldn't. I had never had a porter before except for a few minutes in a hotel. This was going to be an all-day porter. This was going to be a glimpse of the old Africa previously only experienced in safari books and Hemingway stories and Dark Continent movies. I was self-conscious and embarrassed. I wasn't any bwana. I didn't believe in a world of white bwanas and black porters. But here was my porter expecting employment. And in this economy, I was sure he was thankful for the job.

We handed Taylor's backpack—containing not only our rain gear but also our bottle of Evian water—to Lesley's porter whose name was Joseph. But we didn't have anything to give to my porter whose name was Aton. So we started our hike with my porter porting nothing. I was secretly pleased. It was my silent protest against the world of bwanas and porters.

We first walked through fields of pyrethrum which looked like scrawny daisies. This land was once a part of the gorillas' national park, but several years ago Robert McNamara and several other rich men who thought they knew what was best for the poor people of Africa came up with a plan to cut the park in half. As head of the World Bank, McNamara funded a program that turned many square miles of jungle and rain forest into these fields of pyrethrum from which an insecticide is made. Coincidentally, at just that moment, an English scientist was discovering how to make pyrethrum in a test tube for one-tenth the price.

We hadn't even reached the jungle yet and I was already asking myself: How do I feel? Am I tired yet? Am I going to make it? Will I fail?

The pyrethrum fields canted slightly upward, and I started breathing harder. But we were still just walking through farmland. We walked single file. There were eight tourists, the maximum number allowed to visit a group of gorillas on a given day. The line was lengthened by our guides and porters. One young man balanced a large picnic cooler on his head. When we reached a low stone wall, Lesley's porter took her hand and helped her over. Then my porter took my hand and helped me.

At the edge of the jungle, we paused for a reading of the rules. One of the French-speaking guides handed the English-language version of the rules to a woman named Viki Gascoyne who read them aloud. Don't leave any food or paper or anything else in the park because a gorilla might pick it up and catch a disease from you. Don't talk loudly when you are near the gorillas. Don't point at the gorillas. Don't shake the trees or move the branches. If a gorilla charges, crouch down, don't take a picture, and don't run. Don't defecate—but if you must, ask a guide to dig you a hole a foot deep. (Human fecal matter is an even graver threat to the health of gorillas than human gum wrappers.)

Always keep your head lower than the gorillas'. Don't take pictures with flashes. AND DON'T TOUCH THE GORILLAS.

After the reading of the rules, the guide named François wanted to tell us something about the group we were going to visit, but the only European language he spoke was French. So François gave his short lecture *en français*, and I translated into English. He said Group 11 contained ten members—a silverback, five females, two subadults, and two infants. Meanwhile, the other guide, Jean, was using his machete to cut bamboo walking sticks for everybody. The speech ended, the canes were passed out, and our adventure began in earnest.

In the beginning, we walked through a beautiful bamboo forest. The bamboo plants were as tall as trees. Their stalks were the size of posts. The canopy of leaves high above was so thick that it blocked out the sun, so no underbrush grew below, which made the walking relatively easy. We might have been ants walking across a birthday cake crowded with candles. The ground was even relatively level. Of course, I was going to make it. I might not feel at home, but I was beginning to feel more comfortable and optimistic.

"Let's tell Derek it was all straight uphill," Lesley said.

The air smelled new and fresh and green. (The atmosphere left behind in Kenya had been red and old.) The humidity kissed our faces with moist lips.

"Vous êtes fatigué?" asked François.

"Pas du tout," I said.

But gradually the earth underfoot began to tilt upward. Breathing got a little harder. Should I be worried? My porter, Aton, reached for my camera which was hung around my neck. I let him take it. I suddenly felt so much lighter I thought I could walk forever. No sweat.

I was toward the back of the line, but my energetic

daughter was at the head of the column, walking right behind the lead guide. She was having a lighthearted good time until she heard a rustling in the bushes. She was even more alarmed when she saw Jean the guide take out a bullet and load his gun.

BANG!

The report of the rifle shot reverberated through the bamboo. I suppose any gunshot is unnerving, but this one in the jungle seemed particularly so. It definitely wasn't a backfire. We weren't in backfire country. We heard some giant monster crashing through the bamboo.

"It was a buffalo," Taylor called. "Don't worry. He scared him off."

Soon we emerged from the bamboo birthday cake and entered a nettle nightmare. The nettles grew as high as my head so our entire bodies were at risk. We had thought we were well-armed against the nettles, but we were wrong. I felt the first sting just above my left knee. The nettles had penetrated right through my blue jeans and plunged their harpoons into my skin. Then I felt a similar burning on my left side. I zipped up my photographer's vest—the kind with twenty pockets—in an effort to keep out the enemy. Then I noticed that the backs of my hands were stinging. Examining my football gloves more closely, I saw that their fronts were made out of leather, but their backs were cloth. The nettles had no trouble getting in this backdoor. Lesley and Taylor said the backs of their hands were stinging too. Then a nettle hit me in the eye—my sore black eye—and really hurt. I had never felt less at home.

After climbing for about an hour and a half, we finally came to the place where the Group 11 gorillas had been seen the day before. Now the tracking began. Our guides followed a trail of broken limbs and gorilla shit. Lesley, who was walking ahead of me, pointed out some King Kong droppings.

The terrain changed from difficult to almost impenetrable. We had been walking along paths—narrow, crowded by nettles, often steep or muddy—but still paths. Now we were going where no human had ever gone before—at least not in a long time. From now on, the only path would be the one we made.

In the lead, Jean used his machete to cut limbs and vines. He slashed a path through the jungle's interlocking arteries and veins. But he did not chop a very big hole, just one large enough for him to get through, and he was not a big man. Taylor made it through all right, but even Lesley had trouble. And when I came to these holes, I felt like the biblical camel trying to get through the eye of a needle.

Perhaps our diminutive guides really did have a historic chip on their shoulders when it came to big people. After all, the shorter Hutu had suffered all those hundreds of years as the slaves of the taller Tutsi. Were they now getting back some of their own? At my expense? Was I this big person who had been captured and was being tortured by the little victors?

Actually our guide wasn't chopping a hole so much as a dark mine shaft through the thick jungle vegetation. Fighting my way down this tunnel, I was a pig who had been swallowed whole by a python. I was a too big lump of meat moving down its digestive tract. It seemed impossible that I would ever get from one end to the other.

We needed somebody to chop holes in the very air, for it was now thick and heavy with moisture. The humidity, which had been refreshing earlier, was now oppressive. It made every breath an effort. I felt as if I were walking and climbing underwater.

Then I fell. Aton pointed out some sharp twigs at eye level. While I was watching them so as not to get an eye poked out, my left foot got caught under a root. I started falling, thought I had saved myself, and then crashed full-length on the ground. I was embarrassed when everybody rushed to pick me up and ask if I was all right. I said I was fine, but actually I had hurt my problem left knee. If it stiffened up now, I didn't know what I would do. Or rather I was afraid of what I might have to do.

Soon we weren't walking on ground anymore—but on a thick matting of interlocking branches. Taylor said it was like hiking across layers of mattresses. With my walking stick, I could reach down and feel the earth some two or three feet below my feet. In some ways, it was more like climbing a giant tree than a mountain. I had nothing but branches underfoot, and whenever I took another step, I would reach with my hands for another branch or vine to hang on to. Occasionally, I got desperate enough to grab a handful of nettles to steady myself. My big feet were always slipping this way and that. Not only did this landscape not welcome me, not only did it not make me feel at home, it was actually hostile. It fought back.

I remembered James Wild, *Time* magazine's Nairobi correspondent, once telling me, "There's no easy way. You usually have to walk to see the miracles of Africa." But he hadn't mentioned that the walking would sometimes be like this.

I didn't feel at home in this mountain morass, but there *was* something all too familiar about it. The vines were as tangled and snarled as my thoughts had been lately when I sat down and tried to write. The jungle outside was a projection of the jungle inside. As a writer, whenever I fought my way through one obstacle, I would find another waiting on the other side. I tried to hack a passage through the dense growth of doubts and fears and complications, but the climb ahead of me seemed never ending, and I ended up doing a little less each day. I longed for a clear path in front of me, but the jungle simply grew ever more dense. I had all but given up writing, at least for the foreseeable future. Would I be forced to give up my climb up this gorilla mountain as well?

What did the guides think we were? Monkeys? I wished I weren't wearing boots so I could grip the branches with my toes. I wished my legs were shorter and my arms were longer so I could go through the tunnels in the vegetation on all fours instead of bent over and crashing into everything. I became absolutely convinced that humans did not stand erect and walk on two legs until they emerged from these jungles and ventured out onto the plains. Who would want to stand up in a place like this? Who could stand up?

As we climbed higher and higher—almost straight up it seemed—I really began to wonder if I was going to make it. I imagined stopping and sitting down and asking the guides to pick me up on their way back down the mountain. It disturbed me that I could even think such thoughts. I wanted to see the gorillas! I *would* see the gorillas! But what if I broke down physically or mentally?

Worrying about my own physical and mental resilience after only a couple of hours in this high jungle, I could better appreciate what this mountain might have done to Dian Fossey over the years. The constant climbing had been hard on her since her physical health was always fragile. The loneliness had been even harder. She had sought the isolation but surely had not foreseen its eroding effect. I was with a group but nonetheless felt alone for it was up to me—and me alone—to beat this mountain. My thoughts and emotions and doubts grew as tangled as the jungle through which I toiled. I wondered how long it would take me to go completely crazy.

My left knee had stopped hurting, but I was having a

hard time getting enough air. My upper body, which did the breathing, was actually more tired than my lower body, which did the climbing. My lungs were making an embarrassing racket. Except for my breathing, the mountains were quiet. I heard very few birds or insects. I was the loudest animal in the jungle. My lungs were screaming for help.

I was given some slight encouragement by the sight of some shit. It had been dropped by a gorilla and was glistening. It looked fairly fresh. I thought it was beautiful! Then I witnessed another hopeful sign. The guides told the porter who carried our picnic in a huge cooler to put down his burden and wait there. While I had been huffing and puffing and wondering if I was going to make it, he had been striding up the mountain with a refrigerator on his head.

I told myself: We must be close. This was no time to give up. Just a bit farther.

But we kept on climbing and climbing. The ascent was now hand-to-hand combat. Me against the mountain. Me against the vines that snared me. I was a too big Gulliver bound by jungle ropes. But most of all, it was me against myself.

More good news: soft, watery shit!

Aton handed me my camera and took away my walking stick and my hat. All the others were surrendering their walking sticks, too. Now we would have to fight the mountain unarmed.

I climbed a little higher and found the lead members of our party already taking pictures. Taylor had actually been the first of the civilians to see the gorillas. I was the last. We had started our climb at nine in the morning and now, three hours later, it was noon. I was so tired that I had trouble lifting my camera which wasn't heavy.

A couple of feet away, two young gorillas, babies really, were playing with each other. They were wrestling. In describing gorillas' actions, it is extremely difficult not to anthropomorphize. The word *wrestle* is usually applied to human beings. And yet that is what they were doing. No animal word would describe it as well. I saw them wrestling and I thought of a couple of boys playing in the dirt. (When I see young gazelles butt each other, I don't automatically think of boys roughhousing.) The two baby gorillas seemed to be having fun. But fun is what humans have. We don't automatically think of animals having fun, at least not as we know it. But these gorillas were definitely having lots of fun.

At the same time, they looked almost too much like toys to be believed. Toys come to life. Toys romping at midnight under a Christmas tree, only this Christmas tree was decorated with vines and nettles. Half human. Half toy. All gorilla.

When the baby gorillas moved on, so did we. The guides chopped through more brush and we struggled a few more feet up the mountain.

We came upon an adult gorilla sitting in his jungle pantry eating everything in front of him. He would pull down vines from overhead and stuff all the leaves into his cement-mixer mouth. It seemed so incongruous that such a huge, powerful animal should feed on something as delicate and insubstantial as a leaf. Those jaws seemed to be built for crushing rocks. When he finally got up and ambled away, we saw a narrow band of silver fur on his back. He was a junior silverback.

Struggling on, we came across the real thing, The Silverback. His fur had turned white from his shoulders to his hips. He was called Ndume, which means "powerful" in Swahili, and the name fit. He had lost one hand—perhaps to a poacher's snare—but he was still strong enough to rule his high kingdom. He had the calm, assured, unhurried, regal bearing of human royalty, but flies did buzz in and out of his great nose. He stared at me with great, liquid eyes.

And then flies buzzed in and out of my nose. I was the silverback. Perhaps I was overreaching by imagining myself the leader of a gorilla family. But his silver back reminded me of my silver chin. (My hair was still a reddish brown, but my beard was completely white.) Maybe the silver was the bond. Maybe I just wanted to feel like a king. And so I crowned myself king of the gorillas.

Once again, I had escaped from my ragged self and felt glorious. It was as though I had left my old, worn-out psyche behind and had ascended into another realm. I wasn't tired anymore. I wasn't out of shape anymore. I was strong. I had been healed. I had descended evolution's tree to an earlier me, a happier me, a more carefree me, an unselfconscious me, a me who wasn't smart enough for self-doubt or self-criticism or self-loathing. It was pure joy to have broken free of the bars of my own personality, to be outside the cage of self, to have escaped from the tawdry circus where my tricks no longer worked.

Now I looked like and felt like a leader. I had that quality of leadership that suggested I couldn't be flustered or ruffled by anything. Definitely not by anything as insignificant as the comings and goings of humans or flies.

The guides told me to crouch down. I had inadvertently disobeyed the rule to keep my head lower than the gorilla's. The guides didn't realize that I was allowed to hold my head as high as the silverback's because I was him and he was me. And I couldn't really have explained it to them even if my French were better. They had cast me as Anna and the Silverback as the King of Siam. So I played Anna, lowering my head, which pleased the King, who was also me. I thought: We must be related to gorillas, for our customs and even our vanities are so similar.

A baby gorilla, who had also forgotten that his head was supposed to be lower than the king's, climbed a bamboo pole and looked down at the silverback who did not seem to mind particularly. Ndume and I, like the King of Siam, could be indulgent with our children. Soon the baby came tumbling down, then climbed right back up again, a gorilla playing on God's own monkey bars.

I was not so indulgent of an older son who shook the trees and then hit me. I hit back and then chased my son up the hill. Why must teenagers always rebel against their parents?

After the excitement, I took my seat once again on my jungle throne. Then Taylor took my picture and her automatic flash blazed brightly. Would the King of Siam have tolerated such behavior from Anna? He would not! What about a proud silverback like me? I blinked et cetera et cetera et cetera. The guides got even more excited. They told Taylor that she would have to stop flashing or stop taking pictures. She adjusted her camera, the flash stopped flashing, I stopped blinking, and the guides stopped reprimanding et cetera et cetera et cetera.

No sooner was one crisis weathered than another literally appeared on the horizon. A blackback loomed on a bluff above us and started shaking the trees right over Taylor's head. It was interesting to observe the behavior of the twelve-year-old primate when alarmed: She ran straight into the arms of her mother.

Our guides indicated that it was time to move on. Which interrupted the trance—or whatever it was—that linked me to the ruling silverback. Leaving the king behind, we soon found ourselves with balcony seats for a show that might have been called *Bringing Up Baby*. Sitting on a ledge of earth, we looked down into a dell at a mother gorilla playing with her infant. They played just the way a human mother and baby would play, only on another scale of magnitude. This baby's head was as big as a whole human baby. This mother's head was the size of a baby buggy. It was like watching a mother Mack Truck play with a baby Volkswagen. And yet for all their size, they played gently. This mother was indeed a gentle giant—fee, fie, foe, fun. The mom was tickling the baby's feet and playing with its toes. Such behavior must have been based on more than instinct. We were watching recognizable motherly love. We were seeing familiar family life.

The baby, cradled in its mother's valley of a lap, eventually grew tired of the game and tried to crawl away. It had had enough of tickling and wanted to catch its breath. But the mother grabbed the baby and pulled it back. Mom wasn't finished playing yet. Baby didn't really seem to mind.

While we were mesmerized by the jungle madonna and child, we were attacked from the rear. A young blackback came up behind us and was not at all intimidated by finding us in his path. He just kept on coming right at us. Perhaps the guides hadn't read him the rules lately. No knocking down the visitors. No stomping the sightseers. No littering the national park with tourist bones. We all stepped politely aside and let him pass on all fours. Moving at his own unhurried pace, he came within a foot of us and then ambled off into the jungle.

Leaving our balcony, we moved on to the jungle equivalent of the Sistine Chapel. Brushing aside a thick curtain of vegetation, I was surprised to see Lesley seated quite near a gorilla who was sprawled on its back. They were as close to each other as cozy dinner partners. Lesley reached out to move a vine so she could see the ape better. Then the great animal—"thinking" Lesley was reaching out to it—reached out to the human. The gorilla reached back as if it were doing a backstroke. Lesley extended her hand also. The moment was like the one depicted on the ceiling of the Sistine Chapel. The Godlike human was reaching out to touch the humanlike animal.

It was like that moment Dian Fossey described in her book when a gorilla reached out and touched her. This incident was tremendously important to her. It was the reward for all her days and months and years of work. It was a rite of passage. It was an imprimatur of acceptance. She wrote that it was the first time in history that one species had reached out to another . . .

The guides stopped history from repeating itself by shaking a bamboo stick and ordering Lesley not to touch. *"Ne touchez pas!"* So Lesley and the gorilla were both disappointed, but it was still great. The ape is probably still scratching its head wondering why these strange naked apes work so hard to get close, but won't touch.

Why did the gorilla choose Lesley to reach out to? Did it just like blondes? Do blackbacks prefer goldtops? Or was it her personality? Her essence?

We paid a last call on the silverback with whom I so identified. He lay on his back and played with his toes which were the size of mayonnaise jars all in a row. Human babies lie on their backs and play with their toes in just the same way. Then the silverback got up and lumbered off into the jungle without saying good-bye.

Just then we heard a disturbance in the trees behind us. We turned just in time to see a huge blackback "charging" toward us. Was he really charging or just bluffing to see if we would move? We hardly had time to move. I spun as if I were the ape's toy top. Taylor ran behind me. The gorilla charged past us over the very same patch of ground where my daughter and I had been standing a moment before.

"Finis," called François.

Our visit to the gorillas was over. We were allowed only one hour. Otherwise the gorillas might get nervous. So we had to turn and walk away.

We followed Jean and François *up* the mountain. We were still climbing! I had been sure that once we found the gorillas, it would be downhill for us from then on. But I was wrong. We were climbing straight up again. We were tracking the illusive picnic lunch. After we had climbed a heartbreaking fifty yards, we found our quarry resting in a small clearing on top of a peak surrounded on all sides by walls of dense jungle.

When the picnic cooler was opened, I drank some Evian water and a Coke, but I could only eat a couple of bites of cheese sandwich. Lesley and Taylor did not seem to have much appetite either. We gave most of our picnic to the guides and porters, who welcomed it. Their appetites were fine. After lunch, Taylor and I were the only ones who lay down.

"Climbing this mountain is like childbirth," Lesley said. "You labor and labor and suffer and suffer. And then you are rewarded with a miracle and forget all about the pain."

All too soon, the guides got to their feet and started out again. Now at least we were going downhill, but the underbrush was still torture.

I too found the ordeal to be like a birth. My own. The tunnel hacked through the jungle was the birth canal, but I was just too big to pass through. I was sure I was never going to be born. I was an overgrown fetus in panic fighting to get out. But after an hour and a half of unremitting labor, I was finally delivered from my splendid misery.

CHAPTER ELEVEN

LIFE AND DEATH

HAT EVENING, while we were having dinner in the dining room of the Meridien Hotel, a ghost of the sixties appeared out of the mist. He had long, Wild Bill Hickok hair. He wore blue jeans and a green corduroy shirt. We later learned that he had originally come to Africa in 1973 "to save the world." He was Craig Sholley, the director of the Mountain Gorilla Project. We had left a message inviting him to dinner, but had been informed that he couldn't come because he was attending to a baby gorilla injured by a poacher's trap. So we hadn't expected him. But here he was. When he first introduced himself, my first response was: *Oh, no!* I suddenly felt as antisocial as Dian Fossey herself.

Then I noticed that he had someone else with him: Dave Vekasy, the tall Peace Corps volunteer whom we had met earlier. I remembered him well because he was a member of the posse that had caught us trying to smuggle Matthew up the mountain.

After our epic climb, I didn't think I had enough energy to make conversation. I barely had enough strength to breathe, and I was thinking about giving up even that much exercise because every breath hurt. But of course we had no choice but to invite them both to sit down and join us for dinner. I just hoped I wouldn't fall asleep at the table. Searching for something to say to our guests, I sorted through the rag-and-bone shop inside my head.

"How's the baby gorilla?" I finally asked.

"As a matter of fact," Craig Sholley said, "right now she's fighting for her life."

"What happened?"

"A couple of nights ago, the guides radioed down that a baby gorilla had gotten her hand caught in a poacher's snare. Young gorillas are in special danger because they are so curious and reach into everything—even traps."

But can an animal be curious in the true meaning of the word? Perhaps this animal.

The baby gorilla, perhaps with the help of the silverback, had torn the snare loose from the tree to which it had been tied, but the snare's loop was still wrapped tightly around the baby's wrist. And not even a silverback knew how to untie a knot.

"We left the next morning at 4:30," Craig continued.

"We were in the forest by six," Dave Vekasy joined in.

There seemed to be a special bond between these two, both of whom had been brought to Africa by the Peace Corps, Craig sixteen years ago, and Dave, still in the middle of his tour. But short-haired Dave admitted that he hadn't joined the Peace Corps for the same reason long-haired Craig had. Dave had signed up not to save the world but because he thought it would look good on his résumé and help him get a better job later on. Craig, the world saver, sounded like the authentic voice of his generation, and

Dave, the careerist, like the authentic voice of his. And yet here they both were in Africa, for their different reasons, trying to save the gorillas.

They went on with their story: At about noon, they finally reached the Susa Group, the only family of gorillas known by a name rather than a number. Dian Fossey had named the group after the Susa River, which flows through its range. She called its silverback John Philip because she enjoyed puns. Since her passing, the group's name had been retained, but the silverback had been rechristened Imbaraga which means "powerful" in Kinyarwanda. The Susa Group was closed to tourists that day so the rescue team could deal with the emergency.

They began with a "body check" of what was the largest "family" of gorillas in the mountains. High on the side of the tallest volcano, the humans located thirty apes. But one was missing. They couldn't find a baby named Umuyaga which means "wind" in Kinyarwanda. Wind wasn't near her mother or Imbaraga, the silverback. So they did a second check. Maybe they had just overlooked her. But the second time around, they still couldn't discover her. Gorillas are social animals who do not normally go off by themselves. Not unless something is wrong. Craig, Dave, and the others grew more and more worried.

The guides checked all the night nests. Every night, gorillas make new beds for themselves wherever they happen to be. They twist tree branches into circular platforms that look like birds' nests only they are so large they would have to be the nests of pterodactyls. But none of last night's nests contained the missing Wind. All they contained were feces, for gorillas foul their own beds. Craig speculated that the excrement helped to warm the gorillas against the cool of the mountain nights.

Really alarmed now, the search party began back-tracking the gorillas, all thirty of them. Since the various trails would take them in various directions, they agreed to meet back at a certain place at 1:30 in the afternoon. Fighting their way through the jungle, they all had plenty of time to weave dense, tangled fears. There were only about three hundred mountain gorillas known still to exist on earth— and now perhaps one less.

At 1:30 when they were all supposed to rendezvous at the meeting place, they were missing not only a baby gorilla but two guides. Namely Jean Basenarwabo and Joseph Nzabandora. But soon Craig's walkie-talkie crackled with the welcome news that the missing guides had picked up the trail of a young gorilla, a toddler really, traveling alone— very unusual behavior.

Jean and Joseph called in every ten minutes to report. The first call said that they were still on the toddler's trail and it was still alone. The second call was like the first. But the third excited call reported that they had found Wind. This two-year-old still had the snare around her hand, but at least she was feeding.

Then Jean and Joseph did something that was as unheard of as it was natural: They went over and picked up the hurt baby. In the past, humans who wanted to help gorillas had always had to "knock them down" with drugged darts. But this baby gorilla did not resist. For what may have been the first time in history, this primitive ape allowed a more advanced ape to help it without putting up a fight. The guides wrapped Wind in a poncho and covered her head with its hood. Down the mountain, they carried her in their arms like the baby she was, and she let them without a struggle. Unheard of.

The humans carefully removed the cord snare which had probably been set for an antelope or some other small game. Wind was lucky that the snare had not been made of bicycle wire as many are. The park's fifty-five guards cut

2,600 snares last year, but of course they didn't find them all. Often the poachers don't check their traps for days and caught animals are left to die in agony.

Examining Wind's injured hand, the humans noticed some puncture marks on the baby's palm which indicated that her relatives had tried to bite off the snare but had failed. Now she had met some "relatives" who could help.

Two veterinarians—Susan Appleguard (Australian) and Elizabeth MacFie (English)—injected little Wind with long-lasting penicillin and other antibiotics. They were tempted to carry her down the mountain and nurse her until she was well, but they knew from experience that it was best to return the baby to her family group as soon as possible. The longer the injured gorilla was away, the harder it was to assure a warm homecoming.

So once again, Wind was wrapped in a poncho with her head covered by the hood. This time Craig and Dave did the carrying. They took turns. The baby gorilla weighed about thirty-five pounds.

Eventually they located the dominant silverback, Imbaraga. Craig bent down and gently placed Wind at the feet of her father. But the baby just sat there as if paralyzed. And the silverback remained as motionless as Buddha. Would she not be welcomed home after all?

Craig nudged Wind in the back. She got up and started moving slowly forward. But then she stopped and turned back around. She stared at the human.

Craig thought she was saying: *What the hell was I doing with you?*

Then Wind turned and ran into the arms of her father who hugged his daughter home.

Soon other family members—females and juveniles—gathered around and began examining her to see if she was all right. Wind, welcome home.

But the next day, Wind was reported to be depressed. Depressed? Some of the other young gorillas were picking on her because she couldn't defend herself with a swollen hand. Craig was worried.

"But today Liz and I went in and found her traveling with her father," he said. "And she seemed to be doing fairly well. The two of them were feeding together. Imbaraga laid down for a siesta. Wind's mother came over and laid down beside him. And then Wind got in between them."

Lesley and Taylor and I looked at each other. It was a sandwich hug. We knew about those.

Craig said he was still worried about the baby gorilla's swollen hand, but he felt better about her overall hopes of survival. Thanks to him and his team, a new Wind would have a chance to blow through these high mountain jungles for years to come.

BUT CRAIG knew all too well that a happy ending was not certain. The painful memory of what had happened to Josie last year was a constant reminder.

Josie was a young female gorilla who had been named by Dian Fossey. Now the apes were always given African names, but Dian had often given them the kinds of names she might have given her own children—if she had had any. In August of 1988, three years after the murder on the mountainside, Josie had gotten her hand caught in a snare. And a human team climbed up to try to help.

When they found the injured Josie, she was surrounded by her family who were trying to help her but couldn't. Using a drugged dart, they "knocked her down," but they still couldn't get close to her because she was "protected" by her relatives.

So Craig and seven other humans took a deep breath and charged into this gang of gorillas. They shouted and waved their arms and pretended they weren't scared to death. The silverback stared at them, seemed to be trying to make up his mind whether to crush them or not, and then retreated. All the others naturally followed.

Dave and a veterinarian named Mark Kandioti rushed to Josie and started trying to help her. They found a wire snare cutting deeply into her wrist. It seemed to have been there for days. This job was going to take a while and the surrounding gorillas were getting more and more nervous.

Suddenly the silverback charged right at Craig, shaking trees, breaking branches, baring his teeth, an avalanche of muscle and bone and anger. Then the enraged gorilla stopped one foot from Craig's face. He just stood there and looked over Craig's shoulder to see what the humans were doing to his daughter. If he had disapproved, the silverback could have quickly turned the leader of the humans into a broken toy.

"He all but rested his chin on my shoulder," Craig remembered.

They stood there face to face, the head gorilla and the head man, for a long time. The bicycle-wire snare was so deeply imbedded that its removal required forty-five painstaking minutes. Satisfied at last that the humans meant well, the silverback turned and headed back into the jungle, breaking down a tree on his way.

After the terrible snare was finally off, the humans injected Josie with antibiotics and left her in the care of her family. Craig and his team felt good as they walked back down the mountain.

Josie seemed to feel good for several days, too. Then she died. Examining her body, the veterinarian discovered that her injured hand was one massive infection.

In a sense, Dian Fossey had lost another of *her* gorillas to her old and despised enemy: the poacher. But Josie would be the last. The last as of now anyway. The last if Wind lived. Was Craig Sholley finally winning Dian Fossey's war? If so, it would be quite a turnabout, for they had fought their own internecine war when she was alive.

CRAIG SHOLLEY was first introduced to gorillas in the wild in Zaire in 1973. He had come as a Peace Corps volunteer "to save the world," but his job turned out to be helping to save the giant apes. After his two-year tour of duty, he returned home to America.

But he knew he had to get back to Africa somehow. He plotted to get back. He schemed to get back. He was obsessed with getting back. Of course, this obsession with Africa piqued my interest, for I was beginning to feel obsessed, too.

"Why?" I asked.

I was beginning to believe in the magical pull of Africa, but I couldn't just let magic be magic. I had to try somehow to understand it. I wanted to solve the mystery of magic. I was straining for a peek inside Africa's magician's hat.

"Megafauna still exist here," he said. "It's the only place in the world they still exist."

I was a little disappointed. I doubted that *megafauna* was the magic word that would open the doors of this mystery. And yet I loved the megafauna of Africa—the giraffes, the rhinos, the gorillas.

Missing the megafauna—or simply missing Africa— Craig Sholley applied for and received a Louis Leakey grant which brought him back. Leakey, of course, was the famed anthropologist who had dedicated his life to studying early human beings in Africa. But at some point he had come to the realization that early humans could not be properly understood without a better understanding of late apes. So he gave a grant to Jane Goodall who moved from England to Africa to study chimpanzees. And then he gave another grant to Dian Fossey who gave up caring for children in Kentucky in order to study and care for gorillas in Rwanda. They became her new children. In 1978, armed with yet another Leakey grant, Craig Sholley climbed up Dian Fossey's mountain to Dian Fossey's camp where he took up residence. She wanted and needed help, but at the same time jealously hated sharing her gorillas with him or anybody.

Their philosophical differences did not surface right away. They were too busy trying to save the great apes. All the gorillas on these mountains were in jeopardy, but one was in especially grave and immediate danger. A baby gorilla called Lee—Dian had of course named it—had gotten its foot caught in a poacher's snare.

"Back then, we didn't know about tranquilizers," Craig remembered. "We didn't have veterinarians. We watched her dying for two months. Then Dian left for the States."

One day while she was away on a lecture tour in America, Craig went out to observe the group and was alarmed when he couldn't find Lee. So he started backtracking. He eventually found her lagging some fifty yards behind her family. She was following their trail and trying to keep up, but she was so crippled that she was having a hard time.

"I went back to camp," Craig recalled. "I discussed it with the whole crew. We decided to do the best we could to help Lee."

This was a momentous decision. It would be the first time members of the *Homo sapiens* species would reach out to try to help an injured member of the *Gorilla gorilla* species. Up until then, the researchers had only observed. Now they would try to intervene. The whole episode would come to be known as the "first intervention."

The next day, Craig and the rest of the crew climbed up the mountain and found Lee lying face down in the midst of the group. The humans thought she was dead.

Craig and two others decided to try to do something they had never attempted or even considered before: They would do their best to scare the gorillas. The very idea scared them. Always before when they approached the apes, they made calming gorilla sounds. Always before, they approached in a submissive position, as if paying court to the King of Siam. But this time they rushed in shouting with their heads up, standing tall. It worked. The gorillas ran away.

"I grabbed Lee," Craig said, "and ran for my life."

He carried her down the mountain to camp. Then he loaded her into a Land Rover and drove her to Ruhengeri. He pulled up in front of the small hospital run by two Belgian doctors who were latter-day Dr. Schweitzers. They had come to Africa to treat sick humans, but they agreed to do what they could for this baby prehuman. They removed the wire snare and injected antibiotics. Then Craig drove the sick gorilla back to camp.

Several hours later Lee died.

The baby gorilla was buried in a gorilla graveyard near where Dian herself would soon be buried.

In her posthumously published diaries, Dian Fossey gives the impression that she led the battle to save Lee's life. She suggests that she wanted to "intervene" while others opposed her.

"But she wasn't there," said Craig Sholley. "She was in the United States."

So the controversy about what Dian Fossey did or didn't do to save one or all the gorillas continues even after her death. Which I found disturbing. After all, nobody has enough heroes or heroines, so it is always a shame to lose one. Besides, she was my sister. . . .

"**I** HAVE GREAT admiration for what Dian did initially," Craig said. "She is one of the major reasons those animals exist today. But Dian had her problems. She had a lot of problems with tourists."

We tourists at the table felt meek. Of course we already knew from what Dian Fossey had written—and from what others had written and even filmed about her—that she would not have approved of us. We tried not to take it personally. We were aware that she wanted to keep the likes of us away from *her* gorillas. She was afraid that exposure to humans would change the way the great apes behaved. She was afraid we would "contaminate" them.

She was also possessive.

Craig Sholley realized that humans threatened the very existence of the gorillas, but he also believed that only humans could save the apes from humans. And he thought man in the form of tourists could play a role. For he believed that the Rwandan government would only work to save the gorillas if they were valuable. Not of scientific value. Not of historic value. But valuable at the bank. He thought the gorillas would only be allowed to survive if they could pay their own way. And the only way they could pay was by generating a tourist trade.

"Dian came to Rwanda when there was nothing," Craig said. "Back then, vigilante action was all that saved the park and the gorillas."

She used to capture poachers and tie them up and threaten to kill them. She burned down the houses of suspected poachers. She shot at them.

"But Dian was not able to evolve along with the world of conservation," Craig concluded. "That is probably why she isn't around today."

Evolve indeed.

"I'VE BEEN director here for twenty months," Craig said. "In that time, we've lost one gorilla to traps, Josie. But worse than that, last year we had a severe respiratory illness epidemic. Thirty-five got sick and we lost six. We sent tissue samples to the U.S. for tests. We believe one of them may have died of measles."

The evidence was not conclusive, but Craig and the others were concerned enough to take drastic measures. They decided to try to vaccinate all the gorillas on the mountains.

"How do you vaccinate a gorilla?" I asked, not realizing that I was playing straight man.

"Very carefully," he smiled.

It was a new version of an old joke, but it was also accurate. Craig and his team used pistols powered not by gunpowder but by carbon-dioxide cartridges. These guns were loaded not with bullets but with syringes fitted with twenty-gauge needles. They ambushed the big apes and attempted to shoot them in the rump. They vaccinated seven groups of animals, leaving out infants under fifteen months of age and potentially pregnant females, because in these cases the medicine might have done more harm than good. Some seventy gorillas were inoculated in all.

"Usually they just turned around, pulled out the needles, and dropped them on the ground," Craig said. "But some of them got very angry. Group 11, the group you visited today, were very unpleasant. They all got mad."

I had new respect for our group.

Lesley asked, "What's the most amazing thing you've witnessed in the time you've been with the gorillas?"

Craig thought a moment. "Actually, it has to do with what we were just talking about," he said. "Last year when we were vaccinating the gorillas, I came to believe—strongly to believe—that gorillas communicate in a way we don't understand. There is something there that allows messages to be passed. Maybe they make sounds we can't hear. At any rate, I believe messages are conveyed."

"What kind of messages?"

" 'Hey, watch out for the guy with the dart gun!' "

Dr. Dolittle was right, as I had long suspected. It would be hubris to believe that humans are the only animals who have worked out a means of communication. And wouldn't the gorillas be one of the most likely animals to have pulled off that trick? After all, we really are very much alike. Less than 1 percent of our DNA is different from their DNA. They have forty-eight chromosomes while we have forty-six. In this particular case, less seems to be more.

David Attenborough once said, "There is more meaning and understanding in exchanging a glance with a gorilla than with any other animal I know ..." But what if you could exchange more than a glance? What if you could actually talk to a gorilla?

"What do you think gorilla heaven would be like?" I asked the sleepy children.

"No poachers," said Matthew.

"No shots," said Taylor. She thought a moment before adding, "Actually that's my idea of heaven, too."

Smiling, I remembered Ogden Nash's definition of a

"wise child": one who "knew a hawk from a handsaw and a vaccination from a vacation." My daughter was a wise girl.

As I went to bed that night, I was almost too tired to go on living, but at the same time it had been such a magical day that I reminded myself how glad I was not to be extinct.

CHAPTER TWELVE

INSPIRATION

EXT MORNING, the climb got a lot harder a lot faster. Even the pyrethrum fields at the beginning went straight up. Then the bamboo forest at the edge of the park proved also to be a difficult test. This mountain was steeper than a gorilla's forehead. And the chart of my heartbeat and breathing went up even more sharply than the mountain. We took more rest stops today. We had to.

In the morning light, Craig Sholley, who had offered to join us on our climb today, was again a resplendent ghost of the sixties. He had tied a red bandanna around his wild Bill Hickok hair. Again he wore jeans and a green corduroy shirt. He had on low-cut Gore-Tex hiking shoes. Over them, he wore blue, waterproof canvas spats.

We had been assigned to search for Group 13 on our second and final day in the mountains. We weren't particularly superstitious, but we couldn't help wondering if 13 might not be hard to find, which would mean a long hike.

As we passed a patch of nettles, our guides—Fidèle and Leonidas today—explained that the gorillas consider these stinging plants a delicacy. Perhaps they serve the same function in the big ape's diet as jalapeños do in our own.

A little later, Leonidas held up a stick with a huge earthworm draped across it. Everything grew big in this jungle—apes, worms. This worm was as big as a snake.

"The earthworm has only one enemy," Craig said. "Ants. They will gang up on one of these worms and sting it to death and have a picnic."

Which was foreshadowing although I didn't notice it at the time.

I realized that I missed the sky. Locked in this jungle, I got only occasional glimpses of it. Back home in Washington, I could see more of it, but I was still hemmed in by buildings and trees. Back at my first home, back in Texas, the infinite sky had suggested infinite possibilities. Back then, I could see forever and nothing was in the way. Now everything was in the way, vines, thorns, nettles, the knotted jungle, stories I couldn't write, problems I couldn't solve. Half-formed ideas tantalized me like small slivers of a larger sky which I could not quite see.

Fighting my way into a small clearing, I saw Fidèle using his machete to hold up something for us all to admire: a large garland of gorilla droppings. It was lovely. The steam rising from it was beautiful. The trail was warm.

"Merde, merde," Fidèle smiled. *"Le gorille était ici."*

I slipped and fell on my hands and knees in the mud. *Merde!* Getting up embarrassed, I brushed myself off as well as I could. Then I plunged ahead once again into the ensnaring vines.

Today I wasn't the pig in the python but the buffalo in the boa. Either I was bigger than yesterday or the tunnel through the vegetation was smaller. While others walked, I got down on my hands and knees and crawled. And I still had trouble.

The pain was all but forgotten when after a three-hour climb we came across a mother gorilla and her baby. In order to take a picture with no branches in the way, I had to lie down on my stomach. I sprawled and aimed my camera at the photogenic mother and child.

At first, I didn't understand what the guides were saying. Actually, I wasn't paying much attention. I was concentrating on focusing on the baby's face. But eventually I recognized a word that was being shouted over and over.

"Ants! *Ants!* ANTS!"

I looked down and saw that the earth had turned into ants. I was lying stretched out full length in a cauldron of ants, boiling and toiling angrily. I was frightened and yet I kept on taking pictures. I was like a soldier who at first doesn't realize he has been shot because the pain hasn't hit him yet.

But then it did. Now I knew how the earthworm felt when it was being stung to death by an army of ants. This mountain had found yet another way to fight back, to make me feel unwelcome, to tell me to be gone.

Craig had given us a lecture earlier about safari ants. He said that if you are bitten by these ants, you should just grin and bear it and continue to enjoy the gorillas. For a lot of swatting makes giant apes nervous. Unfortunately, getting eaten alive by ants makes a naked ape nervous, too. I jumped up and started hitting myself like somebody in a mental institution. Dozens . . . hundreds . . . maybe millions of ants were inside my clothes. Inside my vest. Inside my shirt. Yes, inside my pants. Just like that old childhood rhyme. The guides were amused. Dian Fossey would surely have loved it: The tourist was getting what he deserved.

As I ran out of this dell from Hell, Taylor was just

coming in. I tried to warn her, but perhaps I wasn't very articulate. I had an ant on my tongue. Soon poor Taylor was swatting, too. My heart went out to her—my stung heart.

Retreating en masse, we hurried and slashed our way to another vantage point. And then another and another. We were following the peripatetic mother and baby from place to place, but they were always behind leaves and vines and branches. While we were tracking the gorillas on the side of the mountain, I was tracking safari ants up and down my body. I was attempting to carry out a search and destroy mission, but I was about as effective as our troops used to be in Vietnam.

Eventually, the mother and baby took pity on us and paused to pose in a clearing. We all lumbered and crashed into position to take pictures. The photos were great, but I was having trouble holding the camera steady because I jiggled every time an ant bit me.

The gorilla madonna had lured us into another ant bed. And this time we were all in it. Lesley was swatting at her clothes. Even the guides were doing an energetic dance as they reached down inside their pants with both hands. Only Craig Sholley stood calmly and suavely at ease: His spats saved him.

I took off my vest and was horrified to see it black with ants. I tore off my khaki safari shirt which was as full of ants as a honeycomb is full of bees. I pulled down my blue jeans and was really horrified. From the ankles up, I was naked except for my underwear and the ants that covered me. I was too frightened and in too much pain to be embarrassed.

Lesley and Taylor helped me brush ants off my body. Then Lesley and I helped brush them off Taylor. We had a terrible time catching one that was in her belly button. Then

Taylor and I tried to pick the ants off Lesley. Suddenly the gorillas' habit of grooming each other began to make a lot more sense.

By this time, the mother and baby had moved on.

Soon we found ourselves fighting our way through the worst thicket I had ever been in. I had to lie down on my stomach and wriggle like the Serpent in the Garden. And I was too hot. And ants were still stinging me. And I felt trapped, claustrophobic. Would I ever get out? Imagine that you have been buried alive on the hottest day of the year and there are ants in your coffin. Could anything be worth this agony?

Then I burst through a barrier of pain and found myself watching the whole family of gorillas feeding peacefully in a steep meadow. I suppose we disturbed them, because they soon got up and marched out of the clearing single file, like circus bears. The last was a baby gorilla who somersaulted all the way down the hill.

A guide called me over to see a domestic scene. A silverback was seated beside one of his wives who held a baby in her arms. She was nursing. It was as if they were in their living room with trees for walls. I was an intruder looking through their picture window. Growing restless, the mother climbed a tree with her baby and took a crap.

"It's raining bowling balls," Lesley said softly.

Getting a little upset, the silverback stood up and shook a couple of trees as if he were Samson trying to shake down the jungle on all our heads. The mighty patriarch soon calmed down, but then I braced my camera against a tree and accidentally shook it, upsetting him again. He gave me such a look! I had wondered before if the gorillas were looking at *me* or just generally in my direction. (It was the same question you often asked yourself about a newborn baby.) But this time I knew that the silverback was looking directly at me personally. He was sizing up the tree shaker. I saw his eyes focus and change color. They turned from chocolate to gunmetal gray. I waited for him to shake more trees and charge.

But he didn't. He evidently didn't consider me much of a threat.

"Look at his head," Lesley whispered. "It's so much larger than you think it's going to be. It reminds me of one of those giant stone heads on Easter Island."

"This silverback's name is Mrithi," Craig said in a low voice. "That means 'successor' in Swahili. The former silverback died and this fellow had to take over while he was still a blackback."

"The boy king," I said.

But by now age and responsibility had turned Mrithi's back to silver.

Near the end of our visit with the behemoths, a mother gorilla with a baby clinging to her stomach approached the silverback. When she got close enough, he put his arm around her to comfort and protect her. It appeared to be such a caring courtesy. I found it such a moving gesture. The gorillas never seemed more "human" to me than at that moment.

I felt: I've done that. I know about that. That hasn't changed in a million years or more.

It was almost as if the silverback had put his arm around me. I felt a real kinship.

I felt more. I felt myself inside a hairy hide. I looked out through bittersweet chocolate eyes. As if she realized that I had changed, the hairy mother pulled away from me. She and her baby disappeared into the brush. I sat down in the middle of a narrow trail and did my Buddha imitation. I thought I might be falling asleep.

Then the human me had an idea: Perhaps I could actually influence what the gorilla me would do. Maybe I could *inspire* the huge ape to act as I wished—as I willed. Back when I had been working on the Rio movie, the screenplay I couldn't finish, I had become fascinated with inspiration. Where does it come from? How does it work? In the story, the young songwriter was supposed to discover that inspiration "rides" an artist the way the gods "ride" a believer. After all, inspiration does seem to come from nowhere, grasp the reins for a time, and then dismount and return to nowhere. Just like the gods of *macumba* . . . the ancient gods of Africa. But I hadn't been able to write about inspiration "riding" a songwriter because I didn't believe it. Or perhaps inspiration simply wasn't riding me.

Now I was ready to try to assume the role of inspiration. I hadn't been able to inspire myself, but perhaps I could inspire a gorilla. Maybe I could think the thought and the ape would do the deed. And if I could somehow be the inspiration that rode a big monkey, would it give me enough confidence to allow some higher inspiration to ride me?

I concentrated with all my flagging energy: Stand up and beat your chest! Come on, stand up and bang your chest! Pretend you're Tarzan! Make believe you're a Hollywood gorilla! Overact! Ham it up! Hammer your chest!

The big silverback slowly rose to his feet and then started pounding his breast as if he were auditioning for a role in a jungle movie. It was thrilling. It was great. Boom, boom, boom! God's own drummer boy.

A S WE sat around in a clearing drinking Cokes and picking at our picnic lunches, Craig removed his walkie-talkie from his belt and started calling the Susa Group on another mountain.

"Écoute," he said into the radio. *"Écoute."*

When they finally answered, Craig talked to somebody for several minutes in French. We could only hear his end of the conversation, for the replies were too low and laced with static to be understood. Still worried about Wind, he asked in French: How is she doing? How is her hand? Is she depressed? When the call was finally over, he noticed us all staring at him.

"Her arm is still swollen," Craig said, "but she's doing well psychologically."

The trip down was a little shorter than the trip up since we weren't following gorillas but simply taking the shortest route "home." As we neared the bottom of the mountain, Lesley's porter Joseph found an African porcupine quill, as long and beautiful as an eagle feather, which he presented to her. A real bond had grown up between them.

When we finally emerged from the jungle into the pyrethrum fields, a group of children got in line behind us and followed us down the mountain. They joined our parade, our triumphant procession, down the slope. What was the nature of our triumph? We had beaten the mountain in the sense that it hadn't killed us. And the kids were helping us celebrate.

CHAPTER
THIRTEEN

CHARM
OF
AFRICA

HE NEXT day was our day of rest. We needed it to nurse our wounds and sore muscles, sore everything. Lesley and I went for a stroll around the hotel's lovely grounds—and she fell! We were walking along a sidewalk and she didn't see a step. She went down hard on her hands and knees on the concrete. She had been surefooted on the side of the volcano, but she fell and hurt herself on a sidewalk. She just sat there and cried, cried because her knees hurt, cried over all the emotion expended yesterday when she had worked so hard for a miracle. By the time she had stopped crying, had washed her face, and I had soothed her like a good silverback, it was time for lunch with Rosamond Carr.

Rosamond Carr had been Dian Fossey's great friend in Rwanda. She had a Helen Hayes quality: old, elegant, easy to talk to, anxious to help. Years ago, I had interviewed Helen Hayes about her friend Scott Fitzgerald. And now I was going to talk to Rosamond Carr about her friend

Dian Fossey. But we began by listening to our guest's own story.

"I grew up in New Jersey, but I married a Brit who had been a white hunter in Uganda," she said. "He was twenty years older than I was. It didn't work."

She sat at the table in the dining room of the Meridien Hotel wearing a simple kelly-green sheath with an ivory and malachite bracelet. Her white hair was puffed up and coiffed. She smiled easily and looked right at you with soft, wide-open eyes. Craig Sholley had described her as "the most charming person I've ever met," and it was easy to see and feel why.

"I lost my heart to Africa," she said. "After I'd been here three years, I went home to South Orange, New Jersey, with the idea of never coming back. But my husband persuaded me to come back. Two years later when we separated for good, it was too late. I couldn't go home."

"Why not?" I asked. Perhaps she would be the one who would explain the magic of Africa to me. Perhaps she would know how it wove its spell. More and more, I felt a compulsion to discover how this magician of a continent did its tricks. I worried a little that learning the answer might ruin the trick, but I couldn't help myself. I had to know—or at least to try to know.

"When I decided to stay," Rosamond Carr said, "the people back home thought I had an exciting lover. But it was just Africa. Africa was my lover."

"But what was it about Africa?" I persisted.

"I think it was the people," she said. "That was the difference between Dian and me. She didn't care about the people except to keep them away from the gorillas."

I found her answer fascinating, but I suspected that my quest was still not over. I would have to keep looking for the answer if there was one. But I loved Africa being her lover. I felt I knew what she meant even if I didn't yet understand it.

"I didn't plan to stay all my life," she continued. "I just kept putting off going. Then I had the chance to buy a plantation. That was 1955. I thought maybe I would stay two more years. It was a pyrethrum plantation, fifty acres with two hundred workers."

Some years ago she switched from pyrethrum, the flower grown to kill bugs, to roses and daffodils, flowers grown for their own sake. And she reduced her work force to a tenth of what it used to be.

"Now I pay the twenty more than I paid the two hundred," she said.

She sells cut flowers to hotels and restaurants all over East Africa. She is one of the very few whites to make her home in this country.

"I didn't know the gorillas were here until Dian came," she said. "I met her not the way it shows in the movie. I met her in Kigali. She had just escaped from the Congo where a revolution was under way. I was invited to lunch by the military attaché at the American Embassy. His wife warned me that I was going to meet a really weird woman and cautioned me not to have too much to do with her.

"When I got to the house, Dian came to the door. She was as tall as Sigourney Weaver. She was wearing a mauve dress. Her hair was done in a French twist. And she was wearing tennis shoes, size ten.

"We went in for lunch and there were three wine glasses at every place. Everything was arranged perfectly. But it was the weirdest luncheon I have ever been to in my whole life. The host and hostess didn't say a word."

Dian Fossey got out a notebook and proceeded to cross-examine the plantation owner who lived at the foot of the volcanoes.

"Now, Mrs. Carr," she said, "I have a few questions to ask you. Number one . . ."

She went right to work trying to find out if there were gorillas in the mountains along the western border of Rwanda. She knew there were gorillas across the border in Zaire, the old Belgian Congo, but she had been chased out of there at gunpoint. So now she was looking for the gentle giants in a more gentle country.

"There are no gorillas on this side of the volcano," Mrs. Carr said.

"I know there are," declared Dian Fossey.

Mrs. Carr felt as if she were on trial and had just been called a liar by the prosecutor.

"I began to see what the military attaché's wife had meant," she told us. "I answered all her long list of questions and then told her that she could come to my plantation, but she wouldn't find any gorillas."

Dian came and lived on her land. Of course, Mrs. Carr was right. There weren't any gorillas on the big volcano that towered above her plantation. But there were great apes on the neighboring volcanoes down the range. So in a sense they were both right. Once she had found the gorillas, Dian Fossey left Mrs. Carr and moved to her own camp high up on the side of a volcano that did have gorillas. Rosamond suggested that Dian build a cottage on the pyrethrum plantation, so she could get away from the mountain occasionally.

"Never," Dian said. "You see too many people."

Dian Fossey didn't care much for people or the languages they spoke. On the other hand, she spent years studying and translating the "pant-hoots" of the gorilla.

"When Dian came here, she didn't know a word of Swahili or French," Mrs. Carr continued. "She learned a very funny Swahili. Much funnier than mine. She had no ear for language whatever. But she had to do a lot of writing in French to the government. She would take four hours or more to write a letter. And there would be very few mistakes. I think she was born writing."

I had been thinking for some time that there was something familiar about Rosamond Carr's voice. Finally I recognized it. She sounded like Eleanor Roosevelt. I still couldn't help wondering: What was this delicate flower of a woman doing raising flowers in darkest Africa?

"Dian did everything in a dead-straight line," Mrs. Carr said. "She was totally inflexible. I was very concerned about her one-person war against the poachers and shepherds. Especially the shepherds. I told her, 'You don't have any right to chase the shepherds out of the park.' She had no sympathy for them whatsoever. She didn't care if they starved to death."

Mrs. Carr disapproved of some of Dian Fossey's tactics, but she never came to disapprove of the woman herself, as so many did.

"I adored Dian," she said, her voice rising. "I miss her every day of my life. We were close by correspondence. And she would come to me when she was sick. Which was often. In the last years of her life, I was the only friend she had in this country."

"Was she your child?" I asked the childless woman.

"She was the most unchildlike thirty-five-year-old you could imagine. I was almost a generation older, but she was much more grown up than I in many ways. Her mother never loved her."

But Rosamond Carr did.

"A producer bought the film rights to her book *Gorillas in the Mist* while she was still alive," her old friend continued. "He paid her a lot of money. She was in ecstacy. 'Somebody will play me,' she kept saying. 'They'll be up here at camp.' The producer arrived in Kigali on the day after Christmas. He had come to talk to Dian about making the movie. He was going to stay a week or so and spend New Year's Eve with her. But she was killed the night he landed in Rwanda, December 26. They never met."

On the morning of December 27, Dian Fossey's cook unlocked her tin cabin—jokingly called the Manor—and found a mess. Furniture was upset. Lamp chimneys were smashed and the floor was dangerous with broken glass. Only the Christmas tree remained untouched. Stepping carefully to keep from getting cut, the cook made his way through the living room into the bedroom. He found drawers and closet doors standing open. He found books and papers and clothing thrown on the floor. He found a table overturned. He found Dian Fossey with her head split open from her forehead to her mouth.

Trying to understand why her friend had died, Rosamond Carr recalled all the problems Dian Fossey had had with the Rwandan government.

"Dian had such trouble with her visa," Mrs. Carr said. "She had no car. She had emphysema. But she would have to come down to Kigali every two months to get her visa renewed. Then the head of tourism wouldn't see her. He would make her wait for days.

"A friend of hers in the government said, 'Why don't you go to the office of the president and get a longer visa.'

"She did. She got a two-year visa. She was so happy, telling everybody that now she could go up the mountain and not come down. But that visa was her death warrant. She got it on the sixth or seventh of December, the month she was killed."

After the murder, Rosamond Carr made the difficult trip up the volcano one last time. In the early days, she used to go at least once a year, but she hadn't been up for six years, not since 1979, because she was getting weaker as she grew older. But now she summoned the strength for one last assault on the mountain that had helped to kill her friend. For she remembered Dian talking about wanting to be buried in the lofty mists of her "gorilla cemetery" where she had laid to rest so many victims of poachers.

"Everybody who worked for Dian was arrested," Mrs. Carr remembered. "So no one who loved Dian was at her funeral, no one but me. It was just pitiful."

Of course, Dian Fossey was buried beside Digit, her favorite gorilla, so named because he had lost a finger, perhaps to poachers. He was killed trying to save one of his sons from poachers. The son died too. So many poaching victims. Was Dian Fossey another?

"Who do you think killed your friend?" I asked.

"I hope it was the American boy," Rosamond Carr said without much conviction. "He was terrible. He broke into her cabin after her death—while the guards were eating—and took some papers. She wrote to me that he was quite nice but so stupid. Whenever he went into the bush, he got lost. In three weeks, he hadn't learned to light an oil lantern."

Mrs. Carr was talking about Wayne McGuire who had come from the University of Oklahoma to study gorillas. He arrived shortly before Dian Fossey was killed. He had a full beard and glasses and looked like a cross between a mountain man and a nerd. Nine months after the killing, the Rwandan government charged Wayne McGuire with the murder of Dian Fossey. The United States embassy, suspecting the Rwandans might simply be looking for a scapegoat, helped McGuire flee the country.

"Dian was found with European hair in her hand," recalled Mrs. Carr. "A Rwandan captain told me about it on the morning of her death. The hair—along with a sample of Dian's—was sent to a laboratory in Belgium. The results didn't come back for five months. Finally the lab reported that the hair wasn't Dian's. If that's the truth, it more or less points to Wayne.

"A Rwandan official said it couldn't have been a poacher or any other Rwandan because the murderer didn't take anything. He left money, a pistol, cameras, family jewelry."

Rosamond Carr was closer to the murder victim than the rest of us, lived closer to the scene of the crime, but she nonetheless remained just as puzzled as we were. This mystery has no neat solution, which is one reason why it stays with us, pursues us, still disturbs us. Dian Fossey's blood has turned out to be an indelible stain. Picking at her lunch and at clues, Mrs. Carr seemed to have convicted the American—then changed her mind.

"Maybe there was a Rwandan cover-up," she speculated. "Her tracker, Emmanuel Rwelekana, whom she had recently fired, was arrested after she was killed. He died in jail. They said he hanged himself, but what if he was killed? Maybe he knew who murdered her."

After all, Rwandan officials wanted to exploit the gorillas by turning them into tourist attractions, and Dian Fossey stood implacably in their way. A lot of money was at stake, and money has often been a motive for murder. She departed and the tourists began arriving.

So perhaps we killed Dian Fossey—*mon semblable— ma soeur*—

"THE ONLY person I ever let read Dian's letters is Sigourney," Rosamond Carr said. Sigourney Weaver, who would play Dian Fossey in *Gorillas in the*

Mist, came to stay with Mrs. Carr just as Dian had. "She read the letters aloud into a tape recorder. I think it helped her."

"What did you think of the movie?" I asked.

"I loved it," she said. "And I didn't expect to. I had the feeling I had been watching Dian."

One afternoon, the gorillas on the mountain had had the same feeling.

"Before she went up to see the gorillas, Sigourney was afraid. She asked me what she would do if she just froze. When she got there, she was dressed exactly as Dian with her hair done the same way. One of the gorillas came up and leaned its face against her. A baby gorilla jumped on her head and grabbed her hair. Others gathered around. I'm convinced the gorillas thought Sigourney was Dian.

"Sigourney had tears in her eyes. She felt it was a gift from Dian.

"But when the gorillas smelled her hands, they knew it wasn't Dian. She was gone."

I liked Dian Fossey much better for having a friend like Rosamond Carr. Perhaps Dian hadn't liked many people, but she had been wise enough to like Rosamond. And Rosamond had loved Dian, which was a moving recommendation. In death, Dian Fossey had become a martyr to some, a monster to others, but one charming woman still adored her simply as a friend. Rosamond Carr added warm light and softening shadows to my picture of that friend. Dian Fossey, flawed, sometimes drunk, maybe a little crazy, was once again my heroine: the wise fool on the mountain. I would have been proud to call her "sister."

We would feel sad to leave this land of beauty and butchery, but we would actually be getting out just in time. For the age-old war between the tall Tutsis and the short Hutus would soon begin again. In the fall of 1990, a rebel

Tutsi force, which had been training in neighboring Uganda, crossed back into Rwanda and attempted to overthrow the Hutu-led government. Battles raged on the slopes of the very volcanoes where the last mountain gorillas on earth are fighting for survival. Bombs and artillery shells shook the gorillas' world beneath their huge feet. It was a war that pitted not only tribe against tribe but also species against species. It was a civil war in which brothers battled brothers and latter-day sons imperiled their ancient Pleistocene parents. Guerrillas invaded the last home of the gorillas and threatened to define a new horror that would rhyme with genocide: "specicide." The park was closed—the movement of researchers and rangers restricted—so we don't know how much the great apes have suffered. At worst, they may have been caught in a killing cross-fire. At the very least, they must have been frightened almost to death. Just when the gorillas were beginning to trust humans, humans turned out to be as bad as they had always supposed. In the spring a "cease fire" was declared, but it did not stop the fighting in this last refuge of the gentle giants.

Moreover, murder in these lush mountains would soon be echoed by murder on a desert plain: Another legendary animal lover was about to be slain.

CHAPTER
FOURTEEN

WHAT'S
IN
A NAME

GORILLA on wheels was racing in circles around the airport waiting room. This mechanized ape was chased by Matthew who was in turn pursued by a little black boy. Round and round the not so happy merry-go-round. Since Matthew hadn't been able to climb up to see the real gorillas, Derek had bought him this toy which he pushed around in circles. We had all been going around in circles for hours. Our flight was supposed to depart Kigali for Nairobi at 2:40 in the afternoon, but it was hours late. We were trapped in a modern bureaucratic jungle of paper and promises. When we finally crowded onto a plane at 7:30 in the evening, we felt we were participating in a jailbreak.

After a three-hour flight, we landed in Nairobi and made our weary way back to the old, half-timbered Norfolk Hotel where British colonialism had gone to die, but wasn't quite dead yet. Inside the Norfolk, it was still 1930, or perhaps 1940, or 1950 at the latest: The Mau Mau rebellion and independence still lay in the complicated future. While our reservations were being sorted out—there had been some confusion—we stopped for hot-chocolate nightcaps in the Lord Delamere Bar.

This bar was named for the man who invented colonial Kenya. In 1891, Hugh Cholmondeley, third Baron Delamere, made his first trip to East Africa. He came as a hunter. In Somaliland, he killed two lions. He enjoyed it so much that he returned almost every year. In 1894, he was mauled by a lion who would have killed him if his gunbearer had not grasped the beast by its mane and tongue. It was not until 1897 that Lord Delamere ventured beyond Somaliland into a new land that would one day be Kenya. He came riding on the back of a camel. Discovering a country that reminded him of Australia, he decided to return as a settler and raise sheep. He did so in 1903. His sheep did not do well, so he tried cattle, which did poorly, too. So he tried crossing his cattle with cattle kept by the Africans. These animals did much better. Other settlers soon followed his lead and he became the leading citizen of British East Africa.

About the time Lord Delamere was "discovering" Africa, an African boy was born who would have an even more profound impact on the history of Kenya. A bar is named after the English nobleman, but the main street in Nairobi bears the name of the African child who had less than no advantages.

H E WAS an orphan named Kamau wa Ngengi. But he was not satisfied with his name or his lowly lot or his country. So he remade them all. He rechristened himself Jomo Kenyatta. Some say he named himself after his country. Others say he named himself after a beaded belt. Before he had finished, he had also renamed his native land. Most people stopped saying, "Keenya" and started saying "Kenya" in his honor, so the country's name would sound like his name. Whether or not he named himself after his native land, his native land eventually renamed itself after him.

Nobody bothered to mark down the exact date of his birth, but it was probably sometime in 1890. The place was the Kikuyu (sometimes spelled Gikuyu) tribal area near Nairobi. He was ten years old before he ever saw a white man. Then at the turn of the century, the missionaries came. Kenyatta, who had lost his parents by this time, was cared for and educated by clergymen from the Church of Scotland.

Then he went to work as an interpreter in the capital, but he soon came to hate the fact that his skills were needed in Kenya. What was wrong with these white people? Why couldn't they learn the Kikuyu tongue? Why couldn't they at least study Swahili? Why did native Kenyans need an interpreter to talk to the people who ruled Kenya?

Nor were African languages all that the British did not understand. Jomo Kenyatta realized that the white rulers did not begin to comprehend and therefore were indifferently destroying African cultures—especially the Kikuyu culture. But perhaps he was most furious about the land. The British Crown ordained that no African could own land in what was called the "White Highlands." Which meant that natives were excluded from the best land in their native land.

Joining forces with others who felt as he did, Jomo Kenyatta helped form the Kikuyu Central Association, which began as a defender of Kikuyu tribal customs, but grew into a champion of all Africans suffering under white rule. Kenyatta was elected its general secretary in 1928.

Then in 1931—the year Lord Delamere died—Jomo Kenyatta left Kenya. As if intent on getting to know his enemy better, he went to Britain where he studied anthropology at the London School of Economics. Later he continued his studies in the Soviet Union. The academic phase of his career culminated in the publishing of his classic work, *Facing Mount Kenya: The Tribal Life of the Gikuyu.*

As the unofficial ambassador of Kenya's black population, Jomo Kenyatta traveled from one European capital to another, pleading the case of his people. But unlike most other ambassadors, he often worked as a day laborer to finance his mission. And all the while, his reputation—his legend—continued to grow back home.

In 1946, Jomo Kenyatta returned to his native land where he spoke out loudly against British rule, addressing rallies that sometimes swelled to 30,000. He persuaded his people to boycott British hats and even British beer.

The British colonial government accused Jomo Kenyatta of leading the Mau Mau uprising in the early fifties. He denied this and there is little reason to doubt him. The actual leader of the Mau Mau—to the extent this diffuse movement had one—was Dedan Kimathi. He and his Kikuyu followers attacked white settlers with machetes called *pangas* and left behind horrible scenes. When the British sent soldiers after him, he retreated with his men into the Aberdare Mountains where they wore skins as if they also wanted to retreat in time. When Kimathi was finally taken, his favorite tree is said to have fallen in the forest.

Although Jomo Kenyatta had little or nothing to do with this rebellion, the British arrested him in 1952, put him on trial, convicted him, and locked him up for nine years. But prison simply added to his legend.

In the early sixties, the British finally agreed to give

Kenya and Kenyatta their *uhuru*—their freedom. In the summer of 1963, even before independence, Jomo Kenyatta, who was still in custody, was elected prime minister. After independence, which came on December 12, 1963, Kenyatta was elected president.

In his native land, Jomo Kenyatta had the historic stature of a George Washington, the moral authority of a Martin Luther King, Jr., the touch with the masses (called *wananchi*) of a Huey "the Kingfish" Long. Like "the Kingfish," Kenyatta was known to everybody by a nickname: "Mzee" which means Old Man. He would end all his speeches with the loud cry of *"Harambee!"*—his trademark—which means "Let's all pull together!" And he did try to bring together the various tribes and races who shared his land. For example, when he took power, Kenyatta appointed as his personal bodyguard the policeman who had led the hunt for Kimathi, the Mau Mau leader. Meanwhile, he named a main thoroughfare in Nairobi: Kimathi Street.

Pulling together was all well and good, but Kenyatta never forgot he was a Kikuyu and his fellow tribesmen usually had more pull than others. He also expected Kenyans to pull together in *one* party, his party, the Kenya African National Union (KANU). But his one-party system allowed more competition than some. A dozen candidates—all members of the KANU—might run for a single seat in the parliament.

Kenyatta didn't mind if lesser politicians competed against each other, but he didn't want anybody competing against him. He made it a crime—punishable by life in prison—even to discuss who might replace or succeed him.

The only other figure in Kenya whose fame in any way competed with Kenyatta's was a man named Tom Mboya, the most powerful labor leader in the country. He wore custom-tailored Western suits, had a debonair style, and drove a white Mercedes Benz. He was a member of the Luo tribe, but his popularity transcended tribal boundaries. In 1968, Tom Mboya was shot to death on the streets of Nairobi. His assassination ignited riots. A triggerman was arrested, tried, and convicted . . . but Kenya's attorney general secretly paid this triggerman's legal expenses.

As he got older and sicker, Jomo Kenyatta also grew more vain, paranoid, and greedy—and his government grew more corrupt. One symptom was what happened to Kenya's animals. Hunting was outlawed, but poachers could kill what they wanted if they could afford the bribes. Some even felt that the hunting was prohibited not to help the animals but to aid the finances of pliable government officials.

In spite of the prohibition against discussing succession, a group of plotters formed a secret paramilitary police commando unit that planned to seize power when Kenyatta finally died. It called itself "Ngoroko," and it drew up a list of a dozen people, including Vice President Daniel arap Moi, who were to be assassinated when the time came.

In late summer 1978, Jomo Kenyatta, a gravely ill leader in his mid-eighties, insisted upon making a trip to the coast so he could lie once more beside the Indian Ocean. Here his condition worsened. In Mombasa in the early morning hours of August 22, Jomo Kenyatta died, setting in motion a riot of vultures.

As news of his death spread, Western-style coat tails flapped in the wind like black wings. The race was on. Vice President Moi got the word first in the middle of the night and so got a head start. He left his rural farm in darkness and sped toward Nairobi. The Ngoroko conspirators were right behind.

"**I** WAS right over there," Derek said, pointing out into the night, "when I heard that Kenyatta was dead."

Still seated at a table in a bar named for a white supremacist, Derek went on to describe how he learned of the passing of one of the greatest black leaders in the continent's history. He had gone swimming in the YMCA pool which was down the street from the Norfolk Hotel. He remembered the day not only for what ended then but also for what began then. He had just met a young woman, born in Ireland, named Elizabeth who was blonde, pretty, and married. He was already falling in love. So a critical moment in his life coincided with a critical moment in the political life of his country. The news of the Old Man's passing swept across the pool like a wave. Everybody stopped what he or she was doing and waited for the world to change.

But Kenya's ambitious politicians could not afford to stop or even pause. Hoping to kill their rival, the coup leaders hunted Vice President Moi through the night the way game used to be hunted in the old dark days—the way it still was by bribing poachers. But Moi outran his hunters, won the race to the capital, and was sworn in as acting president. The former schoolteacher had thoroughly outmaneuvered the military men.

Still the Ngoroko plotters did not give up. Trying to topple Moi by stirring up tribal rivalries, they told Kikuyu politicians, who had been favored by the old regime, that they could not afford to allow a Tugen tribesman to run the government. But they failed. Soon Moi began arresting the Ngoroko conspirators—more than two hundred of them.

As temporary president, Moi had ninety days to consolidate his power and to campaign for a full term. Of course, running as the incumbent, even the acting incumbent, had its advantages. He could put his rivals in jail and reward his friends with jobs. He soon wrapped up the nomination of his country's only party, the KANU, which led more or less automatically to his being elected to a five-year term as president of Kenya. Moi said his watchward would be *nyayo,* which means "footsteps," implying that he would follow the course set by his predecessor.

His new presidency got off to a good start with the failure of the Brazilian coffee crop. World coffee prices soared and so did Kenya's fortunes. Moi was so euphoric that he released all political prisoners.

But by 1982, coffee prices had once again collapsed. A New Year's Eve terrorist bombing in the Norfolk Hotel scared away much of the tourist trade. There were even food shortages. Corruption seemed to be getting worse. And Kenyans began calling their new president by a nickname just as they had called their Old Man by one. But this new moniker did not connote fondness as in the past. Kenyans started referring to their president the "Headmaster."

And the Headmaster was having trouble with his schools. In Nairobi, university students began demonstrating in the streets. In rural schools, students rebelled against taking an oath of allegiance to Moi. Instead of the oath, they chanted, "Moi gives us milk and it gives us diarrhea!" Even young girls in a girls school ran amok and did tens of thousands of dollars' worth of damage.

Moi reacted to all the unrest by beginning to jail political prisoners once again. Rumors of plans for a coup spread through the country.

O N AN August night in 1982, Elizabeth awakened Derek at four in the morning. Since their initial meeting at the YMCA pool, she had dissolved her first marriage and plunged into a second. Moreover, Mr. and Mrs. Dames's gardener had planted a Kamba fertility plant beside their front door and the new wife was expecting.

"I heard gunfire!" Elizabeth said. "Shots!"

"That's just *Diwali,*" Derek said, referring to the Indian holiday that features fireworks. "Go back to sleep."

Taking his own advice, the husband and expectant father dropped off again. But when he woke up at 6:30 A.M., the celebration still seemed to be going on, which was unusual.

"That's not *Diwali,*" Elizabeth said. "Something's wrong."

Then they heard Joseph, their cook, celebrating and were even more puzzled. Going to investigate, they learned that he had heard a broadcast on Voice of Kenya radio announcing a coup and a new government. Joseph danced for joy in the kitchen.

President Moi also learned of the coup by listening to the radio. He had gone to Nyeri to attend the Mount Kenya Agricultural Show where he had been entertained by a precision-flying routine staged by the air force. Afterwards, driving back to Nairobi late at night, Moi heard on the Voice of Kenya that he had been deposed by a coup—once again staged by the air force.

At Nairobi University, students began celebrating. In the streets, citizens started looting. The main target of the looters were the stores owned by Asians who control 55 percent of Kenya's industry and 90 percent of its commerce. Some $50-million worth of goods were stolen.

But the leaders of the coup made some mistakes. For instance, they took over the studios of the Voice of Kenya, but they neglected to seize the transmitter. Forces loyal to

Moi pulled the plug and the rebels founds themselves talking to themselves.

The plotters also failed to take into account interservice rivalry. The air force had counted on the army to follow its lead, but instead the army declared war on the fliers. Hundreds were killed in brief but vicious fighting. When the shooting stopped, the army had won and Moi was still in power.

The Headmaster closed Nairobi University—which he suspected of teaching reading, 'riting, and rebellion—for many months. He also arrested more than 3,000 plotters, mostly air force officers and students.

In 1983, Moi was elected to a second five-year term, and his policy of "footsteps," which originally meant following in Kenyatta's footsteps, began to evolve a new meaning. Moi started insisting that everyone in his government—everyone in the country if possible—follow in *his* steps exactly. Soon his yes-men became known as "the footsteps group." Moi said he wanted everybody "to sing like a parrot after me."

Many believed that "footsteps" came to have an even more sinister meaning: for the political assassin once again walked the land. During Kenyatta's reign, Tom Mboya had been gunned down. During Moi's, the victim was a rising politician named Robert John "Bob" Ouko, Kenya's charismatic foreign minister. Like Mboya, Ouko was polished and stylish. Like Mboya, Ouko was a member of the Luo tribe. But unlike most of his fellow politicians, Ouko wasn't corrupt.

Bob Ouko had long feared that his life was in danger. An American friend noticed a pistol in his briefcase. When the same friend invited him for a drink at the Norfolk Hotel, Ouko first said no, then changed his mind, but insisted on sitting with his back to the wall. The assassin, whom he had been expecting for years, finally made his appearance in 1990, in the spring.

A friend of his declared: "Bob Ouko was Kenya's Thomas à Becket."

The killer cut out his tongue, gouged out his eyes, broke his legs, burned his body with acid, and shot him in the head. His disfigured remains were found near his home in Koru in the western part of the country. As news of the assassination spread, demonstrations erupted, as they had in 1969.

"Moi murdered Ouko!" the people chanted. "Moi murdered Ouko!"

Stores were looted. Cars were set on fire. The police retaliated by firing tear-gas canisters. Helicopters flew through giant clouds of smoke and bromine gas. The police shot into crowds, injuring many.

Ever since, Moi has alternated between arresting his opponents and letting them go, then arresting them again. . . . Demonstrations alternate with repression. . . . The cycle seems as unbreakable as wet seasons giving way to dry seasons.

CHAPTER
FIFTEEN

MURDER
IN
THE DESERT

"THEY KILLED George Adamson," Jeff said.

"What?" I asked.

"George Adamson," Jeff repeated. "He was murdered."

"How did it happen?" I asked.

We were in a minibus headed down Uhuru Avenue. With our luggage and cameras stacked all around us, we were just passing the soccer stadium.

"I'm just reading the story now," Jeff said.

He held up a copy of the *Daily Nation* with a front-page banner headline that shouted in huge type:

**GEORGE ADAMSON,
2 AIDES SHOT DEAD**

There was a photograph of a white-haired man who looked like Uncle Sam with bushy white eyebrows and a white goatee. He was shirtless. There was also a picture of a Land Rover with its windshield shot out.

"Read it out loud," Lesley said.

"OK," agreed Jeff. "Let's see: 'World-famous conservationist George Adamson, 83, and two of his employees were murdered here at high noon on Sunday as he rushed through this thornbush wilderness to rescue his driver and a young German girl who was staying with him.'"

"That's terrible," said Taylor. "Isn't he the one the Craigs sent their orphan lion cubs to?"

"That's right," I said.

" 'His death,' " Jeff continued reading, " 'came nine years after his ex-wife Joy Adamson, the author of *Born Free*, was murdered in another remote Kenya game reserve.' "

"That's amazing," said Lesley. "Imagine, the husband and wife were both murdered in separate crimes. What are the odds against something like that happening?"

We arrived at the airport and had to turn our attention to our luggage. Soon we were all carrying bags and cameras. We were also weighed down by concerns about just how dangerous was this country where we found ourselves. Shortly before we had arrived in Africa, a woman from Connecticut had been murdered by poachers in Tsavo National Park, which was near where we were going. Now George Adamson had been killed. And we had children with us.

We boarded the now-familiar, twin-engine Cessna and took off. My stomach felt uneasy in part because of the unstable air and in part because of the unstable situation. We were flying south this morning to Amboseli, the country's oldest national park, which lay at the foot of Mount Kilimanjaro. On the way, we would pass over the place where the Connecticut tourist had been shot to death.

"Gad, is it going to be a rough flight?" I called, raising my voice above the roar of the propellers.

"It'll smooth out pretty soon," our pilot said.

"Gad flew up and got the German girl," Derek said.

"What German girl?" I asked.

"The German girl who was visiting George Adamson," he explained.

"Gad, you were there?"

"Yes."

"What happened?"

"I'll tell you what I know."

A young German woman named Inge Leidersteill had gone to stay with George Adamson in his compound that stood at the heart of the arid Kora Game Reserve in northeastern Kenya. Bwana Simba, as he was known, often had such visitors who were interested in him and his lions. His home was an unusual place in many ways, including its memorable latrine, where elephant jawbones served as toilet seats. Bwana Simba kept his beloved pride of sixteen lions near him—and helped them to survive in this harsh land—by feeding them camel meat every day. But he was a prisoner of his own "pets" and passion. His compound was surrounded by a high chain-link fence to keep his lions from eating him or his staff or his guests.

In spite of his precautions, George Adamson and several of his men had been mauled. One of the victims was the camp cook, named Stanley, who was clawed by a lion named Boy. As a cub, Boy had played the young Elsa in *Born Free*. Of all the animals in the pride, Boy was Bwana Simba's favorite. Hearing cries for help, Adamson came running and shot and killed his best-loved lion. But the cook died anyway.

On the last day of his life, George Adamson had grabbed his gun and run to the rescue once again. The tragedy started to unfold when his driver and the German woman drove three miles to an airstrip where they were to meet an inbound plane bringing more guests to visit the old man and his lions. While they were waiting, they were surprised by three Somali bandits armed with automatic weapons. The armed-robber problem in Kenya had gotten worse as the poacher problem had gotten slightly better. As the Kenyan government had stepped up its efforts to protect the animals—especially elephants—many poachers had evolved into bandits. Rather than taking ivory from elephants, they took money and other valuables from tourists. The by-product of the one calling was often the same as the by-product of the other: dead bodies.

These robbers amused themselves by breaking Adamson's driver's legs with a tire iron. Then they turned their attention to the young German woman. They started pulling off her clothes and fondling her and firing in the air in their excitement.

Hearing the shots, Mohammed Maru, who had served the old man and the lions for eight years, ran to George Adamson's room. He found the white-haired figure bending over his typewriter tapping out a letter that would never be finished.

"Did you hear the shots?" Maru asked.

"Get the rifle," Adamson said, "and the other men."

The old man picked up his pistol and stuffed it in his belt. The butt nuzzled against his flat, bare stomach. He never wore shirts.

Bwana Simba led the way to the Land Rover. Maru followed behind carrying the old man's bolt-action .303. And then came Angala Solala and Ongetha Dikayo bringing up the rear. They all jumped in the battered vehicle and rode to the rescue. The old man was at wheel of the old war-horse.

When they were about a half mile from the airstrip, they rounded a curve and saw what the bandits were doing to Inge. They also saw the machine guns.

"Stop!" Maru screamed.

But the old knight, who was on his way to rescue his last fair maiden, just drove faster.

IN 1972, George Adamson had ridden to the aid of another distressed damsel. Her name back then was Joy Bally, and she was distressed by her marriage to botanist Peter Bally. He was her second husband, but she was already looking for a third. Mrs. Bally found number three when she and Mr. Balley went on a camel safari led by George Adamson. So in a sense, her new knight rode to her rescue on a dromedary.

George and Joy Adamson were married the following year. They tried to have children but endured one miscarriage after another. In 1956, they adopted a lion cub that had been orphaned when George was forced to shoot its mother who was preying on Turkana tribesman. The husband and wife both loved Elsa, but in different ways because they were very different people.

Once George Adamson had given his heart, it was for good. He loved one woman, Joy, and one species, the lion. But Joy Adamson tended to move from man to man and species to species. After Elsa died, Joy left George and turned her back on lions. She took in a cheetah cub named Pippa and raised and studied it. Later, she moved on to the leopard, adopting an orphan named Penny, which she brought up. Meanwhile, she also had a succession of romances which were the talk of Kenya.

But George Adamson remained true to the lion. Forced

to relocate Elsa's cubs in Tanzania, he wanted to stay with them and feed them. But his estranged wife, who believed the lions should be returned fully to the wild, refused to finance such an operation. She was the one who had the money since she was the one who had written *Born Free*. George and Joy quarreled bitterly.

Joy Adamson quarreled with many people. As she grew older, she had fewer and fewer human friends. Like Dian Fossey, she came to prefer animals to people. And the lover of cats, like the lover of gorillas, was murdered. One of her servants, whom she had recently fired, was convicted of killing her.

George Adamson was his estranged wife's heir. With her dead, he could finally do with her money what she had refused to let him to do while she was alive. He could feed lions.

THE BANDITS looked up and saw a maddened car bearing down on them. One frightened passenger jumped from the charging Land Rover and rolled into the bushes, but the others kept coming.

"Don't shoot to stop the car," ordered the leader of the outlaws. "Shoot to kill."

The bandits opened fire with one AK-47 and two G3 assault rifles. They shot out the windshield and the two side windows. A bullet hit George Adamson in the thigh, but he kept coming. Another bullet struck him in the left side of the chest and the Land Rover swerved off the road into a thornbush. A third bullet tore into the old man's back. He never had a chance to draw his pistol this high noon.

Maru, the jumper, who still clutched the old man's old rifle, watched the bandits flee. Then he rushed toward the ravaged car where he found nothing but bodies—Adamson, Solala, and Dikayo. He could easily have been one of them.

George Bwana Simba Adamson was an Irishman born in India and killed in Africa.

Another conservationist had been martyred.

WE FLEW until Mount Kilimanjaro was in clear view. Rising 19,340 feet, it is the tallest solitary mountain in the world.

"Look," said Lesley, "that patch of snow on top looks like a frozen leopard."

Gad broke off his story in order to talk to flight controllers. We were approaching a small, isolated landing strip much like the one where George Adamson had been murdered. We couldn't help wondering what we would find waiting for us there.

CHAPTER
SIXTEEN

SHADOWS
OF
KILIMANJARO

W HEN OUR small plane finally touched down on the dirt airstrip, something actually was waiting for us: Derek's Land Cruiser "Double Decker." It had been driven to this rendezvous by a Ker & Downey driver. The plane taxied to a stop in the middle of a windy wilderness while dust blew across the runway. We got out and stretched our legs and stared up at Mount Kilimanjaro. Its top was as white as old Papa Hemingway's beard.

Deplaning, I smelled that familiar smell again, the scent of Africa, old and red, dry and peppery. Looking around, turning and facing all points of the compass in turn, I began to relax in spite of all the disturbing headlines. I felt the tension draining out of me like sap descending in a tree. It seemed to flow out of me and into the welcoming earth of Africa. I once again felt at home. Here at the foot of Kilimanjaro, I celebrated a homecoming 7,000 miles from home. And yet all I had actually done was to climb down out of the jungle-bound mountains and to place my feet once more on the level plains.

We all clambered into our high-rise Land Cruiser and began our exploration of Amboseli National Park, which rested on the southern rim of Kenya. Just across the border—a line drawn arbitrarily a hundred years ago by European powers—lay Tanzania. This dotted line across the grasslands originally separated a British colony from a German colony. But after Germany lost World War I, this German land became British land, so the dots dividing this wilderness in half made even less sense. Nonetheless the border remained. Although the colonial powers were eventually forced out of Africa altogether, the lines they had drawn in the sand and through the bush and across the mountains remained as if indelible. The struggles of independence are over, but the struggle to make sense of the borders still lies ahead. One day Africans will surely want to draw their own map of Africa. Unfortunately, some of those lines will surely be—are already being—drawn in blood. The Somalis who had crossed into Kenya and killed George Adamson had not been stopped by any dotted line in the desert.

While the search went on somewhere for Bwana Simba's killers, we continued our own more peaceful quest on a peaceful morning. We drove off in the general direction of our new camp, but we took our time in order to appreciate any wildlife we passed along the way. Having grown accustomed to working hard to see our animals, we found Amboseli to be a welcome surprise. We stopped so often to stare and take pictures that the ride from the landing strip to camp took three hours. We made a list of all the different kinds of animals we were seeing on our drive and it turned out to be thirty species long. Each of the animals seemed to welcome me back as if I were a Noah who had somehow wandered off and gotten lost, but had now returned to the Ark.

Studying this crowded plain, I found myself, quite in character, trying to read it as if it were a written page. The warthogs with their tails pointing straight up in the air reminded me of exclamation points: !!!. Reading on, I noticed that the wildebeests' horns resembled parentheses: () () (). Of course, the zebras were slash marks: /////. The oryx's long, straight horns, viewed from the side, were a single reverse slash mark: \. The waterbuck's horns were also slashes, one turned one way, one the other: \ /. Vultures were vees: v v v. The ostriches' round, fluffy bodies were asterisks: * * *. The vervet monkeys had curled tails that looked like question marks: ???. Two male impalas, butting heads for the honor of mating with the females, were ornate brackets: {}. The little Thomson's gazelles had horns that resembled quotation marks: ˝˝. Giraffes, far away on the horizon, were lowercase aitches: h h h. And the acacia trees were still capital tees: T T T.

```
         T h        TTTH  T     TT  T h
    T   T      TT         TTT       T    T         T
      !  !  !      ( )( )( )              T         TT
  T   \ / \  /     {}       *  *  *       \   \   \         TT
    //////        ! ! ! !    vvv( )vvvvv      *  *  *  *  *
  TTT    ////        ˝˝˝      vvvv  ˝˝˝ //////( )( )\  TT
  ! ! ! !  \/  ? ?  ??? ?     {}   /////( )( )/////˝˝ ////˝˝˝ ///
```

It was a crowded page. The herds were all mixed up together, an animal salad. The far-off h h h had spots that looked like dried leaves, which identified them as Masai h h h. The large number of * * * * were probably descended from a single set of remarkable parents who somehow managed to raise an incredible thirty-nine chicks in one nest.

We also saw many smaller birds . . . Namaqua doves . . . black-necked herons . . . big-footed jakanas . . . African fish eagles . . . pied kingfishers . . . sacred ibis . . . and Kory bustards, nature's 747s. . . . We were entertained by a troop of black-faced ? ? ? who jumped on the hood of our Land Cruiser and played with our windshield wipers. In a swamp, we discovered a large herd of buffalo and a small family of hippopotamuses. We kept looking for George Adamson's favorite animals, but all we found were the bones they left behind.

In the early afternoon, we rolled into a grove of dark green acacia trees where we were reunited with our peripatetic kelly-green tents. We were modern nomads who moved our homes from place to place. Our camp felt familiar in that the beds and tables and canvas chairs were the same, but it also felt new because it was in a fresh setting. The roof of leaves and limbs over our heads was different from the roof we had left behind. In Lewa Downs, we had camped beneath a relatively rare sort of acacia trees that were light green with irregular tops. Now we had a roof that was dark-green and as flat on top as a pueblo. But as at Lewa, our nearest neighbor was miles and miles away, as if we were pioneers.

We hungrily descended on the mess tent. Chef Kaptano had prepared Scotch eggs which were unfamiliar to us. On the outside, they were balls of corned-beef hash, but they contained secrets within. I cut one open and found a hard-boiled egg at the center of the globe of ground beef. These Scotch eggs reminded me of the "thunder eggs" we used to find back home in the American West. When we cut open these ugly rock balls, properly called "geodes," we would find bouquets of beautiful crystals inside. The adults loved the Scotch eggs, but the children refused to try anything new, which may be an inherited defense mechanism:

Kids who don't eat anything they haven't eaten before will rarely poison themselves. Put another way: That race of kids who will try new foods is by now almost extinct.

After lunch, a band of a dozen Masai warriors came calling. They were all "kitted up," as Derek said, wrapped in what looked like red tablecloths. They had beaded earrings from the tops of their ears to the bottoms of their earlobes. And they carried double-ended Masai spears: one end javelin tipped for throwing, the other end a sword for work at close quarters. They had colored their hair with red pigment from the bark of acacias. They smelled like a forest, like trees.

They were *moran*, the elite fighters of their tribe, who once would have spent all their time raiding other tribes and stealing cattle, but who now occasionally varied their routines by invading safari encampments. They offered to dance for us.

While we sat all in a row in camp chairs, the Masai warriors danced several dances, but they all seemed to be the same dance. At the beginning, a "rapper" would begin chanting a story. The storyteller was the tallest and best-looking warrior. One of the stories he sang was about a lion who had eaten their village's witch doctor. The village warriors went out to hunt the lion, and killed it, which happened to be against the law in modern Kenya. The rapper chanted the word *simba* as often as his counterpart back home would have chanted *girl*.

While the rapper rapped, the other warriors hummed an accompanying harmony and bobbed up and down. From time to time, one of the warriors would step forward and jump straight up as high as he could. And his red-dyed hair would jump even higher. If these locks happened to strike a maiden during a dance, she was supposed to be the warrior's true love. But this time they had left all their Masai maidens back home in the village. After three or four jumps, the warrior would take his place once again in the chorus line. When everybody had had a chance to jump, the warriors would march back and forth in single file in front of us. They snaked to the right, then snaked back to the left, using their spears as walking sticks.

Although they were warriors—*moran*—their dances did not seem at all warlike. The dancers didn't work themselves up into a frenzy, and their songs were more melodic than martial. There was actually a sweetness to their music. And the rapper's voice was falsetto.

After the story of the lion hunt, the Masai warriors sang other songs that none of us could understand at all. But some of them surely told tales rooted in the history of their people. For the Masai remember their yesterdays the same way the ancient Greeks remembered theirs. They compose whole *Iliad*s and set them to music to recall the glories of their gory past.

Perhaps the band of young *moran* were singing about their primal ancestor, called Kidonoi, who was a hairy "man" with a tail. He lived at Donyo Egere—Mount Kenya—but one day he explored the land to the south of his home. He shook a calabash as he walked along, making music. The people whom he discovered south of the great mountain so admired him that they brought him females as presents. When these women bore children, they had no body hair and no tails. They were a new people: the Masai.

Historians believe that the Masai did indeed come from the north but by a somewhat different route. At about the same time Europeans were descending upon the New World of America, the Masai were descending from northern spheres upon what was to them a new land: East Africa. The Europeans drove out the red man as they advanced across America. The Masai displaced hunters-and-gatherers and agriculturalists and even other herders who had been there before them.

Tradition has it that a Dorobo hunter—taller than a pygmy but smaller than other men—saw a band of tall men coming down from the north driving great herds of cattle. Fearing these giants, the little man hid, but he was discovered and captured by the Masai. They forced him to guide them to water because they and their cattle were thirsty. These invaders were not only taller but also lighter-skinned and finer-featured and fiercer than the people they found in their way. They were striking and handsome and proud to the point of arrogance. That first Dorobo never forgot them. Nor would anyone else who encountered them down through time to the present.

By the middle of the seventeenth century, the Masai had reached as far as the Ngong Hills where Karen Blixen would later have her farm. Sometime around 1640, tribesmen discovered a boy in the Ngong whom they believed had come down to them from the sky. He became their first great *laibon* or medicine man. From that time on, the Masai would be led by a succession of these witch doctors.

Moving on farther south, the Masai—armed with spears and buffalo-hide shields—fought some epic battles, which are still celebrated in song and dance. They were as unstoppable as time. By the nineteenth century, Masai Land was 150 miles wide from east to west and 500 miles tall from north to south. And the area over which they raided was considerably larger still. Their attacks have been recorded from Lake Victoria to Mombassa, which is to say the full breadth of Kenya. They were so fierce that Arab slave traders and European adventurers shunned their land, which would be one of the last places on the Dark Continent to be explored. The Masai in East Africa were like the Comanches in West Texas who were so feared that their stronghold in the Texas Panhandle was one of the last parts of the United States of America to be settled.

The Masai speak a tongue that belongs to the Nilotic family of languages. Their particular version of the language is closest to the Bari tribe in the Sudan. The various Nilotic peoples share more than similar ways of talking; they also have many customs in common. They shave their women. They extract two middle teeth from the lower jaw so their cheeks look sunken. They remove the foreskins of young boys, and in the old days they cut out the clitorises of young girls. They typically stand on one leg, like herons, leaning on their spears. They spit for good luck. They believe important men turn into snakes after death. And they never bathe.

The Masai men usually dress in red togas, like Roman senators, which are tied in a knot over their right shoulders. The women wear small leather aprons which have been cured in human urine. For beautification, men and women make huge holes in their earlobes. They punch these holes with the thorn of the desert date and then stretch them by inserting wooden pegs. (In modern times, they sometimes pass up the pegs in favor of film canisters dropped by tourists.)

They live in *bomas:* corrals made of thornbushes surrounded by squat, primitive dwellings. The circular piles of thornbushes not only keep the cattle in but also help keep predators out. The cattlemen of East Africa came up with barbed wire long before the farmers and ranchers of West Texas. Their hogans resemble igloos, but are built of cow dung rather than ice.

The Masai believe that all the cattle on earth belong to them, so they have every right to rustle them. The cattle were a gift to the Masai from God. Never mind that the supreme being originally intended to give the cattle to the little Dorobo. A fabled Masai ancestor named Le-eyo tricked both the Dorobo and God and got all the cattle for his people. So the poor Dorobo were doomed to eke out a living by such degrading activities as hunting and gathering and the lordly Masai live honorably off their herds. Their cattle are the basis of their sense of being aristocrats, just as land is the basis of European aristrocracy. The aristocratic Lord Delamere admired the Masai because they looked down on him.

The Masai do not kill and eat their cattle—any more than a mizer eats his gold—because they would be destroying their own wealth. Rather they live off the milk and blood of the cattle which they mix together. After milking the cow, they open a vein. Not only do most Masai not eat the meat of cattle, they generally won't consume the flesh of any animal whatsoever. Since they do not hunt for food—they despise hunters—they have helped to preserve the wildlife in Masai Land. The vast herds of grazers in the Masai Mara and the Serengeti are their gift to our time.

The only Masai allowed to deviate for a time from the taboo against meat eating are the young warriors. Bands of these *moran* wander for a few years taking lovers, stealing cattle, and eating meat before settling down. (If a woman sees them eating flesh, she is flogged.) In the old days, they were supposed to kill another warrior and a lion to earn their manhood. Nowadays, such activities are proscribed, so the bands of *moran* have time to dance in safari camps, where they look down on the poor cattleless people who photograph them.

The Masai traditionally believe in a connection between death and the moon. In the beginning, death was unknown, but then God gave tricky Le-eyo, the man who had fooled Him about the cattle, an order that was disobeyed. The order was to throw away the body of a dead child while chanting, "Man dies and returns again, but the moon dies and remains away," which would bring the little one back to life. Unfortunately, the first child who died was not a member of Le-eyo's family, so he didn't bother to do what God said. God got angry and punished mankind by decreeing: "The moon dies and returns again, but man dies and remains away."

When a Masai is dying, he or she is moved outside the *boma* so death will not infect it. Which is just what the Navaho in our own Southwest traditionally do. When death comes, the body is carried away toward the setting sun. It is placed on its left side with its head to the north and its face to the east. Its knees are drawn up fetally. The right arm crosses the body and the left arm is a pillow for the head. It is left in this position for the hyenas and jackals and vultures and marabou storks. If a Masai dies inside a dwelling, the whole village is supposed to be moved. They listen for the howl of a hyena and walk in that direction until they find a place to establish a new home uncontaminated by death.

As the nineteenth century was drawing to a close, there was a lot of dying in Masai Land. Humans and cattle both. The Masai were weakened from within by the constant civil wars which they so enjoyed. Then in 1869, their Samburu cousins infected the Masia with cholera. In the 1880s, they were further reduced by a smallpox epidemic. Meanwhile, their herds were devastated by rinderpest—a cattle plague from Asia.

As if matters weren't bad enough, a comet crossed the heavens, which according to Masai tradition was a portent of disaster. The tribe's great *laibon* named Mabtien had an inkling of what that catastrophe might be. He drank honey wine which brought on a vision filled with strange pink humans.

The first white man to cross Masai Land and return to

write the tale was Joseph Thomson, who made his historic journey in 1883. He walked. "We soon set our eyes upon the dreaded warriors that had been so long the subject of my waking dreams," the explorer wrote in *Through Masai Land,* "and I could not but involuntarily exclaim, 'What splendid fellows!' as I surveyed a band of the most peculiar race of men to be found in Africa." But these splendid fellows soon began behaving in a warlike fashion which also impressed Thomson. He decided to alter his planned route in order to avoid as much as possible this peculiar "race of men" who might run a spear through him for the fun of it. He took a detour through Amboseli and around the south side of Mount Kilimanjaro.

Soon other Europeans literally followed in Thomson's footsteps. The Masai called them *l'Ojuju* or Hairy Ones and looked down on them.

About the same time, another debacle occurred. Mbatien the *laibon,* leader of the Masai people, fell fatally ill. As he lay dying, Mbatien bequeathed his title not to his elder son, Sendeyo, but to his younger son, Lenana. In the middle of a heathen African wilderness, the ancient biblical story of Isaac and his two sons, Jacob and Esau, was reenacted. Like Esau, Sendeyo felt that his younger brother had tricked him out of his birthright. Like Jacob, Lenana was indeed devious. And as in biblical times, this quarrel between brothers led to a schism of the tribe. One Masai faction followed Lenana while the other followed Sendeyo.

Lenana's Masai were so weakened by human disease and cattle disease and schism that he sued for peace with the British invaders. Sendeyo's Masai held out longer, but finally made peace, too. After twelve years of civil war, Sendeyo also made peace with his brother, Lenana. The Masai were once again united into one tribe, but too late. They were already a conquered people.

Some Masai were jailed, but they promptly died in captivity. So the British turned to fines rather than incarceration as a means of punishment.

The Masai are still a proud and handsome people, but they are also a troubled people. Their birthrate has declined and their alcoholism increased. They reminded me of the proud but troubled Comanches and Apaches and Navahos. They live primarily on reserves, like the Indian reservations back home.

"Epwo m-baa pokin in-gitin'got," the Masai say. "Everything has an end."

Songs end. Dances end. When the visiting warriors finished their last dance, finished their last historical drama set to music, they all plunged their spears into the ground in a row. I wondered if this was some sort of challenge, but it turned out that they just wanted to know if we wanted to buy any spears. We didn't. But Lesley and Taylor were interested in some bracelets and necklaces. They haggled and eventually bought a few. The Masai sold them right off their bodies.

Then we got our Polaroid and took their pictures. They were thrilled and kept staring at themselves. Then I let them look at their dance played back through the viewfinder of my video camera. Some knew exactly where to look and what to expect, but others didn't. The tall rapper was so confused that I had to guide his eye to the eyepiece. Then he was completely amazed! Every one of them had to take his turn. While they looked, I shooed the flies off their faces. They never took the trouble. Flies were beneath their notice.

Then I brought out my miniature portable VCR, which was the size of a paperback book. Now they could see themselves in color and *hear* themselves chanting and singing. This was truly magic. They might have seen some of my other toys before, but they had never seen anything like this tiny television studio in my palm. When I turned it off to save my batteries, they seemed on the verge of rioting—and they were armed. I turned the little VCR back on again and let it play until the dancing stopped.

We thanked them and they drifted away still staring at their Polaroid portraits. The encounter between the Stone Age and the Sony Age was over.

Then we turned our attention to another ancient ritual, afternoon tea, before we got organized and went out for our afternoon game drive. Derek drove us to the top of a rocky hill and we scanned the panorama for game. The land was mostly flat and dusty. In the distance, a dry lake bed stretched to the horizon.

We were surrounded on all sides by dust devils which climbed high up into the sky. These miniature tornadoes reminded me of growing up in West Texas. We kids would chase these whirlwinds whenever we got the chance. If we could catch them, we would play in them and get dust in our hair and our teeth and our eyes. There were so many whirlwinds here in Amboseli that they appeared to be the pillars that supported the vast vault of the African sky: the columns holding up the cathedral.

Looking within, I felt little storms stirring across my interior landscape. These inner whirlwinds were not the terrible storms that sometimes seemed to blow through my head laying waste to dreams and hopes and even sanity. Rather these swirling winds seemed a rebirth of mental activity. Thoughts chased themselves in circles. And I felt myself running and playing in those tiny twisters the way I had as a kid.

Through my binoculars, I couldn't see any game at all except for a couple of white vehicles parked beside each other far out on the plain.

"Look," I said, pointing. "I think I see a couple of

Tourista tourista abercrombie and kenti. And they appear to be mating."

I had referred to these beasts by their scientific name. Their common name was Abercrombie and Kent minibuses. A&K was of course the chief competitor of K&D. Whenever anybody mentioned the enemy, Ker & Downey's own Derek Dames could be counted upon to respond.

"They're not *Tourista tourista abercrombie and kenti,*" he said with disdain. "They never come out this far. No, they're baboon researchers. There's a big baboon research project here."

Deciding to see if the researchers knew where he might find interesting game, we drove down the hill for a closer look at the baboon people. One of the white vehicles drove off—a shy animal not accustomed to tourists. But the other white car was not so skittish, and we soon caught up with it. What we found was a young woman behind the wheel of a white Land Rover with a baboon painted on its side.

"I'm in kind of a hurry," she said, "because I've got a date with a drugged baboon. We knocked him down with a dart. Now I've got to get a cage to him before he wakes up."

"Why did you knock him down?" I asked.

"We're going to take a blood sample."

"Why?"

"We want to study his DNA. We've been able to construct family trees for all the baboons in the park. But we've only got the mothers and grandmothers on these charts. We'd like to know who the fathers and grandfathers were. But that's hard because baboons aren't monogamous. So the only way we can do that is by looking at the DNA. I've really got to go."

The baboon lady sped off to her rendezvous with a sleepy primate, and we went looking for animals of our own. Soon we stopped and got out of the car to do a little tracking.

"Let's have a look at these," Derek said. "Who can tell me what these are?"

He pointed to some tracks so large and so far apart that they could only have been made by some colossus. Perhaps a giant mistook a dust devil for a beanstalk and climbed down to hunt some humans. Or perhaps a dinosaur had been frozen in the snows of Kilimanjaro but had thawed and woken up hungry. Or perhaps. . . .

"They're ostrich tracks," Derek announced.

Moving on, we found where an elephant had passed. Derek pointed out how its back foot always stepped in the track made by its front foot.

"If his front foot doesn't get hurt," he explained, "then he knows the ground is safe for his back foot. That's how he avoids punctures."

A little farther on, Derek stopped again to show us a track that appeared to have been made by a huge snake. It wound back and forth in the dust.

"Who made that?" Derek asked.

"A boa constrictor," I said confidently.

"No," he said. "Look again."

We studied the continuous track carefully. Maybe it was made by God dragging his walking stick. . . .

"It's an elephant track," Taylor said. "He was dragging his trunk on the ground."

"That's right," Derek said.

We drove on until we came to a pond wearing a necklace of bright green grass. The necklace was set with lovely black-and-white zebras and black-and-white sacred ibis. A great white egret was a single large pearl.

Derek explained that there were so many ponds dotting this otherwise arid landscape thanks to Mount Kilimanjaro.

The snows of Kilimanjaro melted and fed underground streams. And these streams surfaced again as springs that fed the ponds encircling the great mountain. These ponds formed a sparkling necklace around the neck of Kilimanjaro.

A veil of clouds lifted and Africa's tallest peak posed for a postcard. We watched the sun go down behind it. Its snowcap turned from white to pink. Perhaps Kilimanjaro was blushing at being so damn beautiful. The East African sky had always reminded me of the vault of a towering cathedral, and now sunset lit up the stained-glass windows.

Staring at the colors, I was light-headed with a euphoria that made me slightly nervous. How long could it last? The higher the climb, the farther the fall, right? At the moment, I felt as though I were as high up as that frozen leopard, found near the top of the western summit, which served as a metaphor for overreaching in Ernest Hemingway's "The Snows of Kilimanjaro" story: "No one has explained what the leopard was seeking at that altitude."

Although I didn't quite trust my mood, I was nonetheless very happy. While my eyes discovered the beauties of this new African landscape, my mind explored the wonders of a vast inner panorama that rolled on and on forever inside my head. Just as the African scenery was new and yet somehow familiar, the plains and mountains inside my skull were both new discoveries and old friends. I knew that I had walked this inner Eden before. I had been happy here before, but it had been such a long time ago that I could barely remember it. I was discovering a new landscape and revisiting it at the same time. I found hidden groves of joy. I stumbled upon gurgling streams of happiness. I rested upon a great plain of peace. New and old, remembered and forgotten, Shangri-la and home sweet home.

I felt a chill as Kilimanjaro cast its shadow over us and enveloped us in night.

I N THE mess tent after dinner, we sat around the table in canvas chairs and played a game, a parlor game. We took turns naming famous couples. They didn't necessarily have to be human couples. They could be animal, vegetable, or mineral couples. They could be anything so long as the two names merged into a single phrase, almost a single word, like saltandpepper or Romeoandjuliet. You couldn't think of one without the other.

"Sherlock Holmes and Dr. Watson," Lesley said to get us started.

"Watson and Crick," I said.

"Dagwood and Blondie," said Matthew.

"Milk and cookies," said Taylor.

"Ferdinand and Isabella," Derek said.

"Ferdinand and Imelda," said Jeff.

"Imelda and Bruno Magli," said Lesley.

"Pride and Prejudice," I said.

"Abbott and Costello," said Matthew.

"Who's on first and What's on second," said Taylor.

"Turnbull and Asser," Derek said.

"Hepburn and Tracy," Jeff said.

"Bogart and Bacall," Lesley said.

"To Have and Have Not," I said.

"Birds and bees," said Matthew, knowingly.

"Wisdom and magic," said Taylor.

CHAPTER
SEVENTEEN

ELEPHANT
MEMORIES

OR MONTHS, I had had a hard time getting out of bed in the morning. On some days, I simply didn't. Occasionally, I succeeded in sleeping as much as a male lion, which is some twenty hours a day. I would have slept longer if I could. I was depressed. So I was surprised to find myself getting up early, very early, on my first morning in Amboseli. I was out of the tent in time to see the dawn turn the zebra's stripes pink.

Waking from a dream-filled night, I checked my wife's watch—I don't own one—to see what time it was. The digital face said 5:35. I knew our wake-up knock on the tent flap would not come until seven. But instead of turning over and going back to sleep, I was anxious to get up. Moving as quietly as I could, I got out of bed and got dressed. Then, still working as silently as possible, I began unzipping the tent flap that served as a door, but it gave me away. The zipper monster roared and woke up my wife, but she turned over and went back to sleep. Our roles were reversed: Back home, she would have been the one to get up early, and I would have turned over and gone back to sleep.

When I emerged from the tent, I saw a band of pale light stretched out, as if asleep, on the eastern horizon. I splashed some cold—very cold—water on my face from a basin. I was anxious for the day to begin, which was a new experience.

I felt energetic, which was an even newer experience— or rather it had been a long time. I had always admired people with energy, in part because I did not have a great amount myself. I coveted energy. I was jealous of energy. But this morning I had energy of my own.

In the east, the sleeping band of light got up slowly, stretched, and blushed. The huge sky turned pink and rose and violet. God had sent Michelangelo down to paint our morning ceiling. A family of zebras, seven in all, strung out single file, marched across our vast front lawn. They seemed a striped wagon train crossing the plains. When the lead zebra suddenly stopped, the one behind ran into him. Then the first zebra kicked the second in the nose. The light from the pink clouds turned the whole family into a variation on a children's joke: black and white and pink all over. They moved steadily from somewhere to somewhere. They had a resolute, relentless, persevering energy, the kind a writer needs. I seemed to feel this striped train moving without me and within me. I felt nature teeming inside of me and outside of me. I sensed energy flowing out there and in here.

The sun peeked over the eastern rim of the earth. It warmed me. It warmed the zebras. It warmed the flat-topped acacia trees. It warmed the yellow grass. We all absorbed energy from this vast ball of energy. God's bright marble.

I found myself thinking of an old woman, a *macumba*

priestess, whom I had met in Brazil. I could still see her, miniaturized by age, sitting in a child's chair in a small house with a tin roof. Her home clung like a barnacle to the side of a steep hill.

"People like to complicate *macumba*," she told me, "but it's really simple: We worship the energy in every particle of nature."

I had been impressed with her at the time, but I understood her better now. I seemed to comprehend not only with my mind but also with my own energy. It wasn't so much an understanding as a feeling. I was warmed by it from within and just as the sun warmed me from without. For a moment, I was a pagan sun worshiper. I was also a zebra worshiper. And an acacia worshiper. And a tall grass worshiper. I even worshiped the giraffe who had just emerged from the trees in our back yard: He was a tower of energy, a steeple of energy.

Rather than plastic flamingos, we had three giant Kory bustards in our front yard, peacefully eating seeds. I walked out toward them to see if I could get them to fly. When I was fifteen or so yards away, they flapped and flapped and finally got off the ground. But they didn't fly very high or very far. I sometimes identified with Kory bustards, but not this morning.

"Energy," a friend of mine used to say, "is better than talent."

I hadn't believed him at the time, had considered the statement pure cynicism, but now I felt he may have had a point. I realized that most of the truly larger-than-life-sized people I had met in my life had had this one trait in common: a high energy level. In this category belonged a billionaire and a famous journalist and a producer/crook and a great magazine editor and my wife. And me this morning.

Lesley and Taylor finally got up, and I showed them

the zebra chorus line in our front yard. Then we went to breakfast. Derek suggested *huevos rancheros*. They turned out to be eggs scrambled with bits of chopped green peppers and tomatoes. They weren't like *huevos rancheros* back home because they didn't have any hot peppers. But if you put on enough Tabasco sauce, it took your mind off the missing jalapeños. That tiny bottle contained an almost atomic charge of energy.

After breakfast, we gathered up our gear, piled into Double Decker, and went for a morning game drive. We followed a double track, faintly marked, across the grassy plain.

"What's your favorite animal?" Lesley asked.

"The elephant," Derek said.

Newcomers always wanted to see cats, but the leader of our safari had developed more subtle tastes when it came to viewing animals. He loved elephants for their look and their complex social structure and their personalities and their being the largest land mammals left on earth. He even loved their being a little dangerous.

We soon located two old bulls in a grove of acacias. They were busy tearing trees apart and devouring them. Derek said their tusks probably weighed about sixty pounds apiece. But they only owned three tusks between them. One bull had lost one of his ivories. We sat back and watched the big mammals browse. Soon we heard a third elephant inside the grove, thrashing about, breaking up the forest into little pieces. But we couldn't see him.

Derek said the bulls were probably using this little wood as a men's club. Of course, male elephants spend a certain amount of their time running all over the place looking for females, but other times they simply retreat to their men's clubs. I thought the two bulls in the grove might fight each other, but when they came close, they were old buddies. They touched but didn't tangle. They were used to each other. Clubmen.

Derek opened the door of Double Decker and got out. We all followed. He bent down, picked up what looked like a brown volleyball, and began tearing it apart.

"If we break this open," Derek said, "we can tell exactly what the elephant has been eating. So what has he been eating mostly?"

"Grass," Taylor said.

"It looks like grass," Derek said. "But it looks like some sticks as well, some twigs. What else do we know about this type of droppings? Has it been rechewed?"

By this time, the children knew that some grazers and browsers chewed and swallowed their food, then belched it up later and chewed it all over again. This double chewing was a very efficient way to eat. But did the elephant like its food well enough to eat it twice?

"No!" yelled Taylor.

"We've got some very good trackers," Derek said.

"Let's find some more droppings," Taylor said.

We all went on a droppings safari and soon found several kinds of animal waste. With great excitement, each new discovery was delivered into Derek's hands.

"These are giraffe droppings," he said, holding up large black ball bearings. "These are gazelle droppings." They were small tan marbles. "Both these animals rechewed their food." He broke open the feces and we could see how finely textured they were. Then he picked up what looked like a gray Brazil nut. Cracking it open, he continued, "This is coarser because it's from a zebra and zebras don't rechew their food." Finally he held up the volleyball again. "And this is coarser still because the elephant only chews it once and eats much rougher material." Sticks and twigs, for God's sake. Wouldn't they hurt?

Leaving the old bulls to the privacy of their private club, we moved on in search of whatever lay in our way. As the sun heated the air, whirlwinds, so characteristic of Amboseli, began to spin all around us once again. Since we were below the equator, they spiraled counterclockwise. What were these dust devils but almost pure energy? They were a reminder of the power that hung in the air all around us. My thoughts were spinning too, as they rarely had of late, but did they turn clockwise or counter?

WE PAID a visit to the elephant woman. Cynthia Moss, the author of *Elephant Memories,* was petite, not at all like her favorite animal. She had been getting acquainted with the behemoths of Amboseli for over two decades. Her Amboseli Elephant Research Project had its headquarters in an isolated tent since no permanent buildings were allowed in the park. The closest thing to a permanent structure was her *choo,* Swahili for outhouse, which may well be all that remains at the foot of Kilimanjaro for future archaeologists to puzzle over. After a park warden almost fell through the *choo*'s rotting wooden floorboards, he made an exception and approved the building of a concrete floor. When Cynthia is alone at her secluded headquarters, she is kept company by the "camp ghost," Melanie Fuller, a researcher killed by a lion in 1972. But the place was crowded today because we descended upon it without an invitation—the same way the elephants often entered the camp.

"When I first came to East Africa," Cynthia Moss told us over a spaghetti lunch, "I had this very strong sensation that I had come home. I felt that my body belonged here. I had a physical love affair with Africa. It was a heart feeling."

I told her I had a similar feeling. I had experienced that same mysterious sense of homecoming. I thought that perhaps I felt at home in East Africa because the landscape was so similar to the one where I had grown up. Kenya was so much like Texas that it even had a few old-fashioned windmills just like the ones that had clanged all through my youth. But Cynthia Moss hadn't grown up in West Texas. Her home had been in Connecticut. And Texas and Connecticut have very little in common, and Connecticut and Kenya resemble each other even less. And yet Cynthia Moss had felt at home in East Africa even though it didn't look anything like the place where she had actually grown up.

We had more than a love of Africa in common. Cynthia Moss graduated from Smith College. I graduated from Amherst College which was just a few miles down the road. Her first job was as a researcher for *Newsweek* magazine. My first job was as a reporter for the *Washington Post,* which owns *Newsweek.*

"Back in the 1960s, I was one of the only East Coast members of the Sierra Club," Cynthia Moss recalled. "I was interested in the loss of wilderness areas. I had grown up riding in Westchester County. I rode on the Rockefeller trails. I wanted to go to one of the last wilderness areas left on earth. One of the last true wild places. The animals were just the icing on the cake. I took a leave from *Newsweek* to do some traveling. I spent some time in Europe which was OK. Then I came here and fell in love right away."

Cynthia Moss and a girlfriend named Mariana Gosnell who also worked for *Newsweek* went on an African safari together. One of the first places they visited was Amboseli. They also took a look at the Masai Mara. And they journeyed into Tanzania to explore the Ngorongoro Crater and the Serengeti plains.

"It was a fantastic trip," Cynthia Moss remembered.

"The skies were the best part. The hugeness of it all. The landscapes. A Tommie was new and exciting. A giraffe was new and exciting. I saw a lion kill in the Serengeti. She went and got her cubs and brought them to the feast. I hadn't been in Africa a week."

I was jealous.

"I was a typical tourist," she admitted. "I wanted to see big cats. I thought elephants were boring. Didn't they just eat all the time? But I had Iain Douglas-Hamilton's name. Somebody in an airport had said to look him up. So we did look him up even though I don't usually do that sort of thing."

The year was 1968 and Iain Douglas-Hamilton was in the third year of his pioneer study mapping the social structure of the elephant herds. He had begun his research by getting to know each and every elephant in Tanzania's Lake Manyara National Park. There were 420! Needing a system to recognize individual animals, he noticed that elephant ears are as distinctive as human fingerprints. The pattern of rips and notches and scallops is unique. So he decided to photograph *all* his subjects. Naturally he wanted to have both ears visible in his pictures, but the elephants would only spread their ears and "pose" when they were angry. So Iain Douglas-Hamilton had many close calls. When one particularly determined bull charged his Land Rover, he jumped out just before the collision. The living tank killed the inanimate car. He showed his visitors a photograph of what an elephant could do to a Land Rover: Nothing was left but a heap of twisted metal bones.

"He took us to see his elephants," Cynthia reminisced. "He made them charge to frighten us."

That was when a love affair began, Cynthia Moss and elephants. She decided to stay on and do research on the world's largest mammals. Which meant that she wouldn't be returning to *Newsweek* to do research on the smallest details in news stories. Iain Douglas-Hamilton was delighted to have an assistant to help him with his work.

"That's when I got hooked on elephants," Cynthia Moss recalled. "Once you get introduced to individual elephants, well, that's the difference between two-dimensional photographs and real life. I just loved it."

Iain Douglas-Hamilton explained that he started out trying to be unemotionally scientific: He just numbered the elephants. But he soon found he couldn't remember the numbers. So he gave in and began giving them names like Queen Victoria, Oedipus, Clytemnestra, Jezebel, Cyclops, and Jagged Ears.

Douglas-Hamilton told his new assistant that he believed elephant social life was organized around a matriarchal hierarchy. A typical elephant family might consist of the matriarch with a baby and a couple of adolescent children in tow; plus another female, perhaps the matriarch's younger sister, and her kids; and perhaps a third cow, say the matriarch's grown daughter, and her newbown baby. When the male calves reached late adolescence, they would be driven out of the family to wander alone. Or they would join one or two other males to form "clubs." Unlike their human counterparts, elephant females have no desire to join these all-male bastions, for the cows already run the society. The highest-ranking female in the family is normally the oldest and largest. If America worked the same way, we would be led by Barbara Bush, which might not be such a bad idea.

Cynthia Moss found herself not only studying elephants but also studying Iain Douglas-Hamilton, who sometimes seemed to be a wild animal worthy of observation. She noticed that he was always trying to frighten people—especially himself. He dared elephants to charge. He dared Land

Rovers to wreck. He dared lions to attack. He dared planes to crash and they sometimes did. He seemed to believe that he would survive so long as he didn't care whether he survived or not. Anybody with a differing philosophy got scared or angry or both.

WHILE CYNTHIA was learning about individual elephants—and the elephant man—her girlfriend Mariana was learning to fly which was remarkable because she had always been a terrified flier. But on their safari, the two young *Newsweek* researchers had been ferried around Africa by a twenty-two-year-old female pilot, a latter-day Beryl Markham. Mariana, the fearful flier, had an epiphany: If this young woman could fly a plane, so could she. So Cynthia's friend learned to fly in Africa. And when she went home, she bought her own plane.

"Africa has this effect of changing people's lives," Cynthia Moss said. "It certainly changed my life. It opens people up. It's such a grand place. It enables you to have a bigger vision. A grander vision of life, of self, of possibilities."

Which reminded her of Kenya's early British pioneers whose correspondence she had recently been reading. She paused to take a bite of spaghetti and then told us what she found in those letters.

"They had a lot of hardship, but they were indomitable. Those early settlers wouldn't be defeated. Like our own pioneer experience back home. The opportunities were so vast that they felt they could try almost anything. Some of that atmosphere is still here. But now the black Kenyans are the ones who are excited. They are building a new country."

AFTER WORKING as Iain Douglas-Hamilton's assistant much longer than she had intended—her own pioneer days—Cynthia Moss returned to Nairobi. But she still didn't go home to America. She couldn't. Having discovered her "home," she couldn't leave it now. She wanted her own animal-research project, but she wasn't trained. It took a long time—and a lot of patience—to get started. She worked as a research assistant on various projects and lived on practically nothing.

Then she got a job with a company that wanted to make a documentary film about elephants. Her assignment was to read everything ever written about elephants and condense it into a report for the filmmakers. She began by reviewing Iain Douglas-Hamilton's observations. And then she went on from there to study every scientific paper no matter how obscure. Finally she wrote up a seventy-five-page report that summarized all that she had learned.

"When I was finished," she remembered, "I thought that I would like to do this for all the other animals. So much new research was being done. Old beliefs were being overturned. I thought it was something that needed to be done."

In 1971, Cynthia Moss went back to America, to New York City, to try to sell her idea. There she met an agent who suggested that she put her proposal in writing. So she sat down for a month and transformed her seventy-five-page elephant synopsis into a sample book chapter.

"My new agent sold it to Houghton Mifflin for $4,000. I went 'home' and went to work. It was an education. I read a hundred scientific papers. I went to see scientists. It was like getting an advanced degree in ecology."

The result of all that work was *Portraits in the Wild* which is not only a classic but the bible of every safari guide in East Africa. She profiled not only elephants but also giraffes, rhinos, zebras, all kinds of antelope, baboons, lions, cheetahs, leopards, and hyenas.

"The hyena was my favorite chapter," Cynthia Moss said.

Most people consider the hyena to be an ugly animal with a questionable character—it is a scavenger, after all— but she turned it into something quite fascinating:

> What is not well known about the hyena and should be of particular interest to women . . . is that the hyena has taken women's liberation to an unexpected conclusion. Somehow in its evolution the female hyena has developed external genitals that are exactly the same in appearance as the male hyena's: her elongated clitoris is the same shape and size as the male's penis, and she has a sham scrotum. . . .

"That was seventeen years ago," she said. "Today guides ask me about obscure points in the book that I don't even remember. They know the book better than I do."

In 1972, while she was still working on *Portraits in the Wild,* Cynthia Moss started what she called the Amboseli Elephant Project. She went to Amboseli, set up a primitive camp, and started photographing and identifying individual elephants. But she didn't insist on being charged by them all the way Iain Douglas-Hamilton had done. There were less self-destructive ways to take pictures of both ears.

In the beginning, she only worked part-time on her elephant project because she couldn't afford to make it a full-time obsession. From 1971 to 1974, she commuted between Amboseli and a small house in the suburbs in Nairobi. Then in 1975, she set up her more or less permanent camp in Amboseli and began devoting most of her waking hours to elephants.

She continues to go home to America occasionally, but she doesn't stay very long.

"I get hungry for the sky when I'm back in the States. After three weeks, I get homesick for Africa. I miss the vistas. I miss the continent—the physical placement of things."

When she is away in America, she also misses her family. Well, actually, her families. Her families of elephants.

"Elephants are such a major part of my life. I can't even consider not being involved with elephants. I have an extremely strong emotional tie. They're my friends. They're glorious beasts. I've known some for seventeen years."

In 1988, Cynthia Moss published her book about her memories of her friends with extraordinary memories. She called it, of course, *Elephant Memories* and subtitled it *Thirteen Years in the Life of an Elephant Family.* She was now two for two, two books, two classics of animal literature.

"In your book, you wrote about elephants burying their dead," I said. "Do they really?"

I asked because this aspect of elephant behavior was so extraordinary to me. Almost unbelievable. For I had been led to believe by long-ago professors—and lots of books— that humans were the only animals who buried their dead. In college, I had been taught that burial ceremonies were the beginning of art and heralded the beginning of civilization.

"They really do," Cynthia Moss said. "They cover the body with soil and rocks and branches."

"That's just amazing," I said. "I suppose it was just species hubris to believe we were the only ones who buried our dead."

"That's right," she said. "Also, if an elephant kills a human being, it will bury him or her, too."

"Elephants bury people?"

"If they kill them."

Which makes elephants more civilized than humans who mow down these magnificent animals with machine-guns, chop out their tusks with axes or cut them out with chain saws, and then leave the bodies for vultures.

Elephants not only bury, but they also mourn their dead. Cynthia Moss watched one young female who regularly visited her mother's skull. Cynthia called the daughter Agatha and the mother who died Annabelle. Just as humans tend family graves, Agatha would "tend" Annabelle's great head bone. The daughter would curl her trunk through her mama's empty eye socket and gently rock the skull back and forth. Agatha has been remembering her dead mother in this fashion for years.

I found myself thinking: Elephants knew how to grieve. Why didn't I? I remembered that I had only visited my sister's grave once and felt ashamed. Shamed by Agatha. I was beginning to realize that I hadn't mourned well. I had attempted to shun my sister's memory in the same way I had avoided her grave, just not quite as successfully. I had botched my grief, not because I felt too little, but because I felt too much, so I tried to deaden all feeling. I had anesthetized myself to the point where I wasn't living anymore. I had felt the loss of her life so keenly that I was throwing away my own. I now knew I would have to learn to mourn better, would have to allow grief to run its full course, would have to experience the full arc of sorrow. But I would have help. The elephants were teaching me to remember.

CHAPTER
EIGHTEEN

ELEPHANT
CHARGE

HAT AFTERNOON, we were thinking about elephants and so we saw elephants. We found them in large numbers and on the move. We drove into their midst and traveled with them. There were long trains of elephants to the left of us, elephant trains to the right of us, gray trains up ahead of us, and trains behind us. Each train was headed by a huge matriarch who pulled eight or nine gray cars. We must have been surrounded by eighty or more elephants all moving in the same direction on parallel tracks.

"Where's Elie?" Taylor asked. "I've got to find Elie."

She searched around among the jackets and sweaters and camera cases until she found what she was looking for.

"Here he is," she called.

Climbing up onto the roof of the Land Cruiser, Taylor carefully placed Elie in a sitting position facing the nearest gray elephants. Elie himself was a white elephant with red and blue spots. He was about two feet tall while his wild relatives stood ten feet tall. He smelled like cotton while they smelled like the cows of my childhood.

"It's a reunion," I said. "Elie's being reunited with her loved ones. She's found her roots."

"*His* loved ones," Taylor said. "Elie's a boy."

"How can you tell?" I asked.

"Well, female elephants have very square foreheads," Derek interjected, "whereas male heads are more rounded. Also, female elephants have cylindrical tusks whereas male tusks are oval shaped."

Actually Elie didn't have any tusks. More and more elephants don't. Perhaps they will be the ones to survive if the ivory poaching continues. Evolution may already be favoring them.

As Elie's African relatives walked, many of them grazed in their distinctive way. An elephant would grasp a clump of grass with its trunk, then kick the clump with a forefoot to loosen the roots, and finally lift the grass to its mouth and chew. Every kick produced a small dust storm. They repeated the pattern over and over. Grasp, kick, lift, eat . . . grasp, kick, lift, eat . . . grasp, kick, lift, eat . . . Derek told us that elephants spend eighteen hours a day eating. Their bodies are huge locomotives that burn a lot of fuel. We moved as they moved, always surrounded by them, always in the midst of them, as if we ourselves were members of the herd.

Remembering what the old *macumba* priestess had told me, I worshiped the energy in the elephants. Remembering also what Einstein taught us about the relationship between mass and energy, I realized that I was watching the largest walking bundles of energy on this earth. An elephant is a cathedral of energy. An elephant is a very Notre Dame of energy—its trunk a flying buttress. I could feel the elephants' energy moving within me and without me.

I felt as if the great behemoths were—to borrow William Wordsworth's formula—half perceived and half created. Half perceived by my eyes, half created by my will. They were one-half meat and bone, the other half pure imagination. They were half the product of the chain of evolution, half the result of a chain of thought. Surely I had a share in God's work, the Creator's work, the first mover's work, evolution's work, the Big Bang's work. I looked at my creations and they were good.

The elephants roamed across the face of the earth and through the infinite vistas of my mind. They moved at the slow, deliberate gait of productive thinking. Inspiration might spring from hiding like a predator, but the work itself is done at a pachyderm's pace, at any rate my work is. When I am actually making progress on a story, it is always step by step, word by word, sentence by sentence, slow thought by slow thought. Elephants are the color of thought, of the best part of the brain. They are walking gray matter. Matter can be converted into energy, and thoughts are energy, so thought must be matter, right? And if thought *is* matter, why couldn't the elephants be a projection of my mind, my consciousness? At the very least, *my* elephants were a projection of *my* thoughts because I saw them as no one else saw them, just as you see them in your own way. Each one to his own elephants.

Then I escaped from myself again. It was a joyous leap. I was the elephants. The elephants were me. I never felt closer to any animal than I did to these animals. I "rode" the elephants, one after another, jumping from back to back. I *was* first one and then the other. Which was strange because almost all of those elephants were females. I remembered that female *macumba* gods rode female worshipers and males worshipers indiscriminately. Male gods did the same. So the sex of the rider had nothing to do with the sex of the "horse." A god named Oxumaré changed sexes each time he/she passed under the rainbow. So I tried not to feel too self-conscious about becoming an elephant cow. But self-consciousness brought me back to myself, to my human self, for elephants do not suffer introspection.

Losing my elephant identity, I decided to pretend to be the next best thing, Iain Douglas-Hamilton or Cynthia Moss, naming the animals. Letting my imagination run where it would—as opposed to its normal halting limp—I called a magnificent old patriarch at the head of a train "Mrs. March." The second in command, probably an eldest daughter, I christened "Jo." Following behind were "Meg," "Amy," and "Beth." Lifting my camera, I took a family portrait of the handsome mother and her little women.

Selecting another impressive train, I named the matriarch "Mrs. Bennet." I called her most beautiful daughter "Jane." I christened the daughter who appeared to be the most intelligent "Elizabeth." Following in their wake were "Lydia" and "Kitty." I imagined them at an elephant ball where a proud "Elizabeth Elephant" offends a prejudiced bull named "Darcy Mammoth" who comes from a very old family.

Reaching a swamp, the elephants stopped for refreshment: Thirst had set all these trains in motion. This was another marsh fed by the melted snows of Kilimanjaro that were piped down via God's own underground plumbing. The great mammals would not have been here if the great mountain had not been there.

We parked on a causeway that bisected the marsh, surrounded by almost a hundred elephants who were spread out in a great circle all around us. Sitting on the roof of Double Decker, we watched them feeding, playing, sparring, courting, defecating, urinating, and generally having a party in a soggy swamp. They were up to their knees in water and mud. Splashing about, they looked like whales with legs. As a former kid, who used to love to run and jump in mud puddles, I wished I could join them.

"Pass the binoculars to your adorable little son," Matthew said to his father.

"You're not adorable," Taylor said.

Right in front of us, a huge elephant spread its legs and relieved itself without embarrassment. It was a gray battleship dropping mines into a harbor. They landed with loud explosions.

"I got it," I announced, lowering my camera.

While the elephants were quenching their thirst and attending to other needs, the pond began to bubble. Then a couple of hippos surfaced. I half expected to see a whale emerge from the muddy water and spout. Then we would have had all of earth's largest mammals together at one reunion.

A "teenage" elephant was sucking mud into her trunk and then blowing it onto her back and sides. She was cooling herself off and just having fun. But then an old matriarch came to the water hole and forced the teenager to move over. Water and mud holes are among the best places to observe elephant hierarchy in action.

The grand old matriarch started using her trunk to rub mud all over her long, curving tusks. She made a real mess.

"What's she doing?" Lesley asked.

"She's cleaning her ivory," Derek said.

"She's brushing her teeth with mud," Taylor said. "Yuk!"

"Look at those two," said Matthew, pointing. "They're fighting."

In the distance, two males with round heads and oval tusks appeared to be wrestling. They stood face-to-face and grappled with their trunks.

"It's not really fighting," Derek said. "It's dominance. One is saying to the other, 'Look, I'm really bigger than you.'"

Like sumo wrestlers, they leaned against each other and pushed. The larger elephant eventually managed to shove the smaller animal backward. The victor signaled his triumph by placing his trunk on top of the vanquished head. Then the defeated animal turned around and offered its rump. It was saying "uncle" in elephant. The winner placed its trunk on top of the loser's behind and followed him around.

Two other elephants approached each other with a more peaceful intent. One was a baby, the other full-grown. The little one placed its trunk inside the big one's mouth.

"If you see one elephant put its trunk inside the mouth of another, that's a greeting," Derek explained. "Also the young do it to find out what the older ones are eating and what tastes good."

Then we witnessed a third meeting which was not particularly friendly but wasn't a fight. It had to do with curiosity about taste but nothing to do with food. These huge animals were coping with giant appetites of another sort. A young bull with his trunk extended approached a young female from behind. She speeded up her pace to get away from him, but he responded by walking faster, too.

"He wants to check her out," Derek said. "He's going to come up to her and check."

Matthew started laughing.

The young bull caught up with the young female and put his trunk between her legs. It was foreplay on a grand scale—as big as romance on a movie screen. The tip of his trunk explored her sexual organ carefully.

"See that," Derek said. "He wants to make her urinate a little bit."

Matthew laughed so hard he was in danger of urinating himself.

The young female opened a fireplug between her legs and urine gushed. She could easily have put out a burning building or stopped a riot, but she couldn't cool or stop the ardor of the young bull.

Matthew almost fell off the top of the tall car.

"He will taste the urine," Derek said. "That's called 'flemen.' He'll know exactly what stage of estrus she's in."

Matthew thought this was the best scene he had ever seen in his life. It was better than the Marx Brothers. It was better than Eddie Murphy *Raw* because it was even "dirtier." The boy was about to laugh up his kidneys.

The young bull sucked some of the female's urine into his trunk and then sprayed the yellow liquid into his own mouth. He savored the urine on his palate the way a connoisseur of wine tests a new vintage. Was it too dry? Was it too sweet? Was she in estrus?

No, she wasn't.

So the young bull moved on in search of another female to taste. He did not have to go far in this singles bar in the swamp. Soon he came upon another female—one with a calf in tow. Once more, the bull reached out with his trunk and explored between the female's hind legs.

"She's old enough to be his mother," Derek said.

"You mean he likes older women?" Matthew choked out through howls of laughter.

"He doesn't care," said Derek. "Look at that calf. It looks like it's sucking."

The baby elephant reached up with its small trunk and drank from its mother. The mother's breasts were located on her chest between her front feet and they were the familiar shape. Meanwhile, the bull was attempting to drink the female's urine. The huge cow had a calf on her nipple and a bull on her vulva.

Suddenly this female's fireplug started gushing urine in the now familiar fashion. The bull again sucked up some in his trunk and transferred it to his mouth.

"He's testing it," I said. "Yum, yum."

Matthew screamed, shrieked, squawked, howled, roared, whooped, wailed, caterwauled, bellowed, barked, yowled, yelped, bayed, and brayed.

"Look at that!" exclaimed Lesley.

The young bull had an erection that was literally as big as a cannon. And it was attached to a couple of cannonballs. No wonder the females were somewhat reluctant to step onto his firing range. A romantic interlude with him would be like the battle of the *Monitor* and the *Merrimac*. I thought that the enormous erection meant that he had tasted something sexy in the urine, but it turned out that he was just young and easily excited. The old cow was not yet in estrus, so he wandered on in search of other urine to drink.

When he finished checking all the females in this particular "family" of elephants, this young bull would probably move to another family. For he probably wasn't a member of any of the dozen families who had gathered to graze and drink together in the great swamp. He would be a loner who was on the prowl. He had probably been kicked out of the "nest" a year or two ago. He might well have been looking for his first sexual experience all that time in vain. For whenever he did find a female who tasted ripe— an older, bigger, stronger male would almost certainly come along and take her away from him.

While we watched, especially Matthew, an older, larger male did appear on the scene, and the younger, smaller would-be lover beat a retreat. Then the old bull approached

our Land Cruiser the same way he had approached the adolescent. He wanted to prove that he was dominant and we
were subordinate. The animate elephant was out to prove
that he was stronger and tougher and meaner than the
mechanical elephant.

"See his musth gland dribbling between his ear and his
eye?" Derek said. "He's in a heightened sexual state. His
testosterone level is high. And, ah, he's extremely aggressive."

"Where did you look to see that?" asked Jeff.

"Between his eye and his ear."

A sticky liquid poured from a small hole in his cheek
and flowed down the side of his face. This odorous elephant
cologne streaked his features. He looked as if he were wearing war paint, which was appropriate.

"Look, see how his penis is dribbling?" Derek said.
"This is known as green-pee syndrome. It just means he's
aroused."

The giant bull stood in front of us, shaking his head,
his musth gland gushing, his pee dribbling, trying to stare
us down. His stomach was also booming. For many years,
this noise was taken to be simply a by-product of digestion,
but modern scientists have recently begun suggesting that
the sound is a form of communication. Perhaps the elephant
was saying: *Fee, fie, you're my foe.*

"Is he mad at us?" Lesley asked.

"Hang on," Derek said in a less playful tone. "Sit
down. I don't like this."

The largest land animal left on earth came charging
right at us. And he kept on getting bigger and bigger. He
was larger than all those elephants in zoos and circuses. He
was larger than the memory of that charging bull in Samburu. Perspective is everything. He made himself look even
bigger by spreading his vast ears. This male in musth, who
was bearing down on us, was about the same size as a

Tyrannosaurus rex. At around eight tons, the living animal's weight was approximately equivalent to the extinct monster's. The elephant's head was actually larger than the deadly dinosaur's and it stood taller at the hip. And its fast-magnifying tusks were a lot longer than tyrannosaurus's fierce teeth.

The bull elephant was so close that I could smell the sourness of its musth. I wondered what it would feel like to touch this viscous stain. And I imagined that I would soon find out. What would it be like to drown in musth?

A magnificent temple of energy was about to fall on us. I no longer worshiped this energy. I feared this energy. Which some gods prefer anyway.

Derek stepped on the gas which made the out-of-gear engine race and snort. The great bull-elephant rex turned at the last moment and veered off to his right. The sound of the car roaring to life seemed to have deflected his charge. We all started laughing.

The bull in musth circled around us. He had examined us head on, but now he wanted to view our defenses from other angles. As his great bulk passed our mobile fortress, I could have reached out and touched him. But I didn't. He was taller than the tallest car in Africa. I thought he might simply pass us by, but he didn't. The bull turned and stared at the rear of the Land Cruiser. Perhaps it presented a more vulnerable target. Maybe he wanted to mount us.

"This may not be pretty," Matthew said.

The ten-year-old boy, whose head had been sticking up through one of the roof hatches, suddenly disappeared back down inside the car, like a prairie dog ducking into its hole at the first sign of danger.

The musth bull charged again. The modern-day dinosaur seemed intent on making us extinct. But again he veered off.

"Whew!" Matthew said. "This is fun."

Then the elephant turned his back on us and stalked off down the causeway leaving us behind. He wanted to cross to the other side of the swamp where he hoped to find a female in estrus. But he had gone only a few steps when he stopped because something was in his way. A minivan full of tourists had just entered the bridge at the far end, blocking the bull's way out. So the elephant turned around and headed back toward us.

But that way was soon blocked too. A second minivan, this one extremely bad-mannered, pulled onto the causeway at the near end. So now the male in musth was trapped between vehicles located at both ends of the bridge. The bull was a book—a thriller—caught between bookends.

Perhaps the driver of the second bus, the impolite one, was late for lunch. Or more likely late for his lunch break away from his tourists. He was determined not to give way to a mere elephant. He was going to drive the bull to the other end of the causeway or get mashed trying.

"I'm pulling for the elephant," said Taylor.

The driver of the rude minivan raced his engine, making it roar and disgorge exhaust. The bull elephant rumbled back, making the ominous sound with his stomach. It sounded like distant thunder, a faraway storm.

"He's going to nail him now!" Matthew said.

But the ill-mannered minivan kept inching forward, and the elephant took a step backward.

"I thought he'd charge by now," Matthew said, "but I still think he's communicating with that bus to get out of the way. This could get ugly."

The crude minivan kept bellowing and belching a dark cloud of smoke. It stank. The elephant kept backing up, grudgingly retreating, but there was no place for him to go. His way off the causeway—his exit—was still blocked by

231

the other bus which just sat there watching. One bookend was passive while the other was aggressive, noisy and smelly. And the thriller in the middle kept getting madder and madder.

The elephant rumbled. The bus rumbled. The elephant snorted. The bus snorted. But the elephant didn't foul the air.

"Come on, elephant!" said Taylor.

But the bull finally turned around—turned tail—and retreated in earnest. Still he had no way out. Fleeing one bus, he was bearing down on the other.

"I hope they have collision insurance," said Matthew.

Just as the elephant reached the end of the causeway, the passive bus backed up and got out of the way. The bull ran past. But once he was off the bridge, he stopped and waited. What was he waiting for?

The rude minibus soon reached the end of the causeway, too. The driver could almost taste his lunch. He was almost home. But then. . . .

"Watch! Watch! Watch!" said Derek breathlessly.

"He's charging!" yelled Matthew.

The bull musth elephant charged the bad-mannered minivan full tilt. This time the bus was the one that turned tail and ran. We all clapped and cheered.

"That driver is nuts," I said.

"The elephant knew which bus to go for," Derek said.

I hoped he not only knew but remembered.

NINETEEN

TRIBAL
MONOPOLY

W E WERE in the air again, flying north over the Great Rift Valley, which stretches from Mozambique in southern Africa to the Jordon River in the Holy Land, in the largest single scar on the face of the earth. As markers along its route, the Rift had piled up stones, one pile called Mount Kilimanjaro, another pile named Mount Kenya. God seemed to have placed them there to stake His claim. We had taken off from the foot of the mountain that was famous for its frozen leopard. We were now flying toward the mountain that shared its name with the country. Our destination was a body of water cradled at the bottom of the Great Rift: Lake Baringo. We were also headed toward something else: trouble.

Flying over a landscape miniaturized by height, we saw dwellings down below that were the size of houses on a Monopoly board. But rather than blocks named Park Place and Boardwalk, Atlantic Avenue and Marvin Gardens, the

squares on this board were called Masai and Kikuyu and
Samburu and El Molo and Luo. The tribes of Kenya.

The symbol of the Kikuyu tribe is not the spear but
the iron hoe. They were always workers first and warriors
second. They were more intent on subduing the land than
on subduing other tribes. In many ways, the hoe proved
to be mightier than the spear, for the Kikuyu population
multiplied vigorously. They became the dominate tribe of
Kenya.

The Kikuyus are believed to have settled in the central
highlands—where Nairobi and its suburbs would one day
spring up—some five hundred years ago. Before they had
lived on the coast, but they were driven inland by an invasion of Galla nomads from the Horn of Africa who in turn
were fleeing an invasion of Somalis. When the Kikuyus
moved west into the interior, they also displaced an earlier
people, the Gumba, who were small and lived in holes in
the ground. The Gumbas disappeared from the earth while
the Kikuyus went on to rule a part of it.

In his book, *Facing Mount Kenya*, Jomo Kenyatta
described a prophecy made by a nineteenth-century Kikuyu
shaman named Mogo wa Kebiro: "In a low and sad voice
he said that strangers would come to Gikuyuland from out
of the big water, the colour of their body would resemble
that of a small light-coloured frog (*kiengere*) which lives in
water, their dress would resemble the wings of butterflies;
that these strangers would carry magical sticks which would
produce fire. That these sticks would be very much worse
in killing than the poisoned arrows. . . . He went on to say
that when this came to pass the Gikuyu, as well as their
neighbors would suffer greatly. That the nations would min-
gle with a merciless attitude toward each other, and the
result would seem as though they were eating one another."
And it all came to pass.

When the white man arrived at the end of the nine-teenth century, he found the nomadic Masai picturesque but the agricultural Kikuyu useful. The whites made servants of the Kikuyus. They also made students of them. And whenever they could, they made Christians of them. Kikuyus worked on Karen Blixen's farm and Elspeth Huxley's family plantation. These whites and blacks got on well in literature, but not always in real life. The European settlers and the Kikuyu were physically closest together but in many other ways the farthest apart. Proximity often led to prejudice. The Kikuyu chafed at being treated as apprentice white people. And they seethed at having lost their tribal lands—the best land—to the new white population. So it was natural that eventually the Kikuyu would mount the Mau Mau rebellion.

When independence came, these hardworking farm builders and village builders became nation builders. Of course, Jomo Kenyatta, the founding president, was a Kikuyu. But so too were most of the bureaucrats. The wielders of the iron hoc had become the wielders of the scepter of power.

With the death of Kenyatta, the Kikuyus lost the presidency, but this industrious tribe, the largest in Kenya, still controls the bureaucracy and the parliament. They set the tone in this most businesslike of African nations.

THE SAMBURU tribe is symbolized by the herder's stick.

The Samburu are so similar to the Masai that they are sometimes known as the northern Masai. The Samburu call themselves *il-Oikop,* the Fierce Ones, but the Masai call them *il-Sampurrum Pur,* the White Butterflies that Swarm

Around Dung. The tall, thin-featured Samburu probably broke away from the tall, thin-featured Masai two or three centuries ago, choosing to tend their herds of cattle in the harsh northern deserts. Perhaps because their lives are harder, the Samburu are not as arrogant as the Masai.

Traditionally, Samburu boys go naked except for beads and earrings made of shells. The girls wear aprons of calfskin and a bright cloth tied over one shoulder which separates their breasts. Unmarried girls are painted red. Married women wear beautiful but heavy collars woven of doumpalm fibers decorated with big red beads. Their necks rise from these collars, long and thin and delicate, like the necks of our old friends, the gerenuk, with whom they share their arid land.

THE EL Molo tribe is symbolized by the harpoon.

The El Molo are the only hunter-gatherers left in Kenya. But their hunting usually takes the form of fishing. Their name derives from the Samburu description of them, *Loo Molo Osinkirri,* the People Who Eat Fish. They are smaller than the Samburu and have bowed legs. The men wear earrings carved from the vertebrae of two-hundred-pound Nile perch. The women wear red cloth skirts over petticoats woven from doum palms. They can be found on the shores and islands of Lake Rudolph which was once a part of the Nile. The El Molo are considered inferior by other tribes—and even by themselves—because they eat fish.

But El Molo will eat more than fish when they get the opportunity. They love crocodile which they kill with a heavy harpoon. They also crave hippos which they hunt with a harpoon made from the saber horn of the oryx. They also use oryx horn to spike their gill nets—woven of doum palm—to the bottom of the lake.

THE LUO tribe is symbolized by the three-pointed sail. The Luo are also traditionally fishermen. They can be found all over Kenya wherever fish are to be caught. They are skilled builders of boats—a craft they learned from the Arab slavers. Adopting the Arab style, they have constructed fleets of lanteen-rigged dugouts. Navies of these Luo boats with their triangular sails make Lake Victoria look like the Red Sea.

IN THE old days, the iron hoe caused a population explosion in this land. In modern times, medicines and medical care have done the same. The declining infant mortality rate plus the lengthening life expectancy (Kenya has one of the highest in Africa, 58.5 years) equals a population problem spiraling out of control. Half of all Kenyans are under fifteen years of age. The average first pregnancy comes at fifteen. The average mother has eight children. Less than 10 percent of Kenyan women use birth control. All of which adds up to Kenya having the fastest-growing population in the world: It increases 4.1 percent every year. The World Bank estimates that by the 2050 the number of Kenyans will have grown from today's 21.6 million to some 120 million.

Much of the burgeoning Kenyan population pours into Nairobi where there are not enough jobs or living quarters.

Wretched slums have grown up around the city. And the majority of the poorest—as the majority of the richest—are Kikuyu.

During Jomo Kenyatta's lifetime, of course, the Kikuyu tribesmen were masters of the monopoly game, virtually cornering the power market, which made the other tribes jealous. Even after his death, the Kikuyus continue to dominate Kenya's only political party, its monopoly party, the KANU. More jealousy. But now other tribes and other would-be political parties are demanding to have their own turns drawing from the Chance deck. Which could lead to an outbreak of tribalism or democracy or both.

Our plane dropped down and landed on this precariously balanced Monopoly board.

CHAPTER
TWENTY

LOST

E HAD traveled by air, we had traveled by land, and now we were traveling by water. Our twin-prop Cessna had deposited us on the shore of Lake Baringo where we transferred to a small, open, aqua-colored boat with an outboard motor. We were now on our way, putting along at about four knots an hour, to a large island in the middle of the lake. En route, we steered around a few living islands, hippo backs.

We moved our bags into Island Camp, a campground dotted with tents that never came down, tents almost identical to "our own" which were on their way by truck to the Masai Mara Game Reserve, our next stop. We would spend a day investigating this part of the Rift Valley while "our" camp went on ahead. The crew needed the time to get it ready.

Matthew was sick; perhaps from the bumpy plane ride, perhaps from something he ate, and so bedded down in his tent. Jeff stayed with his son. But the rest of us were soon on the move again.

After a quick look around Lake Baringo, we set out by boat and then by Land Cruiser, not Double Decker but a substitute, in search of the greater kudu, the antelope Ernest Hemingway had pursued in *The Green Hills of Africa*. Since a few kudu had recently been seen on the shores of nearby Lake Bogoria—where an early missionary had been murdered—we headed in that direction. We planned to spend a few hours looking for corkscrew-horned antelope—and looking at some hot springs—then return to our camp for dinner and a good night's sleep.

Lake Bogoria turned out to be rimmed with pink, as though Taylor had taken her crayons and outlined the water. Upon closer inspection, the pink border metamorphosed into flamingos. Thousands of flamingos. Millions of flamingos. Taylor called them a "flamingo continent." Derek explained that flamingos get pinker as they get older. So the oldest flamingos are the most beautiful, which is as it should be. They often live a dozen years. One old patriarch was actually red. When they wanted to fly, they would flap their wings and run across the water on their long legs. We could actually see their footprints on the surface of the lake momentarily.

We stopped beside a million or so birds and got out to have a late lunch. We picked our way between bubbling springs in which little geysers lifted steamy heads. Lesley had suggested that we try to boil eggs in the hot springs, so we had brought some along. But how would we cook them? Derek started improvising. He placed the eggs inside a small metal toast rack. Then he wrapped string around and around the rack to keep the eggs from falling out. Next he removed the tall radio antenna from the Land Cruiser. Locating a rope, he tied one to the aerial and the other end to the "basket" of eggs. The antenna looked like a fishing pole, the rope was the line, and the eggs were the bait.

Then the adults walked cautiously to the brink of a steaming, bubbling, gurgling hot spring, but Taylor was not intimidated. She marched right up and dropped her eggs into the boiling cauldron. She appeared to be fishing in a small, angry volcano. What sort of monster did she expect to catch in such a demonic broth? Veiled in steam, Taylor looked like an apprentice ghost or witch.

After about four minutes, she pulled her "fish" out of the water. We had a wonderful picnic beside the mean spring. We ate the boiled eggs out of cups with salt and pepper. A pink picnic blanket stretched for miles to the left and right of us.

"Scrumptious," Taylor said.

After lunch, we put the antenna back on the Land Cruiser, got back inside, and drove along the shore. Something startled a couple of million flamingos who flew up into the sky and made it look like sunset.

"What are the chances of seeing a kudu?" I asked. "I mean our realistic chances."

"Well, they're here, but I don't know if we'll see them," Derek said. "They like to stay hidden in the brush."

"Hemingway looked for a kudu for a month," I said. "But he finally got one. He had it skinned and made into a rug. He used to write with his feet on the kudu's back."

"We don't have a month," Lesley said. "Sorry."

I found myself musing about what Africa had meant to Ernest Hemingway. Surely his African safaris were a logical extension of his Nick Adams stories. Northern Michigan had been enough of an Eden for the Adam-like Adams, but Papa Hemingway, full-grown and famous, had sought out the original Eden. I suspected that he had felt a sense of renewal in Africa, just as I had, but in the end he had been badly hurt. He had taken one safari too many and his small plane—not unlike the one we flew in—had crashed. Perhaps the garden resented the intrusion of a machine. Perhaps Africa wanted to prove to the he-man that even he had limitations. Perhaps his luck just ran out. Trapped in a burning plane, Ernest Hemingway used his head as a battering ram, butting the jammed door over and over again, until it finally opened. He escaped but was never quite the same again. A Hemingway character might have described him as "cracked." He went into a mental decline that ended with a shotgun blast, the hunter finally turning the gun on himself.

"Look!" said Taylor.

Right in the middle of the dirt path, right in front of us, stood a greater kudu. Its corkscrew horns spiraled toward heaven. Its big, round balloon ears turned in our direction. It looked straight at us. Derek stomped on the brakes.

"He's beautiful!" said Lesley. "We beat Hemingway. It took him a month. It only took us an hour. And I'll bet ours is bigger."

"His horns look like roller coasters," said Taylor.

The huge greater kudu—the second largest species of antelope on earth, exceeded only by the eland—ambled unhurriedly off the road and then started crashing through the brush. We pulled forward to try to get a better look at him as he moved away from us.

And there they were—two more kudu! One was a relatively small, hornless female. But the other was a giant bull. He was much bigger than the first kudu we had seen.

"That's no ordinary antelope," Derek said.

He might have weighed close to a ton. Take that, Ernest.

Leaving the kudu behind, we drove on and soon found ourselves rolling through a grove of giant fig trees. Their huge trunks and branches were twisted and gnarled.

"I feel like Snow White," Lesley said. "Where's the wicked witch?"

After we left the figs behind, the track got considerably rougher. We bounced over large rocks. We jackhammered across "luggers"—as Derek called them—which were ditches, gullies, or ravines. It was almost 6:30 in the evening and growing dark.

"It's getting late," Derek said. "We've got to be out of the park by seven. That's when they lock the gate. They figure anybody who stays later is probably a poacher. And we don't need that kind of trouble."

"Okay, let's go home," Lesley said.

"We'll have to look for a place to turn around. The road's too narrow here."

"Road" was an overstatement. We bounced and lurched and bruised along looking for a wide place. Derek suddenly jammed on the brakes.

"I don't believe it!" he gasped.

"What?" we asked simultaneously.

"Dogs!" Derek said. "Hunting dogs!"

We jumped to our feet and stuck our heads up through the open hatches of the Land Cruiser. Reaching for cameras, we could barely make out the wild dogs who were the color of gloom. What we could see most clearly were their tails which were bright white flags. These hunting dogs were about the size of coyotes back home.

"These dogs are so rare," Derek said. "I've only seen them four times in my life. And I've never heard of dogs at Bogoria. How many of them are there?"

We counted, which wasn't easy. The only parts of them we could see clearly were their white-tipped tails and their bright eyes reflecting our headlights.

". . . eleven, uh, twelve," Derek said. "I count twelve."

"I think that's right," I said.

"That's amazing. That's a large pack. Imagine, twelve hunting dogs at Bogoria."

The pack turned and ran. White patches danced in the darkness. But after they had gone thirty yards or so down the "road," they turned and looked back at us. Their eyes again gleamed in our headlights, as if they were demons of the night. Our initial excitement was turning into awe, even wariness.

"We can't turn back now," Derek said. "We've got to follow them."

He put the Land Cruiser in gear and we rolled slowly forward. We got so close that the front bumper almost touched the dogs.

"Are they hunting?" asked Taylor.

"Probably," Derek said.

"What do they want to eat?" she asked.

"Kudu," he said.

"No!"

"I'm afraid so."

The pack retreated once again. The dogs ran off down the rocky path, but soon stopped again. Their eyes burned up ahead of us like will-o'-the-wisps which seemed to say: *Follow, follow. . . .* What were they luring us into?

"Shall we keep following them?" Derek asked. "We can't stop now."

We drove forward again, but we didn't reach the dogs this time because we got stuck. Derek put the Land Cruiser in reverse, but it didn't budge. So he tried forward once more, but we still didn't move. The wheels just spun and spat out gravel. We were a beetle on its back waving its legs. Derek got out and looked under the car.

Keeping a wary eye on the hunting dogs, I got out too. The Land Cruiser was stuck on top of a boulder that kept the wheels from getting any purchase. Moreover, we were perched precariously on the side of a steep hill.

Derek started talking in Swahili to Mandiza. The two of them moved to the front of the car and started unwinding the winch. Mandiza took hold of the hook, which was attached to the end of the steel cable, and started walking up the hill. He moved between two huge boulders. Even if we somehow managed to get unstuck, we would then have to pass between these towering rocks. Was there room? There didn't seem to be. The boulders guarded the road like mythic monsters.

"Look," I said, "Scylla and Charybdis."

The whole family had recently read the *Odyssey* because Taylor studied it in school. I walked up—still watching the dogs—for a closer look at Charybdis and Scylla. I paced off the distance between them. Then I returned to Land Cruiser and paced off its width. By my rough calculation, we might be able to squeeze through with an inch to spare on either side if we hit the opening just right and didn't skid. I was worried.

I felt as if I had gotten halfway down a page—the writing seemingly going well until then—only to get suddenly and unexpectedly bogged down. My writing was full of Charybdises and Scyllas. Sometimes I found a passage between them, sometimes not. Lately my work seemed to founder more times than not. A story, like a trip, was no good unless you could get from here to there. When I reached an impasse, I often took a walk, and I was pacing now. But this time deliverance wasn't really up to me or my ingenuity. It was out of my hands. All I could do was stand on the sidelines and watch. Which was often how writing seemed to me. Where did the answers come from anyway? Why didn't they come more frequently? And why did they seem to come less and less often? More and more, writing seemed to be a matter of banging my head against a door that wouldn't open.

One trouble with being a writer is that everything becomes a metaphor for something else. Bad luck now foreshadows even worse luck later on. A stalled car can come to symbolize a stalled story, a stalled script, a stalled career. Ever since coming to Africa, I had felt better, my depression magically dispersing, but now I felt my mood to be precariously balanced, like the symbolic Land Cruiser, on the brink of despair. We had to get going soon before I dropped over the edge. I didn't think I could stand being unhappy in this paradise.

Trailing the winch cable behind him like a kite string, Mandiza climbed up the side of the mountain. He kept going until he found a boulder the size of a car. He wrapped the steel cable around the big rock and hooked it in place. Now we were ready to try to winch ourselves off one rock and between two others with the help of a fourth rock. It promised to be some ride.

"Everybody out," Derek said.

"What?" asked Lesley.

"I don't know what's going to happen," he said. "If the car goes over the edge, I'd rather you weren't in it."

"OK," she said.

"And don't stand too close," he added. "I don't want you to get whipped by the cable if it should happen to break."

"All right, but what about the dogs?" she asked. "Do they ever attack humans?"

"Not unless they're very hungry."

"Do they look hungry?"

"Not particularly."

"You can't tell. It's too dark."

Nonetheless, Lesley and Taylor both got out of the

Land Cruiser and joined me on the ground. At that moment, it started to rain. Then it started to pour. Lesley looked up at the dark heavens in despair. She hated the idea of getting her hair wet almost as much as she feared the wild dogs. The rain grew heavier and heavier. The air was as wet as the lake.

"Aaron, would you get back in here?" Derek asked. "I need somebody to hold the spotlight."

I was glad to have a job to do, to be able to help, but I somehow couldn't forget Derek's earlier warning that the Land Cruiser might end up going over the side of the cliff. I pointed the spotlight through the windshield and tried to see through the raindrops.

Derek simultaneously gunned the engine and turned on the winch. The wheels spun and the winch reel turned. I could hear the tires whirling helplessly and see the winch cable going taunt. Winching was supposed to be like fishing, but in reverse, for the "fish" (in this case the boulder) was supposed to reel in the "fisherman" (the Land Cruiser). Unfortunately, our "fish" was acting more like a real fish than the immovable object it was supposed to be. The great rock shook violently and then started coming toward us. Bearing down on us. The boulder was supposed to pull us out of a hole, but instead we were pulling the rock down on top of us. I shined the spotlight on the boulder as if that would help.

But then the big rock caught and held. It became our anchor. Now the winch worked as it was supposed to work. The "fish" was pulling the reel to it. The Land Cruiser groaned and slipped off the rock that had held it. The wheels caught and churned up dirt and gravel. But the tires slipped and we lurched sideways toward the precipice.

Then the rubber caught and we jerked forward. Now we had to worry about Charybdis and Scylla. Could we get through? Was there room? I pulled in my stomach to make myself thinner as though that might help. Somehow the Land Cruiser slipped between the two monstrous boulders.

"This is better than Tom Sawyer!" Taylor yelled.

Once we had successfully climbed the rocky hill and slipped between Scylla and Charybdis, we were suddenly all in a cheerful mood. Derek chose this moment to change eyeglasses. He said he had a special pair for when it rained. Fishing them out of the glove compartment, he stuck them on his face and turned around. This pair of glasses was equipped with working windshield wipers. Swish, swash, swish, swash. It was a moment of comic relief to mark the end of what could have been a tragedy. Now we could all laugh because everything was going to be all right. Like paper through a typewriter, the road was scrolling beneath our wheels once again.

But the road kept getting bumpier and bumpier. And the luggers kept getting deeper and deeper. I figured they called them that because they could jar the lugs right off your wheels. Then we came to a giant lugger that would have taken the wheels off along with the luggers. Since there was no way to cross it, we would have to go around it. Derek decided to follow the lugger down to the beach and then follow the beach until we found the road again.

By now, our guide had taken off his windshield-wiper glasses and replaced them with his sunglasses. Wearing shades at night might have been amusing under other circumstances, but none of us were amused, especially not the wearer. Derek had brought along only prescription sunglasses—leaving his regular glasses back in his tent— because he expected us to get "home" well before dark.

"If we ever get home again, I want a Bloody Mary," said Lesley, who doesn't normally drink.

"That's a deal," Derek said.

We drove along the beach, just a few feet from the water, where normally only flamingos dared to tread. It was a nice ride—a motorized stroll on the beach—until our left rear tire began to sink into the soft sand. Derek gunned the engine in an effort to escape. The left rear wheel buried itself.

Getting out in the pouring rain, we found the left side of the Land Cruiser sunk up to its running board in the mushy sand. The car was tilting precariously. And what was more, the tilting kept getting worse—as if our Land Cruiser were a fast-action Tower of Pisa.

Alarmed, Derek and Mandiza wasted no time stretching out the winch cable in the direction of a small tree, but the steel line wouldn't reach. So Derek had to do some improvising. He lengthened his winch cable by tying a rope to the end of it. Now it would reach the tree. So he knotted the rope around its trunk. There, that should do it. Hurrying back to the driver's seat, he started the tires spinning and the winch turning once again. The Land Cruiser stayed put, but the tree started moving toward us as if it were on wheels. Pulled up by the roots, the poor acacia was heading rapidly our way.

"Anybody want a Cocalola?" Derek asked.

He got out a chest full of Cokes and beers and soda water. He passed them out—the gracious host in the midst of tragedy. Taylor and I had Cokes, Lesley soda water, and Derek drank a beer. Then Derek put music on his tape deck, a haunting flute melody, very strange.

Taylor was having such a good time that she started dancing. She danced in the tropical rain on a deserted beach on a night that seemed as dark as any the Dark Continent had ever seen. She danced with her father. She danced with her mother. She would have danced with Derek, but he was busy once again.

Having finished his beer, our guide and leader had decided to jack up the sunken left side of the Land Cruiser. The car was tilting so badly that he had to use a machete to dig down to the bumper and then dig a hole under the bumper to make room for the jack. But then the jack, which was sitting in this great hole, wouldn't jack. So Derek went to work fixing it with vise-grip pliers and a ball-peen hammer. He banged the jack like the village blacksmith. He was in a race against time because the car was sinking and listing all the time.

"If we ever get home again," Lesley said, "I want a Bloody Mary *and* a bottle of champagne."

"That's a deal," Derek said.

After half an hour, he finally had the jack fixed. I put a huge rock in the hole under the bumper. Derek put the repaired jack on the boulder and started jacking. But rather than raising the car, the jack sank the boulder, which seemed to be on its way to Australia. I realized I was shaking my head.

Again I was reminded of my writing. So often apparent solutions just made matters worse. The introduction of a new character didn't work, a plot twist seemed false, an attempt to jack up suspense wasn't credible. It had happened so often that I was losing faith in my ability to do repair work on my prose. If it was wrong, which it often was, it stayed wrong.

Giving up on the jack, we tried pushing the Land Cruiser once again, but we knew before we started that it wouldn't work. Which was how I often felt when I sat down to type. The heavy car's wheels spun, the way my imagination so often spun, to no effect. Stuck on this beach, my spinning mind dug itself a deeper and deeper hole. I felt that old familiar sinking sensation that signaled the onset of depression.

Watching the spinning wheels, I remembered a much more terrible night. The monsters who pursued me through that darkness were much more horrible than packs of hunting dogs, much more frightening than possible leopards or lions. Rejections usually came in the form of telephone calls, but this one arrived in the mail. What I had spent nine months writing simply didn't work. Sorry. I didn't know what to do or where to go. I started walking and eventually found myself in the woods near our home. I stayed there all night. It rained. It rained hard. Using a fallen tree as a pillow, I tried to sleep and would occasionally doze off. But these escapes into unconsciousness never lasted long. I spent most of the night turning over and over, first this way, then that, rolling in the dead leaves, rolling in the mud, rolling, as it turned out, in poison ivy. Around and around and around. Going nowhere. I was a useless wheel, a broken wheel. I couldn't go back to that. But here I was stuck again. Metaphors, metaphors, the trouble with writers is that they believe in metaphors.

Matters seemed hopeless. Taylor cheerfully started making plans for where everybody would sleep.

"It would be fun to sleep uphill," she said. "We'll put Derek in the front seat. And I'll—"

"Are we going to die?" Lesley interrupted.

"No," I said. "The worst that will happen is we'll be stiff in the morning."

"Are you sure?" she asked.

"Pretty sure," I said.

Taylor's attitude had amused me and made me feel better, and now I was trying to pass that feeling on to my wife.

"Then why don't we try winching again?" Lesley suggested.

"Okay," Derek agreed.

Once more, he unwound the winch cable and added rope to it. But this time he tied it to two trees. Lesley had recovered enough from her fears by then to hold the spotlight to illuminate his task. The beam reflected off his sunglasses as he made his way back to us through the driving rain. He slid in beneath the steering wheel.

"Okay, everybody push," Derek shouted out the window.

We all got behind the Land Cruiser and put our shoulders into the task. Even little Taylor. The wheels spun throwing mud on us. The winch groaned, but this time the trees remained rooted in the earth. The bending acacias seemed to be fishing poles reeling us in. The Land Cruiser somehow struggled up out of its grave and back onto level ground again.

After reeling in the winch cable, we all piled back into the Land Cruiser and started off again, veering away from the soft beach. Soon we were back on the trackless grass banging over luggers once more. We were bouncing and bruising, but we were elated with our escape.

"I'm cold," said Lesley, who was soaked through. "How about you, Taylor?"

"N-n-n-no," Taylor chattered.

Every few yards, Derek would stop the Land Cruiser, get out, and inspect the luggers on foot. He was looking for the best path through the wilderness. It was slow going. We moved the way I move when I am having trouble finding my way to the bottom of the page. At such times, I always tell myself: Slow writing is just unclear thinking. But a muddled mind is not always easy to clear. Especially when trying to write fiction. When working on nonfiction, there is always a road paved with facts to guide you. This road may be hard to find, may be faint, may have twists and turns, but it is there and goes from somewhere to somewhere if you can follow it. But fiction can literally go anywhere. There is no road in fiction. Or rather there is only the road you see in your mind and impose on the landscape of your story. You guide it rather than it guiding you. Fiction can make you mad, as in angry *and* as in crazy.

Since the road had abandoned us, having been washed out, if it ever existed, we kept on starting and stopping, starting, stopping, looking for a way out of the wilderness. The journey felt like fiction, but it was all too real.

Derek eventually got an idea: He explained to Mandiza in Swahili that he wanted him to ride on the hood of the car and help find the way. So our spotter got out and pretended to be our hood ornament. Derek pulled out some rope and tied Mandiza in place so he wouldn't bounce off. Then our guide handed our spotter the spotlight to help him in his role as pathfinder.

We started off again in the driving rain. Mandiza pointed to the left, then pointed to the right, and Derek did his best to follow these directions. Then Mandiza held up both hands and signaled a halt. Derek slammed on the brakes—we must be on the brink of a cliff!

But we weren't. When Derek got out, Mandiza explained to him in Swahili that the hood was too hot. Our spotter had become a pancake on a griddle. So Derek fetched cushions out of the Land Cruiser and tied them to the hood and tied Mandiza on top of them.

We started off once more. Mandiza signaled to the left, signaled to the right, signaled straight ahead. And Derek did his best to do as ordered, for he couldn't see. There was the darkness. There was the rain. There were his sunglasses. And there was Mandiza sitting on the hood blocking his view. Derek sensed that we needed some cheering up.

"Did you hear the one about Idi Amin wanting to change the name of Uganda?" he asked.

"No," we said.

"Okay, Amin wanted to change Uganda to Idi. He asked his ministers what they thought of the idea. They were all silent. He encouraged them to speak up. Finally one minister got up the courage to ask, 'Do you know that the people in Cyprus are called Cypriots?' "

We were all so rattled we laughed.

"You're the first safari I've ever gotten lost," Derek said. "I'm sorry."

"Th-th-that's okay," Taylor chattered. "Th-th-this is b-b-better than T-t-tom Sawyer."

Derek decided to change places with Mandiza who was drenched and cold. So we tied our leader to the hood on top of the cushions. I offered to drive, but Derek preferred to trust Mandiza, who slipped behind the steering wheel. It was very slow going. Derek pointed to the left, pointed to the right, pointed straight ahead. We bruised and bounced.

Then Derek held up both hands and we halted. He untied the ropes that bound him to the hood and got off to take a closer look. I got out of the car because I wanted to see, too. What I saw was a huge muddy riverbed. It was the ultimate lugger. It was a lugger's lugger. It was a lugger broad enough and deep enough to swallow all our other luggers. It looked like the Last Lugger.

I got back in the Land Cruiser, but Derek stayed out in the rain, walking up and down the bank of the vast lugger. He followed the muddy ditch all the way down to the shore, down to the hot-springs-fed lake, which was smoking. And Lesley in turn followed him with the spotlight. Surrounded by flamingos, bathed in artificial light, swaddled in mist, Derek just stood there, staring at demons in the dark. We kept expecting him to come back, but he didn't. He looked like another strange bird.

"I think he's having a nervous breakdown," Lesley said.

"I think you're right," I said. "What time is it?"

Lesley lifted her watch into the spotlight's beam.

"It's a little after one," she said.

We had been lost and the rain had been falling for six hours. I kept expecting Derek to raise one leg and turn into a flamingo. I wondered if I should go get him, go talk to him, but I didn't. We sat in the car, and he stood on the beach, slowly sinking into the sand. Illuminated by the theatrical spotlight, Derek might have been playing Prince Hamlet among the flamingos, hesitating, hesitating, hesitating.

I thought I knew how he felt. Before we left home, before we launched this safari, I had felt as if I had come to a place where my road was blocked. I hadn't known which way to turn . . . whether to go on trying to write or to give up writing entirely . . . whether to write only nonfiction or to go on cracking my head against fiction's locked doors. I had even considered some solutions that I would rather not get into. So I believed I knew how it felt to stand at the edge of the abyss, even a smoking abyss. I felt that I was Derek and Derek was me. A darkness was gathering that no spotlight would be able to penetrate.

"Here he comes," Taylor said.

After half an hour of solitary meditation on the beach, Derek made his way slowly back to us, walking resolutely through the rain. I got out to meet him because I was anxious to hear his plan, if he had one. As it turned out, he had indeed returned to us with a time-honored solution, of a sort.

"Let's have tea," Derek said.

That was his plan. It was a reflex action in a crisis. His father might have been Dutch and his mother might have been German, but he had lived in a former English colony so long that he automatically reached for tea to get him through hard times. Blood, sweat, tears, and tea had gotten the British through World War II, so perhaps those same ingredients would save us now. At least Derek seemed to think so. Thankfully there was considerably more tea than blood: Only a few drops of the latter had been spilled in nocturnal hand-to-hand combat with acacia trees. Earlier when we had gotten stuck on the beach, Derek had turned to an American solution: Cokes and beer. But now we had really reached the end of the line. The Last Lugger. So Derek turned to an English solution, a Kenyan solution, a solution in which he really believed. Derek poured the tea out of a silver thermos into plastic cups. The rest of us were amused and apprehensive and a little irritated. We had expected more than tea.

"Let's consider our options," Derek said at last.

He put on the flute music once more and listened to it as he sipped his tea.

"Let's consider our options," he repeated.

But he didn't mention any options. Instead, he unfolded a map of Lake Bogoria.

"We could be here," he said.

He pointed to a place about three-quarters of the way around the lake.

"Or we could be here."

He pointed to a spot seven-eighths of the way around.

"What difference does it make where we are?" I asked curtly, beginning to lose my temper. "We're stuck. We're not going anywhere."

Derek sipped his tea and listened to the flute.

"Let's consider our options," he said again.

Now there really seemed to be no way out. I was angry at Derek, even madder at myself. I was the Jonah on this trip. I was the reason we were stuck here in the middle of a rainy night. This steaming lake was trying to tell me something sad about my life.

I thought: I'm always getting stuck. I get stuck when I try to write. I get stuck when I run away from writing, run all the way to Africa, run right to the edge of this damn lugger. I get stuck in the deep ruts of depression. I should just give up and stay stuck. Hell. . . .

But then I felt something else. I sensed the new energy of old Africa moving through me. I had come a long way on this safari. I was no longer paralyzed. I could think and plan and act. My wheels no longer spun uselessly. I had a new confidence in my ability to get to the bottom of the page. In short, I knew what to do.

"Let's turn back," I said.

"OK," Derek said without a moment's hesitation.

Evidently our leader, our guide, had been unable to bring himself to suggest a retreat. But once somebody else suggested it, he leapt at the chance.

Supplanting Mandiza behind the wheel, Derek made an elephantine U-turn and we headed back. We followed our own tracks with Derek holding the spotlight out the side window. Retreating was a little easier than attacking, because we assumed that if we had made it over a lugger once, then we could make it over it again. We didn't hesitate, just crashed right through. But these luggers looked worse than when we had first met them, for they were now roaring cataracts.

We thought tracking ourselves would be simple—almost as easy as pressing the delete key and watching it race backward—but it wasn't. We kept losing our own spoor. The rain and the dark obscured our trail. Fortunately, Derek and Mandiza were good trackers. So they kept finding our spoor again and again.

"What are those?" Taylor asked, pointing.

"Bush pigs!" Derek cried with glee, as enthusiastic as ever. "That's incredible. Bush pigs are as rare as wild dogs. Maybe rarer. What a night!"

The bush pigs looked like pigs back home, but they had long black hair.

Then suddenly there was another corkscrew-horned kudu standing right in front of our headlights. Derek had to hit the brakes to keep from hitting him.

"I don't remember ever being so lucky or so unlucky on a safari," Derek said.

We slowed down as we approached Scylla and Charybdis once again. Once more, I inhaled and pulled in my stomach. Somehow with my help we squeezed through.

We picked up speed but then had to slow again to keep from hitting a couple of dik-diks—their name means "quick quick" in Swahili—who ran and jumped in our headlights. These lovely rabbit-sized deer mate for life. They seemed to want a long-term relationship with us as well. We couldn't shake them or frighten them away.

Then the Land Cruiser stopped dead. Derek got out in the rain, crawled under the car in a puddle, and discovered that the exhaust pipe was crushed shut. The muffler had also been destroyed. Derek got some tools and went to work at two in the morning. By 2:30, he had fixed the exhaust pipe, had removed the muffler, and it had stopped raining. To get warmer, he changed out of his wet clothes into a pair of dry green coveralls.

"Are those your pajamas?" asked Taylor.

We drove into a cloud of moths that blinded us.

"I'm going to throw up," Lesley said.

Emerging from this plague of insects, we passed through the grove of fig trees once more and passed by the hot spring where we had boiled eggs so many hours ago.

And then we saw the park entrance up ahead. It was a gate—which was closed—with a small building attached. Derek stopped and I got out to see if I could open the gate. It was padlocked.

Hearing a door open, I looked up and stared into the barrel of a rifle. I was frightened. I noticed a green-gray uniform behind the gun. The armed guard said something to me in Swahili.

"We got lost," I said.

He said something else in Swahili.

"We aren't poachers," I said. "We're just a lost family."

Unimpressed, the guard continued to point his rifle at me. I was glad to see Derek bearing down on us. He went through the elaborate Swahili greeting ritual . . . *jambo* . . . *habari* . . . and on and on and on. Then Derek took a pack of cigarettes out of his coveralls and shook one out and offered it to the man in uniform. The guard lowered his rifle to accept the smoke.

I thought the confrontation was over and expected the gate to be opened now. But I had forgotten how time-consuming elaborate Kenyan manners can be. Derek and the guard talked on and on into the night in Swahili. They had time to tell each other their entire family histories.

I returned to the car to wait with the others. We were tired and wet and sleepy. Perhaps I should hijack the car and smash through the locked gate and make a run for it. But before I went completely crazy, the guard opened the gate and Derek drove the Land Cruiser through it.

But we still had a thirty-mile ride back to camp. We stopped once when we hit an Abyssinian nightjar that flew in front of us. It turned out to be beyond our help.

We stopped again when we ran out of gas. Fortunately, Derek had brought along extra fuel in a large metal can.

He got out a rubber tube and siphoned gas from can to tank. And then we roared off—the Land Cruiser was deafening without a muffler—once gain. We sounded like the Four Horsemen of the Apocalypse riding Harley-Davidson motorcycles.

We didn't stop again until we reached the shores of another lake: "home" sweet Lake Baringo. Transferring from the Land Cruiser to a motor launch, we thought our troubles lay far behind us, but the outboard motor wouldn't start. Derek got out his tools and patiently went to work again. He eventually got the motor running and we headed off over black water. We sang, "Michael, row the boat ashore," which seemed a distinct possibility.

By four in the morning, we were snug in our tent. We were getting ready for bed when somebody knocked on our tent flap. Lesley unzipped it and discovered Derek with three Bloody Marys, a bottle of champagne, and a pot of the English national drink.

Taylor said, "Ah, four o'clock tea."

CHAPTER
TWENTY-ONE

SECOND
CHANCE

ROWING UP in Texas, I used to wish that I could live back in the old days when the buffalo roamed. I dreamed of great plains covered with a million humped animals. And then one day I woke up from my dreams and there they were. Living. Grazing. Running. Bucking. Acting crazy. Goofy ghosts of a lost frontier.

I was in a new New World with a second chance. I wasn't exactly Columbus discovering an unknown world. I wasn't even Balboa staring from the peaks of Darién with "wild surmise." But I could have been a contemporary of Billy the Kid or Jesse James or Sitting Bull. I was staring out at what America looked like before Buffalo Bill Cody and his gang destroyed the great herds of bison. The buffalo were almost all gone by 1880, but now, well over a hundred years later, I was seeing the great herds again.

I was in a twin-engine Cessna flying over the Masai Mara Game Reserve in the southwestern corner of Kenya. But I felt that I was in the Old West reborn. The Great

Plains unspoiled. An early America with another opportunity to preserve its natural heritage—or ravage it. A New World redux.

I thought: Perhaps that was why I was so moved by Africa. It was an opportunity to time travel, to go back a century and do something right this time. Of course, there were already signs that this new New World was in danger, too. And the new Buffalo Bills were armed with AK-47 machine-gun-action assault rifles.

And I wasn't actually watching great herds of buffalo but vast herds of wildebeests. The bison and the wildebeest have a lot in common. They both have short horns. They both have small hindquarters. They both have large, muscular, humped shoulders. They both have oversized heads. But the American buffalo has a woolly robe draped over its shoulders which is its glory and was its undoing. The mass killers killed it for its skin. But the wildebeest wears no robe and actually looks a little silly.

A wildebeest's face looks like a gym bag with eyes. A wildebeest's physique is right out of *The Hunchback of Notre Dame*. And it runs funny. This antelope is proof that evolution has a sense of humor. It has several other names: Some call it the "clown of the veld," while others label it a "gnu," which is hard to say without smiling, until you realize it is an anagram for "gun."

Wildebeests may not be too impressive individually, but collectively they are one of the most impressive species left on earth. A century and a half ago, the world was the home of two great cloven-hoofed herds, one in Africa, its complement in America. Now there is only one.

It was an illusion, of course, but I felt as if I were being given a chance not only to go back and rewrite a continent's history, but also an opportunity to go back and rewrite my own. Just as America had squandered its buffalo and many other resources, I had squandered days, weeks, months, perhaps even years. Just as my country was running out of oil, I had allowed my own gas tank to run low on energy. For a long time, I had been writing on fumes. But now, here in Africa, I saw the great herds brought back to life, as if by magic, and I once again felt infused with energy, brought back to life in a sense, as if some Merlin were looking after me. This world and I seemed to be partners: We both shared a second chance.

This sense of second chance reminded me of Jay Gatsby, who had been given a second chance to win Daisy in one of my favorite novels. Nick Carroway, observing and narrating, says, "You can't repeat the past." But Gatsby says, "Why of course you can!" The action of the novel seems to prove Carroway right and Gatsby wrong. But I was now on Jay Gatsby's side. At that moment, I almost felt as if I could rewrite history, rewrite my own life, and rewrite Scott Fitzgerald's classic so Gatsby got the girl. Perhaps the altitude was making me delirious. I wondered how long the mood would last.

We were arriving here in late August at the height of the "great migration." Every year, during the dry season when the rains stop on the vast Serengeti plains, a million or more wildebeests start moving north. They cross the Mara River and all crowd into what appears on the map to be a small bubble at the very top of their range: the fabled Masai Mara.

From the air, the wildebeests resembled safari ants, not just because they were so small, but because they moved in the same endless lines. To see wildebeests, even from this altitude, was to be puzzled by these curious beasts. Why do they travel in these long trains—often going in opposite directions or moving on collision courses? Is this any way to run a species?

Besides the great formations of wildebeests, we could also make out a few giraffes. From the air, they looked like clothespins. As we descended, we began spotting bands of zebras.

When we landed, Derek announced happily, "There's my car. It made it!" Then he studied it more closely. "Look how dirty it is. It must have had a hard time."

Lesley had had a hard time, too. She had forgotten to put on her behind-the-ear patch that controls motion sickness, and she had paid the price. She was nauseous. I felt so sorry for her. It is no fun feeling terrible in paradise. She moved shakily from the plane to the waiting car. I felt guilty feeling so good.

The Land Cruiser was caked with mud and was missing a rearview mirror. The driver said a bird had hit it. At Lewa Downs, Derek had saved his mirror from a rhino by unscrewing it, but now he had lost it to a little bird.

The driver had driven all night to meet us here at the airstrip. Our camp crew had also driven over night and were supposedly putting the last touches on a new camp right now. We all piled into the muddy Land Cruiser and started off. Lesley was still feeling terrible. She lay down and put her head in my lap. The road was rough, muddy, and slippery. And this was the dry season.

We drove up to a gate that was set up in the middle of the wilderness. There was no fence on either side. This gate was a Zen gate. It was a door with no walls.

We drove through and immediately came upon a pride of lions. The tawny cats were resting in the shade of a clump of acacia bushes at the top of a rocky hill. Using four-wheel drive, Derek urged the car up the rough slope for a closer look. We inched to within eight feet of the pride and stopped. The lions were so upset by our presence that a couple of them yawned. We counted eleven reclining in the brush.

A fat raindrop splattered on the windshield like a bug. Then another splashed. And then suddenly it was raining hard. The drops were as thick as a plague of locusts. The rain not only fell on our windshield—it fell on us. Our roof hatches were open for better game viewing, so the storm came right into the car with us. Thinking quickly, Lesley put up an umbrella inside the Land Cruiser and we all tried to crowd under. We were laughing, but we stopped when Derek jumped out of the car—right in front of the lions— to replace the hatches. Such behavior was not only dangerous but against the law. Still we were thankful when we once again had a roof over our heads.

Without a roof, the big cats, who hated water as much as most little cats, looked miserable. I felt so good, my sense of euphoria still at work within me, that I felt especially sorry for those poor killers caught in the rain.

"Is everybody all right?" Derek asked.

"Everybody but the lions," I said.

When we finally drove on, we could hardly see through the streaming windshield. The road was a muddy river. We bounced. We skidded. We slid along sideways. We all held onto whatever handles we could find inside the bucking car. We needed football pads for this ride. People often refer to this part of Africa as the Ark since it has preserved so many animals. We were beginning to feel like Noah.

Then the sudden dry-season flood stopped abruptly. We rolled down the dripping windows and looked out at the landscape through which we were sloshing. Kenya still looked like West Texas, but this particular corner of Kenya resembled not so much the Texas of my own experience but the Texas that my grandparents had told me about. Or more accurately, my grandparents told my parents who told me. When my parents' parents came to West Texas in the late 1880s, they had to make their way through savannas of grass as high as the wheels on their covered wagons. In later years, farming and overgrazing destroyed that tall, beautiful grass. But it seemed to have been reincarnated in Kenya. Or rather Kenya had not destroyed its natural heritage. Not yet. Again I had the sense of a second chance. Not only had I found a land where the buffalo—or rather their first cousins—still roamed. I had also discovered a land where the buffalo grass still grew. I felt a twinge of what my ancestors must have felt when they first looked on what Scott Fitzgerald called the "fresh, green breast of the new world."

Much of this tall grass was wild oats. The grazers of Africa have evolved a system for sharing this grass so there is enough for all. The zebras love the oat seeds growing at the tops of the mature stalks. The wildebeests prefer the half-grown grass. And gazelles feast on new, tender shoots just as they are coming up. Impalas also like the fresh young blades, but they are adaptable and will browse on bushes when the grass begins to get tough.

We stopped when we came upon a large herd of female impalas shepherded by a single buck with a large lyre on his head. Derek said that such a male would be able to hold such a herd only for about a hundred days. We watched how hard he worked to keep his wives bunched together. He hardly had time to eat. Evidently being the head of such a household takes it out of a buck. He loses condition and is replaced by another hundred-day wonder. I found myself wondering if perhaps we shouldn't borrow this system for the American presidency, since most presidents do their best work in the first hundred days.

Since impalas are so common, you tend to take them for granted, but they are actually beautiful animals. And they are even more beautiful in motion than they are at rest. Nothing jumps as beautifully as an impala . . . not Mikhail Baryshnikov . . . not Michael Jordan. This herd of impalas crossed in front of us and each jumped the road. Such grace in such a wild place.

We had some trouble finding our tents. Derek had never camped at this site before. Nobody had. At least not since the park service had been watching over this game reserve. So we would be inaugurating a new campsite—if we could ever find it. We bounced along looking for our distinctive kelly-green tents which should already be set up and waiting for us.

Before we found our camp, we discovered a giraffe mother with a newborn baby. It was the newest we had ever seen. Derek thought it was probably less than an hour old. Giraffe mothers give birth standing up and their babies enter the world by falling about five and a half feet and landing with a thud. After fifteen minutes, the new arrival can stand up and look at the world from a height of six feet. This baby giraffe was standing, but it swayed.

"I don't think it's ever walked yet," Derek said.

Seeing us, the mother giraffe started moving away from her calf. She seemed to be intent on saving herself while letting her calf fend for itself. The calf wanted to follow its mother but apparently didn't know how to walk. The mother, who kept getting farther and farther away, didn't even look back. (These were no elephants!)

"Giraffes aren't very good mothers," Derek said. "It's their strategy for the survival of the species. A fertile grown female can have another calf and perpetuate the species. A newborn's chances of surviving aren't as good. So the mom is moving away from the likely target of a predator—the calf."

Screwing up its courage, the baby giraffe did something

273

daring. It took a step. The calf wobbled but didn't fall down.

"That's probably its first step," Derek said.

The baby took another step and still didn't tumble. Gaining more confidence, it took third, fourth, and fifth steps, picking up a little speed. But the mother's legs were longer, and she had more experience walking, so she was faster. The baby giraffe chased its mother but couldn't catch her. She kept pulling away from it.

"We shouldn't stay too long or get too close," Derek said. "Because the calf will imprint on just about anything that moves. We don't want it to think a Toyota Land Cruiser is its mother."

So we pulled away from the baby giraffe just as its mother had.

Eventually we found our camp hiding in a pretty grove of trees on the banks of the Ngorbop River, which looked more like a creek. The crew clapped when we pulled in. The ground of this brand-new campsite was uneven. I tripped on a small stump and almost fell. There were a lot of these stumps where brush and small bushes had been chopped and cleared away. The staff carried our suitcases and took our dirty clothes to wash. All this help was embarrassing but also welcome.

Lunch was Indian cuisine. Tandoori chicken. Curried rice. And something similar to a taco.

Then I let down green flaps over the mesh windows of our tent. I lay down to take a nap in the cool darkness. Lesley joined me, stretching out on her camp bed, ready to enjoy an African nap although she never napped back home.

"I think I like tents," I said. "Maybe it's in my blood. Did I ever tell you that my dad's family lived in a tent when he was a kid?"

"Yes, but that's okay," Lesley said. "That's the definition of being married: hearing the same stories over and over."

"Did I tell you how big a tent it was? The center pole was twelve feet tall."

"Sounds familiar."

"My grandfather and grandmother slept in a brass bed in the tent surrounded by six sons on cots. Did I tell you that?"

"The brass bed's my favorite part. Do you remember your grandfather very well? You never talk about him."

"What I remember best is when he died. I'd never seen a dead person before. My dad told me to take a good look because I'd never see my grandfather again. I looked and later tried to draw Granddad's picture. I thought I remembered him so well it would be easy. But I couldn't do it, maybe because I didn't remember him as well as I thought, maybe because I couldn't draw. I was five."

"Do you think you could draw him now? You're older."

"I doubt it. I can draw better now, but I don't remember him as well."

I settled deeper into the darkness and the bedding, getting ready to doze.

"Do you think you could draw your sister's picture?" Lesley asked.

I was surprised. She never asked about my sister. She sensed my difficulty in discussing this subject.

"I don't know," I said defensively. "I still don't draw very well."

The darkness lay between us.

"Do you think you could paint her picture with words?" she asked. "Words are your brushes."

The darkness between us deepened. I didn't say anything. I felt trapped in our large, comfortable tent.

"I think it might be good for you," she said.

I concentrated and tried to remember my sister in detail, tried to recall every feature, tried to see the face I had avoided facing for so long.

"She had shoulder-length brown hair," I said at last in a low voice. "Her nose was longer and straighter than mine. Her eyes were much bluer than mine." I paused because it was hard to talk. My voice was thick, my tongue awkward. "She was tall, I'm not sure exactly how tall. I should know, but I don't. Probably about five ten." I tried to moisten my mouth. "She looked, well, she looked a lot like Taylor. More every day."

I could feel Lesley studying me in the faint light, as if she were storing up details so she could do my portrait from memory is she ever wanted to. The longer she looked, the stranger her gaze became. She almost seemed to be examining me to see if I might be an impostor.

"You've changed," she said.

"How?" I asked.

"I've never heard you talk like that before," she said. "Do you know you've changed?"

"I know," I whispered.

The sun shone through a crack in the tent flap and hung a curtain of glittering air between us.

CHAPTER
TWENTY-TWO

GOLD

AFTER FOUR-O'CLOCK tea, we got in Double Decker and went back out. We began by looking not for animals but for a way to cross the Ngorbop River. Of course, there weren't any bridges, so we searched for a place where the banks weren't too steep and the water wasn't too deep. We finally found a likely spot, but the ride was so rough that we seemed to be crossing the river on a jackhammer.

On the other side of the water, we found the most beautiful plain I had ever seen. An ocean of grass rippled in waves all the way to the horizon. The waves were golden. I was seeing the gold in the grass for the first time. To me the grass of Africa had always been yellow, or brownish yellow, or just plain brown. Somehow I had missed the gold. Every blade of grass wasn't gold. But some were. Perhaps every tenth strand was golden, perhaps more, perhaps fewer, but the scattered gold blades gave the whole plain a golden luster. They were the gold threads woven through the rich tapestry.

I found myself wondering if the yellow grass of Lewa Downs had really been gold; it probably was. I asked myself if the grass that grew in the shadow of Kilimanjaro had been golden; it probably was, too. I had been blind to the gold. My eyes had been closed to a treasure that waved all around me. For a moment, I regretted the gold I had missed. I wished I could go back and start all over. But then I settled down to enjoying what was right in front of me. I had discovered gold!

Or perhaps had we found heaven, not our heaven, for we were just visitors, but a heaven for beasts? Had we ascended into "The Heaven of Animals"? In a poem by that name, James Dickey described what their paradise would be like:

> If they have lived on plains
> It is grass rolling
> Under their feet forever.

Enjoying the golden grass which seemed to roll forever were a multitude of gazelles and waterbuck and impalas. But these pastoral grazers were not the only animals in paradise. There was room in heaven for killers, too.

> For some of these,
> It could not be the place
> It is, without blood.

Before long, we saw three cheetahs. They were walking in a chevron-shaped formation—the leader in the middle, another trailing on the right, a third following on the left—near the crest of a hill. These lovely animals flowed smoothly through the gorgeous grass. Their limbs moved gracefully among the gracefully swaying blades. They were a beautiful color, golden fur offset with black spots, but of course the grass was golden, too. Until now, my eyes had always gone directly to the exotic animals while missing the rest of the tapestry that held them. Until now, I had thought of the grass as just something that got in the way, something that partially obscured the beasts that we had come to see. But now as the cheetahs slithered through the grass, I saw gold on gold, grace set against grace, beauty in the foreground matched by beauty in the background. Then it started to rain.

Derek put on the windshield wipers. We pulled closer and I photographed the cheetahs through the swish-swashing wiper blades. All three cats appeared to be males, probably brothers. Were they hungry?

"There's a bunch of gazelles up at the top of the hill," Derek said.

The Tommies suddenly started running across the horizon, horns against the sky.

"Do you think they might go for a kill?" Taylor asked.

"They might," Derek said. "Where's the third one? Sometimes when there are three, they'll hide one. He'll lie in ambush."

By the time the two cheetahs reached the top of the hill, the gazelles had scattered. The cats didn't give chase. We pulled forward and saw the cheetahs disappear into a clump of bushes. We circled the brush to see if we could find them again, but they were shy.

"Let's let the cheetahs settle down a little bit," Derek said. "We'll come back and check on them later."

We drove off in the direction of a tall, solitary acacia tree. It looked like the sort of tree favored by leopards. But before we reached it, something else caught our attention.

"Look, hyenas," I said. "No, they're dogs!"

They were hunting dogs. These dogs were *so* rare and yet we kept running into them. Then we realized that we were seeing something even rarer than we had ever seen before: We saw puppies.

"I don't believe it," Lesley said.

Like adult hunting dogs, the pups had huge ears, which appeared even huger on those little bodies. The little dogs looked as if they could fly with those ears. They seemed to have a couple of satellite dishes on their heads. The big ears made them resemble members of the Mickey Mouse Club, so perhaps they were picking up reruns of the Mouseketeers with their cranial dishes. Like the adults, the puppies also had tails with white tips. The rest of their bodies were mottled black and gray. The babies wagged their tails and shook their big ears. They were playful as puppies.

"There's a lot of them," Derek said. "Look at all the white tails. This is probably the first time they've come out of the den."

He explained that two other Ker & Downey guides—whose radio "handles" were Double Whiskey and Bordello Charlie—had seen the dogs the day before but had not reported any pups.

The den was a hole in the ground beneath a mound of dirt. The babies moved in and out of it. When they dived for cover, their white tails were the last things to disappear. When they reemerged, their big ears were the first things to appear.

"I'm pretty sure this is the first time they've ever come out of this den," Derek said. "Mom has regurgitated some food. You can see all the white tails going after it. She must have given birth about six weeks ago."

There were three adults, the mother and two males. The female's undercarriage was heavy with milk.

"Derek, would they go after a wildebeest?" Matthew asked.

"These are incredibly dangerous dogs," Derek said. "They go after anything. A little while ago, there were only 120 hunting dogs in the whole Serengeti-Mara ecosystem. Now they're starting to come back slowly. This is really a minimum-sized pack—three dogs."

"Why are there so few dogs?" Jeff asked.

"There's a whole series of things, they figure," Derek said. "Distemper, rabies, farmers consider them as vermin. You can still hunt them in Tanzania despite the fact that there are so few of them in East Africa."

One puppy stood on top of the den mound—king of the mountain. The mother dog picked up something out of the grass and started carrying it away.

"What's that?" asked Lesley.

"A baby topi," Derek said. "No, it's got to be smaller than that. Maybe a baby duiker."

Running after their mother, the puppies stretched out their white-tipped tails straight behind them.

"One, two, three, four, five, six . . . how many do you count?" asked Derek.

We all tried to count.

"Eight," Lesley said. "There are eight."

"One, two, three, four, five, six, seven, eight," Derek counted.

"Yes, that's right."

"Twelve," Matthew said.

"They all have very fat tummies," Derek said. "And they all look in very good condition."

Which was good news, but Derek was worried about a missing dog. A few weeks ago, there had been a fourth adult dog—and four was supposed to be the smallest viable pack. Could they survive as a three-dog pack long enough for these puppies to grow up?

A topi suddenly burst from the brush about ten feet from the den. It was hard to say who was more surprised—the antelope or the dogs. One of the male dogs gave chase. After all, the supermarket seemed to have followed him home, so why not do a little shopping? But the topi outran the dog. When it was sure it was going to get away, the topi went into a prancing gait as if to say: *Can't catch me! Can't catch me!*

Then another topi came running out of the brush even closer to the den. He almost fell in. Again the dog gave chase and again the topi was too fast for him. The pack was not big enough to tire the topi by running in relays.

We stayed until darkness forced us to return to our own den. I lay in bed feeling good.

"My sister was a great dancer," I said. "She tried to teach me, but I was hopeless."

"I used to try to teach you, too," Lesley said, "but you were worse than hopeless. Now, I don't know, maybe you're finally catching on. What do you think?"

"I hope so. But I still can't dance."

"Who gives a damn about dancing?"

It got quiet in the tent. I lay in the darkness feeling better and better. Back home in Washington, I had come to think of slumber as an anesthetic, which I craved, because life was a toothache. I was always in a hurry to get to sleep and so often had trouble. Tonight in Africa, I was in no hurry. I tried to savor my drowsiness, to make it last. But just when I seemed to be on the verge of understanding what made Africa so special, I dropped off with no trouble at all. Lions roared in my dreams.

CHAPTER
TWENTY-THREE

THE HUNT

E WENT out early, even before breakfast, to look for the lions who had roared us a lullaby all night.

At first, all we found was grass, golden grass, rolling under us forever. Watching it ripple, I knew that the exterior landscape was gilded because my interior landscape was no longer blasted. I saw gold out there because I was no longer made of lead in here. I had discovered Rumpelstiltskin's secret for spinning grass into gold: The magic was in the eye of the beholder.

Then we found them less than half a mile from our camp: two large male lions with magnificent manes. I had always thought of lions as yellow—or perhaps yellow fading to brown—but these were gold. They matched the golden grass perfectly, allowing them to disappear almost at will, gold melting into gold. (Now all those golden lions crouching in dark corners of antique shops made more sense.)

Derek called Double Whiskey and Bordello Charlie on the radio to report the news.

"We've got two woolly heads," he said.

One of the lions limped right up to the Land Cruiser. His back right leg had been badly injured, probably in a fight with another lion, probably over a lioness. Lions don't have too many enemies except themselves—like us. We could see scabbed wounds on this simba's right hip. He walked the way I sometimes do when I get out of a car after a long ride. And yet the crippled lion still led the way while the whole one followed behind. The gimpy lion was thirsty, so he stopped in the middle of the road—actually just a couple of ruts in which water had collected—and crouched down to drink. Not even the ferocious King of Beasts looks very intimidating when he is lapping water. A king shouldn't have to get down like that to drink. Such behavior should be beneath him. And yet there the King was down flat on his stomach lapping like a tabby cat. To me, he never looked more like his distant domestic cousin than at that moment.

When he had finished drinking, the King of Beasts got up, regained his dignity, and took a piss. He was relieving himself and marking territory at the same time. The King did not conduct his toilet the way more lowly animals do. Does any royalty? No, the King pissed backwards. This trick is known as being retromingent. The lion—and other big cats—share this uncommon talent with the rhino. I wondered what Queen Bea, Prince Charles, Princess Anne and other safariing royalty made of such a royal trait.

"He's peeing on his back legs," Derek said. "He's marking territory like the rhino. He's leaving his calling card."

Sure enough, like the rhino, the lion scuffed his feet in his own waste. Now as he walked—or limped—he would leave the scent of his urine on the ground. He was saying: This is mine! He was Donald Trump putting his name all

over his real estate. The King limped off down the middle
of the road. Or rather the ruts.

"Now the vehicles will pick up his scent," Derek said,
"and spread it up and down the road."

"Lions have figured that out?" asked Lesley.

"Sure."

The gimpy lion got tired of limping and sat down in
the middle of the road and stared off into the distance. I
stared too. The cat had stopped at the edge of what seemed
an ocean of molten gold, waves rising and falling. The lion
was studying what appeared to be a string of dark islands
floating in the golden sea. But this archipelago was shambling along at an unhurried pace.

"Are those elephants?" Lesley asked.

"They are," Derek said.

The Crippled King of Beasts just sat there dreaming an
impossible dream. Staring at him, I dreamed, too, and made
the leap. I was him and he was me. I had been crippled by
life, by failures, by my own reaction to those failures, but I
was no longer paralyzed. My crippled mind could still
dream dreams as big as elephants. I got up, limped a few
paces closer to them, and sat back down. After a short rest,
I limped again and sat again. This is how an old, crippled
lion hunts elephants.

"What are those little black spots all over his body?"
Lesley asked.

"Flies," Derek said.

"No!" said Lesley who hates bugs. "They're all
flies!"

"How does he stand it?" asked Taylor. "I'd love to get
the bug repellent and spray him all over."

So even the King of Beasts was not Lord of the Flies.
The flies were lords of him. These pesky insects were on a
lion hunt while the lion in turn was on an elephant hunt. I

realized that I was scratching my back, but I couldn't reach the place where it itched the most.

"Lesley, would you scratch my back?" I asked.

"That's unusual," she said. "You never want your back scratched. I'm the one who likes back scratches."

Her fingernails found the itch. Ah.

AFTER BREAKFAST—I had *huevos rancheros* as usual—we started out again. On the radio, we could hear Double Whiskey and Bordello Charlie chatting about a dalmatian who was walking across the Mara. Then they saw two dalmatians. This was supposed to be some sort of coded guide talk, but we managed to figure out that they probably meant cheetahs. Derek admitted that we were right. So we set off in search of a couple of cats with dogs' code names.

But we took the scenic route. We weren't going to be the kind of tourists who just wanted to see cats. No, we wanted to see everything. We stopped here. We stopped there. But I secretly had a typical tourist longing: I wanted to see cats, especially spotted cats. Nevertheless, we paused to watch a gang of vultures devouring the remains of a wildebeest.

"What kind of vultures are they?" Lesley asked.

"Actually, there are three kinds," Derek said. "Most of them are Repell's vultures. The darker ones with white backs are white-backed vultures. And then there are also Nubian vultures."

Leaving the Nubians et al—God's own garbage disposals—to their work, we rolled on and were soon driving through a herd of wildebeests.

"Uglee!" shouted Taylor who was riding on the roof.

Meanwhile, the chatter of the radio between Double Whiskey and Bordello Charlie about the cheetahs continued. But where were they? Where were we? Wherever we were, the grass had recently been burned over.

While zebras raced across the road in front of us, Derek explained that the fire had been set by a couple of Ker & Downey guides. They burned the old, tough grass so new tender shoots would grow in its place. The fire had clearly worked as intended: The burned areas had sprouted tender blades. Which had drawn an incredible array of animals. The world is supposed to end in fire "next time," but this fire had produced a new Eden. The game on the new grass was as thick as flies on a lion's back.

The bright green plain looked as new and shiny as wet paint. Dabs of brown were wildebeests. Delicate black-and-white brush strokes were herds of zebras. A larger brush had applied a wide black racing stripe to the side of each brown Tommie. These colors didn't just lie motionless on the canvas. They moved the way colors in an impressionist painting sometimes seem to.

Leaving the green fields behind us, we drove back into the gold. Wildebeests raced in front of us, suddenly changing direction, then changing direction again, like a race run by the insane. Zebras rolled on their backs to scratch themselves.

Then we saw them: two Land Rovers seemingly courting. We pulled up beside Double Whiskey and Bordello Charlie. Even though we were right next to each other, the men of Ker & Downey continued to converse with each other over the radio.

"Where are the dalmatians?" Derek asked.

"Under that tree," Bordello said over the two-way—but he also pointed.

The tree was about two hundred yards away at the far

edge of a golden meadow. We looked through our binoculars and saw what looked like kittens under a bonsai tree. We drove up for a closer look. The spotted cats were taking it easy in the shade. We could tell they were living creatures and not pretty toys because occasionally the closest one would wag his tail up and down.

"The Swahili word for cheetah is *duma*," Derek explained as we waited to see if the cheetahs would hunt. "So that's what we started calling them on the radio. The trouble is that pretty soon all the tourists begin to understand the word *duma*. So then the word gets changed to *madoadoa* which means 'the spotted one.' "

"Ahah," said Lesley, "but that could mean a leopard."

"That's right. So you say *madoadoa nchini*—'the spotted one on the ground.' "

"Oh."

"And then when they catch onto that one, you say *kelele kelele*—'that about which much noise is made.' "

"How do you know for sure that that's a cheetah?" asked Taylor.

"Just any spotted cat will keep your clients happy," Derek said.

Both cheetahs were facing us now—two Kewpie dolls who looked exactly alike. Derek explained that genetically all cheetahs are virtually identical. Their genes are 98 percent the same. They are all each other's twins. Which is not considered healthy from the point of view of breeding. They could face extinction brought on by a threat not from without but from within. So cheetahs have been brought in from as far away as Russia in an effort to enrich the genetic mix. These "twin" cats put down their heads simultaneously and closed their gorgeous eyes.

"They're taking a nap," said Taylor.

"Sweet dreams," said Jeff.

Somehow the fastest mammals on earth had become the slowest. I realized that when I thought of cheetahs, I always visualized them in action, running, a blur of motion, but these animals were as sedentary as a couple of writers. I identified with them because I normally spent much of my days doing just what they were doing, lounging about. Even when I was hard at work on a project, I was hardly a blur of motion, but lately I hadn't worked very hard on anything. I had lost my work ethic because I had lost my confidence. I told these cheetahs what I often told myself: *Get up and do something!* But as usual, this command was ignored. Their inaction seemed to be a reproach for my inaction. They wasted time in order to show me how costly the wasting of time could be.

For time was running out. The sun would soon be going down and we would have to head back to camp. And the last days of our safari were fast running out, too. And everybody said that time was also running out for the animals who were being pressed into smaller and smaller corners of Africa. If we didn't see a hunt now, when would we see one?

Illogically, I felt that if I saw a hunt, I would be that much closer to solving the mystery of the African experience. I wanted to drink deeply and completely from that experience and I knew I hadn't yet. So far, there had been no blood in the cup.

"Uh oh, Aaron," said Lesley, "his ear flicked. Did you see that?"

Then one of the cheetahs rolled on his back and pawed the air. Such violence. Who knew what might happen next?

"Do they ever climb trees?" asked Taylor.

"Cheetahs gave up their retractable claws," Derek explained, "and the right to climb trees in exchange for spiked running shoes."

Watching the dozing cheetahs, our eyelids were getting a little heavy, too. And it was almost lunchtime. Double Whiskey and Bordello Charlie had long since headed in for chow.

"I'm hungry," said my ten-year-old nephew Matthew. "Let's go back to camp and eat lunch and take a nap."

Derek said going back to camp was fine with him. We could feast, sleep, and then come back and check on our cats in the late afternoon. But the cheetahs might well hunt before we returned. They were diurnal animals and sometimes killed during the middle of the day.

"Then maybe we should stay," I said.

I wasn't yet ready to give up on the cheetahs. I had given up on too many projects lately. But now I felt that I had the energy, the confidence, the stubbornness, whatever, to see something through to the end. So I convinced my somewhat reluctant family members to help me keep this vigil. Derek pointed to a box of ginger snaps on the dashboard of the Land Cruiser.

"We can have those for lunch," he said.

The kids were good sports. They climbed up on the roof of Double Decker and lay down. Taylor lay on her back and read a Perry Mason mystery. Matthew lay on his stomach and kept asking: "How long have we been here?"

The answer to that question kept getting more and more impressive. One hour . . . two hours . . . three hours . . . four hours with no end in sight. We sat and watched the grass, which was beautiful, but after several hours even I felt the gold was beginning to tarnish.

"He's up!" I cried.

One of the cheetahs got up, then the other. They stretched and yawned the way I often do when I finally get up and head for the keyboard. They rippled over the rocks toward a herd of Tommies. The gazelle hunt was beginning. . . .

But actually the cheetahs turned out to be hunting for a more comfortable place to lie down. They chose a patch of shade cast by boulders and settled down again. Then they went back to sleep. The hunt turned out to be just another false start. I knew a lot about false starts.

"They're never going to hunt," Matthew said. "They haven't moved all day."

"Yes, they have," I said. "They moved about twelve feet. Wasn't it thrilling?"

A line of zebras passed in review before the cheetahs under their tree. One of the striped animals saw the spotted cats, stopped, and faced the danger. Soon another saw and stopped and stared. And another. And another. Until there were seven zebras all in a row. They could have been an exotic chorus line or dishes in a cafeteria. Eventually they got tired of waiting to be killed and moved on.

While we waited and waited to see if the cheetahs would please hunt—the family indulging my obsession—we looked them up in a field guidebook. We learned that these cats weigh from 88 to 132 pounds. So both of those cheetahs under the tree put together weighed about what I weigh, maybe less. I am a heavyweight and they are lightweights, but I still wouldn't want to take them on, not even one at a time.

While we waited and waited and waited for the hunt to start, Derek put a cheetah tape on the car's sound system. Suddenly the jungle rang with chirping sounds. If I hadn't known better, I would have thought it was a bird rather than a killer cat. Lions roar but cheetahs chirp. Maybe that was something else they gave up for speed. A big voice would be too much to carry around. Hearing our taped cheetah, the living cheetahs didn't even bother to open an eye.

We waited and waited and waited and waited some more. Normally on a game drive, you go to the animals, but now we just sat still and the game came to us. Two hyenas ran along the crest of the hill directly above the cats.

Soon a family of topi walked between us and the cheetahs. They were strung out in single file. They moved calmly, resolutely. They seemed unaware of the cheetahs' presence, nor did the cats pay them any attention. Perhaps they were too big for the cheetahs to handle.

Then came a parade of Grant's gazelles. I remembered the saying, "Grant's have pants," which was how one distinguished them from other gazelles. They had lovely white behinds. A male with an impressive crown of horns was followed by half a dozen females. Normally one drives by gazelles quickly, but now the gazelles were passing us by and doing it at a stately pace. I had time to appreciate how beautiful these animals were, especially the females. Normally one's eyes go automatically to the big horns atop the male. But if one studies the smaller-horned females, one sees—women. Of all the animals in Africa, these female gazelles reminded me most of the females of my own species. Which is a compliment to both animals. The female gazelle is so dainty and moves so gracefully on such beautiful long legs. They crop grass the way a woman sips tea from a delicate china cup. Their faces are lovely and fine-featured. They looked so lovely and so much like women that I found myself thinking that they should put some clothes on. These Grant's needed pants.

I paid attention, but the cheetahs didn't.

Then came the smaller Thomson's gazelles—which are one of the cheetah's favorite foods. They didn't parade in front of the cats the way the topi and the Grant's had done. Rather a whole herd grazed closer and closer to the cheetahs. If they kept slowly moving in that direction, a Tommie would eventually fall right into a cat's mouth.

The cheetahs continued to doze, but a Thomson's

gazelle suddenly woke up to the danger. He stood absolutely still and stared at the cats for a long time. Then he wheeled and ran back through the herd, a little Paul Revere. As he spread the alarm, the Tommies, who had been grazing closer and closer to the cheetahs all afternoon, stopped and began to retreat. The chances of the cheetahs hunting seemed slimmer than ever. But one secretary bird started chasing another which was a hunt of sorts.

These kitten faced killers were just two cats ignoring their food. And every cat owner knows how frustrating that can be. They let the zebras pass in peace, let the gazelles alone, let the topi troupe on by unmolested. These felines obviously weren't tempted by these glorious brands of cat food. What delicacy could possibly stir them to action?

"Who wants to see a dead lion?" Derek asked. "One the Masai killed with a spear."

"I do," said everybody.

Everybody but me. I knew the lion wasn't going to hunt, and I still thought the cheetahs might. Unfortunately, they looked dead at the moment, too.

"Well, all right," I said, "if that's what everybody wants to do."

Derek started the engine and we began pulling away, but just then a long line of wildebeests came filing past the cheetahs. It was one of those seemingly endless gnu trains to nowhere. As they passed near the cats, they would break into a run, but the line never stopped coming. One calf broke into a pronking gate, landing stiff-legged on all four hooves at the same time, then jumping almost straight up again. Pronk, pronk, pronk. It was a pretty way to run, but it was also more. When a wildebeest pronks, it means danger.

"Let's wait just a little longer," I said. "Maybe cheetahs like wildebeest meat."

It was just an excuse not to give up, not yet. I didn't

explain—because I didn't think I could explain—that if I gave up now, then it would be easier to give up next time, and pretty soon I would be back in that old rut of abandoned projects. Moreover, I felt the stirring of an old belief, the belief that I could make things happen, that by force of will I could compel movies to be made, books to be published, television shows to appear on the screen . . . even cheetahs to hunt. I once considered my belief in my own powers to be one of my greatest talents. I had lost that ability to believe, but now I was getting it back. Now was no time to call off the hunt.

"What time is it?" asked Matthew.

"A little after five," Derek said. "Let's give them until 5:30. We have to leave by 5:30 if we're going to get home before dark."

We sat and watched and waited and saw spots before our eyes. I believed as hard as I knew how to believe. In my mind, I saw the cheetahs getting up and heading toward the wildebeests. But the cats ignored my dream and didn't move. Once again, I imagined them getting up. Still nothing. I imagined again and again and again. *Move, damn you!*

At exactly 5:30, the cheetahs got up, yawned huge yawns, and stretched with their forepaws extended out in front of them and their rumps in the air. They even stretched their tails. Then they sat and stared at the wildebeests with lowered heads.

Finally the cheetahs started walking down the rocky hill. They strolled over to a lone tree that stood in the meadow and sat down. Oh, no, they were just looking for another shady place to continue their nap. But they did seem a little more awake than before. One of them rolled on his back and did a long wiggle. Then the other seemed to have an identity crisis.

"He's trying to climb a tree!" Taylor said.

The cheetah seemed to have forgotten his Faustian pact in which he had traded trees for speed. He also appeared to have forgotten what sort of spotted cat he was. He was the cheetah who would be a leopard. The tree trunk grew at an incline, so the would-be tree climber got off to a good start, but halfway up his running claws betrayed him. He slipped and fell back to earth. In the cheetahs, I had seen an emblem of myself, so now I wondered: Was my trying to write like a cheetah's trying to climb a tree? But I was feeling too good to dwell on the question.

"What do you suppose cheetah heaven would be like?" I asked the children.

"Maybe they nap all the time," said Matthew.

"Maybe they can climb trees," said Taylor.

Then one of the cheetahs started moving toward a herd of wildebeests off to the right. Soon the other cheetah was up and moving, too, following about ten feet behind his brother. They traveled at a resolute walk. They did not crouch low or make any effort to hide. They just walked straight toward the wildebeest commissary. They might have arisen not from the shadow of a small tree but from the lines of William Butler Yeats's poem:

> . . . such a form as Grecian goldsmiths make
> Of hammered gold and gold enameling. . . .

The goldsmiths had hammered out not only the killers but also the wilderness through which they stalked.

"This could be it," Derek said.

Before I had seen a reproachful reflection of myself in the sedentary cheetahs, but as soon as they started to hunt, I felt something else: I was a cheetah. Call it a daydream, call it vivid imagination, call it magic. I was a quiet-footed hunter. As boy and man, I had always been slow in foot-races, but now I would be fast. Speed meant new freedom. I could out-run old troubles. Now if I could only teach my mind to be as fast as my feet.

I led the way while my brother, as always, followed behind. Through gorgeous cat eyes, I saw the wildebeests suddenly begin bucking wildly. They were a great gnu rodeo, but they had already bucked off all their riders. Or perhaps the riders just hadn't gotten there yet. Soon I would be on one of their backs riding with claws instead of spurs.

I noticed a lone Thomson's gazelle who was between me and the ugly gnus. He turned tail and ran, then turned back to face the danger, then ran again, then stopped again. But I wasn't interested in the Tommie.

I headed straight for the herd of wildebeests at a gradually quickening pace. My walk became a trot, then an unhurried lope. Then I stopped. It was a deadly beauty contest. I was deciding which one would die.

Then I started moving again, picking up speed faster this time, but still not running full-out. I was saving some of my legendary speed for the final charge.

When I was almost to the wildebeest herd, which stood as if waiting for me, I lengthened my stride and picked up speed. I reached way out with my paws and claws. I was frightening and exciting and exquisite.

A terrible beauty is born. . . .

Yeats wrote those words about Ireland on Easter morning 1916, a killing morning. Would this be a killing afternoon? I took dead aim at a wildebeest calf and pulled the trigger of my speed.

"He's after one!" yelled Derek. "He's after one!"

As I became a blur of motion, I somehow lost my identity, like the cheetah who wanted to climb trees. I wasn't the cat any more; I was the calf. I wasn't beauty anymore; I was ugliness. I wasn't the hunter anymore; I was the hunted. And I was afraid. Back to me came all those childhood nightmares about being chased by a big cat who wanted to eat me up. As if in a bad dream, I ran but didn't seem to get anywhere while the killer suffered no such paralysis, quite the opposite, being as fast as he was gorgeous.

While I seemed to hobble along, he reached top speed. A greyhound can run thirty-nine miles per hour, but it is too thin, like an anorexic model. A thoroughbred racehorse can run forty-seven miles an hour, but it makes a lot of noise. A cheetah can silently accelerate from zero to forty-five miles per hour in two seconds. And a few seconds later, it can be running seventy miles an hour. My would-be killer was running fast enough to break speed limits in America.

The cheetah's forefeet stretched out straight in front of him, his hind legs straight out behind, like an Olympic diver, but this diver was diving through the air horizontally. Then suddenly his feet were underneath him again. Then he stretched out full-length again. Seeming not to touch the ground, he raced across the earth with the same trajectory as a bullet. This cat forced you to believe in God and the Devil at the same time, for only God could make such a perfect running machine, but only the Devil would make it run with such deadly purpose.

A terrible beauty is born. . . .

This terrible beauty was out to kill ugly me. Why had I ceased to be the predator and become instead the prey? Perhaps my sympathy had originally been with the cat as the individual pitted against the herd. After all, by a stretch of the imagination, I could be a lone cheetah, but I couldn't be a whole multitude of wildebeests. Moreover, I was a product of a culture that valued the individual rather than the masses, rather than the classes, rather than the mob. But once the cat had chosen his intended victim, an individual wildebeest, then my sympathy had gone over to the hunted, the underdog, the little guy, the unintentional clown, the Masai Mara equivalent of Charlie Chaplin's tramp. My run was as funny as his walk.

When the cheetah launched himself at me, aiming to bring me down, I realized what it was that I was afraid of: It was death. It was a new sensation for me. Or rather it was the rebirth of a sensation that I thought had been deadened long ago. For I had not feared death for some time. I sometimes actually looked forward to it. For instance, when a plane would hit an air pocket causing the other passengers to wince in fear, I would smile because I knew a crash would put an end to considerable mental pain. Once I had been afraid to fly, but no more. Once I had been afraid to die. But no more. Or so I had thought. But now I feared death once again. Why? Was it because I had come back to life? Was it because I once again had the energy to hope, the energy to plan, the energy to believe? Perhaps there was a down side to resurrection. Fear was resurrected, too.

"He missed!" Derek cried out.

I was saved! I survived! I had beaten death! But then I lost myself in the herd of other wildebeests and ceased to exist as an individual. Losing my identity, I returned to the Land Cruiser where I watched the rest of the hunt as a spectator rather than a participant.

Some of the wildebeests changed direction and ran back to the right, which was nothing new. Wildebeests are always changing direction. If there is one thing you can count on about wildebeests—besides their being ugly—it is that if some go in one direction, others will go in the other. They are bewildered and bewildering beasts.

Using his tail as a rudder, the cheetah suddenly changed direction, too. Some of the wildebeests were so confused that they actually ended up chasing the cat. But he paid them no attention. He had a single target in mind which looked like a fleeing hunchback. The cheetah was a deadly version of a story for children: Beauty was out to kill the beast.

"He's going for him!" Derek yelled. "He's got him!"

Lacking retractable claws to grab and hold, the cheetah depended upon tripping to bring down his prey. He simply reached out and knocked the young wildebeest's hind legs from under it. The calf stumbled and fell and the cat attacked with fangs. Beauty had felled ugliness. I was glad I wasn't that poor calf.

We raced the Land Cruiser ahead to see the cheetah on his kill, but when we got there, all we saw was a spotted cat on a termite mound.

"He missed again!" Derek said.

On this particular day, ugliness had beaten beauty. The wildebeest had somehow gotten up and gotten away. The cheetah was breathing hard, its narrow chest heaving, from its profitless race.

We were just beginning to calm down from the adrenalin rush of the hunt when the hyenas appeared. Two of them headed directly for the cheetah, spots against spots. But one spotted animal was beautiful while the other two were ugly. Actually the hyenas were almost as ugly as wildebeests. They too were misshapen and looked like hunchbacks. And they too ran funny. Hyenas and wildebeests would seem like brothers if the former didn't sometimes eat the latter for dinner. Perhaps the hyenas charged in order to defend their territory. Perhaps they just didn't like the cheetah's good looks. Perhaps they were just being dogs chasing a cat. Anyway they came right at him with fangs bared, and they have the strongest jaws of any predator in Africa.

When the ugly spots were only a couple of feet from the beautiful spots, the cheetah jumped to his feet with bared teeth and a hiss. But the big cat did not challenge the spotted dogs. He turned and ran.

Ugliness had defeated beauty again.

While the cheetah was in midflight, a secretary bird walked right through this drama the way the hero of Stendhal's *The Charterhouse of Parma* rode through the Battle of Waterloo without realizing anything was going on.

I was excited—exhilarated—but I still hadn't seen a hunt carried to its logical conclusion. I still hadn't seen a kill.

CHAPTER
TWENTY-FOUR

DEATH
IN
AFRICA

HE MORNING after the cheetah hunt, we went to see a huge herd of wildebeests try to cross the Mara River. The Mara kills more wildebeests than any living predator. A million or more cross it at least twice every year. They swim it once as they migrate north during the dry season, then again as they migrate back south when the rains return. It was dry season now. We were all sitting on the roof of our Land Cruiser on the northern bank of the Mara River on the last day of our safari.

For over an hour, the wildebeests hesitated, playing Hamlet on the riverbank. Then they suddenly became decisive and started hurling themselves at the water—jumping, bucking in midair, belly flopping. They swam with just their heads out of the water—looking like ugly ducks with horns. But when the wildebeests reached the other side of the muddy river, they faced an insurmountable cliff. They tried to climb this vertical wall with wet, slippery hooves, but they never rose higher than a couple of feet before falling back.

I knew something about falling. I was familiar with sinking. I was used to beginning bravely but ending feebly— or not finishing at all. I could empathize with those ugly animals down below.

"Look, some of them are starting back," said Taylor.

A stream of wildebeests had given up on the sheer cliff and were returning to the shore from which they had come. Meanwhile, more wildebeests were still jumping into the river and swimming toward the cliff.

"What would wildebeest heaven be like?" I asked.

"No rivers," said Taylor.

"Just ponds," said Matthew.

Eventually, a few wildebeests discovered a small out-cropping of land where they could get a footing. The cliff looked a little less steep here and might possibly offer a way up and out.

"Where are the lions?" asked Lesley.

"Right up there," said Derek.

He pointed to the trees and brush directly above the few wildebeests who looked like they might make it.

"They're either going to drown," said Matthew, "or the lions are going to get them."

But even the wildebeests on the beachhead were having a hard time scaling the heights. They would climb about ten feet and then fall backward on top of each other. They fell hard. They crashed on their backs and bounced and skidded. They smashed so violently that you imagined ribs and even spines being broken. And when they splashed back into the water, some had trouble swimming. You could see the cripples floating away with the current downstream. Some would find a way to clamber ashore, but many others belonged to the hungry river. The scent of Africa, red and peppery, was intensified by the water. Enlarged, underscored, magnified, it finally identified itself: the smell of death.

"They're lemmings with horns," said Jeff.

"Ow!" said Taylor.

A wildebeest took a particularly cruel fall. It fell on its back and bounced and did a somersault and then splashed. Falling bodies seemed to be everywhere. It was a wildebeest Gettysburg.

"This is the most incredible thing I've ever seen," said Lesley. "This must be ritualistic. They can't be this dumb."

"It's so sad," said Taylor.

I thought of a Robert Frost poem called "Design" that questions the cruelty that often seems to characterize nature. In a few lines, it recounts the story of a butterfly who, caught in the web of fate, unerringly makes its way to the net spread by a spider:

> What brought the kindred spider to that height?
> Then steered the white moth thither in the night?
> What but design of darkness to appall?—
> If design govern in a thing so small.

What brought the wildebeests, who were not at all small, to this river? There must have been a design, for these silly animals had crossed at the same place last year, and had not fared any better then. The design that killed the butterfly fed the spider. One of God's creatures made a meal of another of God's creatures. But the river wasn't hungry. The river did not grow fatter for swallowing dozens and dozens of these funny-looking animals. Was their destruction, like their very shapes, a part of some giant joke? Was the design just cosmic humor? Was the universe laughing at the wildebeests, at all the beasts, particularly at the human beasts who looked for meaning, for designs?

"I saw a bunch die," Matthew said. "They were crying in agony."

"There we go, there we go," said Derek. "They've found a route."

Now a small trickle of wildebeests had discovered a narrow path that actually led to the top of the cliff. A very few were finally making it.

"There's one old bull," Derek said. "He's pushing them to go the right way."

But in spite of his efforts, the vast majority of the wildebeests continued to go the wrong way, to fall, to crack, to drown. It was too sad to keep on watching. I felt a pressing need to do what so many wildebeests were failing to do: to escape from this river with all its depressing devastation of life and limbs.

"Who wants to go now?" asked Lesley.

"I'm ready," I said.

Although we had seen a lot of death, we still hadn't seen a kill. But what we had witnessed was more chilling than a kill, I told myself, for the destruction was so inexplicable. I felt like that man in *The Maltese Falcon* who believed "somebody had taken the lid off life and let him look at the works."

But I was wrong about one thing: how it would actually feel to see a cold-blooded kill.

LEAVING THOSE poor animals to their fate, we started up the engine and headed for camp. Rounding a clump of acacia, we came face to face with a lioness whose teeth were clamped on the back of a baby wildebeest's neck—its brown body limp as a shroud. We all gasped. The lioness studied us a moment, then dropped her prey and ambled back into the brush.

"It's alive!" Lesley said.

The wildebeest's ear was twitching.

"Just a reflex action," I explained.

I knew that this wildebeest had already gone to its riverless heaven.

But then the baby lifted its head. This had to be more than a twitch. This was Lazarus. With all of us straining to help, the small animal staggered to its feet and wobbled on its legs. It looked just like a newborn calf getting up for the first time in its life. And indeed this baby wildebeest was being reborn. It took a few tentative steps and almost fell down. This "newborn" was learning to walk all over again.

"Now there's a will to survive," Lesley said.

Her saying it made me feel guilty, for my own will to survive had been weakening for months. I compared myself to that little wildebeest calf—ugly, ungainly, downright funny-looking—who had beaten a lion by brute force of will. All I had faced was an empty page. And yet I was the one who had given up, who had been broken, who wanted to lie down and sleep with death. I felt humbled, unworthy. I knew I had been not only a coward but a stupid coward.

As if acting out a parable for my benefit, this Lazarus of wildebeests actually started running. James Dickey's lines about what happens to prey animals in paradise had literally come to life, had come to pass, right in front of us:

They fall, they are torn,
They rise, they walk again.

Then another young wildebeest emerged from the trees at the edge of the river. It must have had a strong desire to survive, too, just to have saved itself from the jaws of the Mara. Here was another spindly legged prophet come to teach the power of the will to live. To be. To keep going no matter what. . . .

Then as if in midthought: The lioness rushed out of the brush. I felt as if I had fired the predator at the wildebeest. Hadn't I wanted to see a hunt? An attack? A kill? Had I willed this violence? Now that it was too late, I was sorry. But at the same time, I wanted to see what would happen, so I wasn't sorry enough.

"Uhhhh!" grunted Derek.

The lioness overtook the wildebeest and pounced on its haunches. The claws of her front paws sank into the meat of its rump. The lion kept her hind legs on the ground to act as a brake, an anchor. She was trying to tackle the wildebeest the way a linebacker brings down a running back, but this was the ultimate tackle. The lioness jerked the wildebeest sideways, but it didn't go down. The lion gave another hard pull and the beast flopped to the ground. The wildebeest kept trying to get up—its head and shoulders would rise—but the lioness would always pull it back down.

"She's playing with it," said Derek.

And then the wildebeest was up! But it didn't run away. The lioness had it by the throat. They just stood there, the prey and the predator. Neither made a sound. The victim did not seem to struggle. The lion did not rip out the wildebeest's jugular as I had expected. There wasn't even any blood. The lioness contented herself with strangling her victim—a form of killing that I had thought was practiced only by humans. She clamped her teeth down on the wildebeest's windpipe and held on.

Ten seconds passed.

They were statues standing in a grassy field, but one of the statues was dying. The scene was incongruously gorgeous, the blue unblemished sky, the blades of gold. It might have been a canvas by Vincent van Gogh, the vivid colors, the bright hay in the fields, the profound peacefulness, the insanity of the universe.

Fifteen seconds.

I remembered the only blood sport I had ever witnessed. It was a bullfight in the ancient Roman coliseum in Nîmes, France. It had been the perfect setting for life-taking since those stones had deadly memories. The Romans too had enjoyed watching lions kill their victims. And they enjoyed gladiators. Was I in the cheering stands turning my thumb down on the poor wildebeest?

Nineteen seconds.

The wildebeest fell over on its side—dying without a bang *or* a whimper. Dying utterly silently as if in a painting.

When we pulled forward, we saw the lioness hunched down behind the fallen wildebeest. She lifted her head and stared at us. The lioness was out of breath from the effort of killing while the wildebeest didn't breathe at all. She looked to the right, then to the left, then got up and calmly walked away from a couple of hundred pounds of very fresh meat.

We pulled up for a closer look. The wildebeest lay quite dead without a mark on it except for a couple of flecks of blood on its haunches.

"Daddy, I hope you're happy now," Taylor said accusingly. "You wanted to see a kill."

Tears ran uncontrollably down my face. I *had* wanted to see a hunt. I *had* wanted to see a kill. But I didn't anymore. The wildebeest didn't look so foolish now that it was dead. Death had somehow ennobled it. Still I felt silly crying over the death of an animal, embarrassed. But I couldn't help it, couldn't stop. Trying to cut off the tears just made me choke and cough and feel sillier. I knew now that I had been wrong to wish for death. For an animal's. For my own.

"I'm sorry," I blubbered with everybody staring at me. "I'm really sorry."

I was sorry that I had ever wanted to die. I was sorry

that my sister had died. I cried for myself because I had been such a fool. I cried for my sister because . . . because . . . well, because crying for her was long overdue. I had been afraid to face my grief for her, been afraid for over twenty years, been hiding all that time. My grief was still a blank page, a page I feared to touch, a page on which I had long feared to write. Now tears fell on that blank page. I knew that I somehow had to get to the bottom of it. I had to write my mourning on it in language so clear it hurt. And I had to begin now. . . .

"I'm sorry," I said again. "I should have called. I meant to call."

"What?" asked Lesley.

"My sister," I said. "Von Sharon." I had not said her name in years. If I had to mention her at all, I simply called her *my sister* which was somehow easier. "I intended to phone her that night," I continued in a hoarse voice. "But I forgot. If I'd called, she'd have been talking to me instead of driving in her car. Von Sharon would still be alive."

"You can't know that," Lesley said.

"I'm sorry," I said. "I'm sorry I'm crying."

"That's all right," Taylor said. "You'll be OK."

Maybe I would be now. When I stopped sobbing, I felt a little better, the way you do right after you throw up. But I knew the pain would return. This page could not be written quickly, not at one sitting, not in one day, perhaps not even in a lifetime. But I had made a beginning. I said over and over to myself: *Von Sharon, Von Sharon, Von Sharon, Von Sharon.* . . .

"There's another dead one over there," Lesley said.

It lay at the edge of the trees. Soon we found a third body hidden among the bushes. All were dead but unmarked and untasted. The lioness had been killing purely for sport. Which was something I thought only humans did. Humans like Ernest Hemingway.

As we drove back to camp for lunch, we saw our two cheetahs on top of a freshly killed wildebeest calf. Beauty could not be denied forever.

Von Sharon, Von Sharon, Von Sharon. . . .

CHAPTER
TWENTY-FIVE

THE ANSWER

E TOOK off into a sky that looked as ominous as Africa's future. The continent is sometimes said to suffer from three plagues: population, tribalism, and backward economies. The sky was only troubled by dark boiling clouds and machine-gun rain. Buffeted by strong winds, we flew toward a black wall. We seemed about to crash into a mountain of coal, but then the coal turned into black cotton candy. We slipped inside the blackness and bounced up and down. Our Cessna was a paper airplane. Our safari was over and we were flying back to Nairobi as best we could.

Coming in for a landing in the capital city, I felt a sinking sensation, not only because we were losing altitude, but also because we were returning to a world of politics, of growing graft, of shrinking freedoms, of problems multiplying beyond control. Urban Africa could be as depressing as wild Africa was exhilarating. Why did such bad governments spring up in such a good land? Africa's rulers generally reminded me of the flies on that limping lion's back. The best that could be said for Kenya was that it was not the worst-ruled country on the continent.

That evening, Derek took us for a tour of nighttime Nairobi. We came across an overturned *matatu*—a public minibus—lying on its side. The dead body of a man lay uncovered in the middle of the street. I suddenly remembered the bodies of the wildebeests killed by a lioness for sport on the north bank of the Mara River. And I could still see all those other drowning brown bodies floating downstream. I recalled the two cheetahs tearing hungrily at the flesh of their prey. I had a vision of a landscape of brightening bones. I was remembering a wilderness killing ground. But Nairobi was a killing ground, too.

And so was America. I recalled another killing street, the one where my sister was crushed to death. She died exactly one month short of her first wedding anniversary. Her body was taken to a mortuary where her husband worked part-time to pay college expenses. Von Sharon had often visited him there. They courted there. And when she came to him there one last time, he would not let anyone else touch her. He prepared her for eternity and laid her out in a room where they had once whispered and kissed. My heart ached for the man who lay dead in the Nairobi street and for his family and for my own. We drove on, leaving the body behind, but taking with us our memories.

After another night in the Norfolk Hotel, the rest of the family flew home. But I stayed on to continue to try to find an answer to my question about why Africa meant so much to me, to us all, why it moved us so deeply.

I hoped Richard Leakey, Kenya's wildlife czar, a member of one of the country's most prominent families, might be able to help me. His father was, of course, the late Louis Leakey and his mother is Mary Leakey, so he grew up with *two* giants, *two* larger-than-life heroes of anthropology. Louis Leakey was evidently the better organizer while Mary Leakey was the better fossil-finder. In 1948, when Richard was four years old, his parents took him along on an expedition to Lake Victoria where his mother found a remarkable skull and jaw of an apelike animal who lived 20 million years ago. It was the first important fossil to be discovered in Kenya and was named *Proconsul africanus*. In 1958, in Olduvai Gorge in what was then Tanganyika but is now Tanzania, Mary Leakey made the most important discovery of her life, one of the most important anthropological discoveries ever. It was a hominid skull with enormous humanlike teeth that was 1.7 million years old. The Leakeys christened it *Zinjanthropus boisei,* but they referred to it familiarly as "Zinj" or simply "Dear Boy." Later other scientists renamed it *Australopithecus boisei.* Following in the footsteps of his parents—who themselves had been trying to follow the million-year-old footsteps of dawning man— Richard Leakey himself made a major anthropological discovery in 1972. He found a 2-million-year-old skull at Kooba Fora near Lake Rudolph that was the earliest known bone that could be labeled *Homo*—human. Richard Leakey had shown us that we were all older than we thought, and he had helped substantiate his father's long-held belief that East Africa was the place where humans arose. The real Garden. He certainly had the credentials to answer my question if it were answerable, but I was beginning to worry that perhaps it wasn't.

I drove a small, white, rented Fiat toward Richard Leakey's office located in Nairobi National Park, which sprawls just beyond the capital suburbs next to the international airport. In this surprisingly good, almost-urban wild animal park, zebras and wildebeests, giraffes and warthogs, ostriches and eland, lions and cheetahs listened to 747s take off and land. I drove through the park's elaborate wooden entrance which resembled the facade of a church. I stopped in a small parking lot surrounded by drab official structures made of stucco.

Getting out of my rented car and shambling toward the headquarters building, I was nervous. I had been warned that Richard Leakey was a businesslike busy man who hated to have his time wasted. I had been cautioned not to attempt to make small talk or to create an atmosphere. If I knew what was good for me, I would dispense with all prologue and get right to the point. Unfortunately I was unaccustomed to frontal assaults.

The headquarters building looked as if it belonged in a small shopping center in the American Southwest. It was the sort of structure that usually houses dentists. And yet in this unimposing edifice, Richard Leakey was trying to save the elephant and the rhino and other species being pushed off the edge of the earth. It wasn't just a park headquarters but the headquarters of a war being waged against poachers. I opened unimpressive doors and walked in.

A guard behind a pane of glass directed me through a turnstile and down a hall. Finding a door with Richard Leakey's name on it, I knocked warily, but no one came. Slowly and nervously, I opened the door. I discovered a secretary who told me that the head of wildlife was still at lunch. I took a seat.

As I waited, I was made more uneasy by what I knew of Richard Leakey's relations with his only brother, Philip. The two of them had fallen out in the late sixties and had not spoken for over a decade. Richard, the more aggressive of the two, had made a point of being unfriendly not only to his brother Philip but also to his brother's family. It was a terrible Cain-and-Abel feud. And Richard was Cain. Having had a sister taken from me, I couldn't imagine voluntarily giving up a brother. What kind of man would cast away a member of his own family? And yet hadn't I done something similar? Hadn't I cast out my sister's memory? Hadn't I removed her from my life? Perhaps I had better not throw the first stone.

Something very like design had eventually brought the two brothers back into contact with each other. In 1979, Richard's kidneys failed and he faced death ... unless he could persuade his brother Philip to give him one of his healthy kidneys. The elder brother had trouble even bringing himself to open communication with his younger brother. How could he ever force himself to ask for such a sacrifice? But to save himself, Richard finally humbled himself and Philip responded generously. Abel saved Cain's life. But Cain still had not mellowed. I reminded myself for the thousandth time to get right to the point.

Then Richard Leakey walked in and filled the room. He was taller than I expected, well over six feet. He was slightly overweight. He reminded me of one of my oversized Texas uncles. In all the pictures I had seen of him, Richard Leakey had worn outdoor safari clothes. Khaki shirts. Even khaki shorts. But now he wore a coat and tie and white shirt. He had brown hair and a handsome weathered face. Apologizing for being late, he ushered me into his small office.

"What can I do for you?" Richard Leakey asked, getting right to the point.

"How is your campaign against the poachers going?" I asked, not exactly getting to the point. Of course, I was interested in Kenya's struggle against the murderers of elephants and other game. But I was more interested in my own struggle to comprehend the "African experience." Unfortunately, I was afraid he might consider such an interest trivial.

"There were some people making a living shooting elephants and holding up tourists," said the head of Kenya wildlife. "If they couldn't find any elephants, they would look for tourists. An American woman from Connecticut was shot to death during a robbery. Two Frenchmen also died. The poaching gangs had the run of the place. Something had to be done."

A man of action, Leakey wasted little time coming up with a solution that just might work. He called it "sort of a war." But it was more "war" than "sort of." He had cast himself as the commanding general of a hot shooting war being waged relentlessly against the poachers. His game wardens had been transformed into an army.

"In the past, we tried to apprehend poachers with good luck," he explained. "But all that has changed. Now if men are found in the parks under arms, they are treated as an enemy and are fought. The poachers haven't fought back as hard as I thought they would. We have killed or captured large numbers of their team."

So no longer did game wardens with bolt-action rifles ask poachers with AK-47s: Please, put down your weapons and surrender. First of all, the wardens weren't using guns with bolts any more. "They're using G3s," Leakey said. "They're NATO issue." These machine guns were the West's answer to the East's AK-47. But the wildlife department did more than just pass out new guns. "Training has improved," said Leakey. And most important, the orders had changed: Wardens kill armed men first and read them their rights later.

"We've stepped up aerial surveillance and ground patrols," Leakey continued. "The aircrafts see poachers and radio to our men on the ground. We make plans to ambush. There is an exchange of fire. We've won most battles."

Leakey was reluctant to talk about poachers because

he believes that any news about them, even good news, eventually turns to bad news. For it only serves to remind potential tourists that there is a war going on. Nonetheless, he was proud of what his army of wardens had accomplished.

"We are not in this business to play games, not against poachers armed with automatic weapons," Leakey declared. "So far, there are fifty-one dead on their side, ten on our side. And the poachers who are killed or captured are not being replaced. We are mopping up the residue."

Kenya is winning the war of the body counts. Critics of the new shoot-first policy—shoot first with a burst from a G3 assault rifle—say an elephant's life is not worth a human's life, not even a poacher's life. But perhaps that depends on whether the human is armed with an AK-47 and prepared to shoot first himself if he gets the chance.

Richard Leakey leaned back in his chair and assumed a position that was supposed to signal that our talk was at an end. He was a busy man who needed to get on with the saving of the animals. Realizing I was being politely dismissed, I felt an almost irresistible urge to get up and hurry out of the office. But I clenched my will and remained seated.

"Just one more question," I blurted a little breathlessly. "I was wondering if you could tell me why Africa has such a profound effect on people. I've asked a lot of people, but nobody seems to know."

"Genetic memory," Richard Leakey said succinctly. "That's your answer. There's no basis in science. But people come here from China, people come from Japan, people come from America, and the vast majority of people who come here feel something they feel nowhere else. It's not just the wildlife. It's the place. If, as I believe, it is a memory, almost a familiarity, it is very primitive. It is the capacity homing pigeons have, salmon have, to recognize, to go back. You feel it's home. It feels right to be here. The feel of the air. Everything. And yet geneticists say there is not a shred of evidence. So how does it work? What is the genetic basis for instinct? What enables a swallow to find Capistrano? What allows a salmon to go home to its birthplace?"

I didn't hear church bills ringing. I didn't see fireworks bursting. I didn't say *Eureka!*, not out loud anyway. But I liked his answer.

THE NEXT day, I called on Hugh Lamprey, the head of the World Wildlife Foundation, the leading conservation organization in the world. His office was at the center of downtown Nairobi. Traffic was terrible as usual. It was almost as difficult to make my way through the car-clogged streets of Kenya's capital as it had been to fight my way through the interlocking vegetation on the gorillas' distant mountains. Some of the downtown office buildings resembled barracks. Some others looked like high-rise motels. The city is dominated by a cylindrical skyscraper with what appears to be a huge cup of tea sitting on top. I somehow managed to find a parking place in a municipal parking lot and then walked down Harambee Avenue to Embassy House. It is so named because it houses both the French and German embassies. The World Wildlife Foundation is located on a floor between the French and the Germans.

Hugh Lamprey, a conservation legend in East Africa, turned out to be a handsome, dignified man dressed in safari shorts. He reminded me of an older, more conservative Indiana Jones. Like the movie hero who combines academics and action, Lamprey is a scientist, actually a botanist, who has chosen to make his mark in a larger world. He is a pilot and spends much of his time acacia-hopping over the African wilderness.

"Do you have an explanation for the so-called 'African experience'?" I asked. "Why does this part of the world affect us so?"

"First of all," Lamprey asked cautiously, "have you felt this experience?"

"Yes," I confessed. "Very much."

Seeing the elegant man relax slightly, I had the feeling that I had passed a first test. This careful scientist was uneasy discussing anything so parascientific as "the African experience." I had the sense that he would not have indulged in such a conversation at all if I had given the wrong answer.

"Well, I may know what you're talking about," he said, "but I'm a scientist and scientists don't . . ."

"Richard Leakey says it's 'genetic memory,'" I interrupted.

"Does he really?" Lamprey smiled warmly for the first time. "That's very interesting."

I felt that I could read his thoughts: Well, if Richard Leakey can talk about what can be felt but cannot be proved, why can't I?

"Isn't it?" I prompted.

"If you go into this beautiful country," he said gravely, "it will impress you. You may be emotionally moved. Africa does have a special appeal."

"Yes."

"Now we know very well that people like to relax by getting out into the countryside. Especially people who live in cities. Why do we get so much enjoyment and so much relaxation from going into the unspoiled country. Perhaps it is because that is where we came from. That was the world of our primitive ancestors. It is relaxing to go back to what must have been the normal human habitat. Man as a species comes from those surroundings. Our ancestors came from Africa—from the very surroundings that we see in East Africa. Our ancestors lived in this country in a habitat that looked like the Masai Mara and the Serengeti. We may have an ancestral memory in our genes of what our earlier habitat really was. I can understand why people are more spellbound by Africa than they are by the beauties of Paris."

I HAD HEARD that Cynthia Moss, the elephant woman, was back in Nairobi and I got in touch with her. We talked in an Italian restaurant in the middle of downtown Nairobi across the street from the American embassy. We both wore jeans while almost everybody else was dressed in skirts or suits and ties.

"We naturally like savanna landscapes because we evolved here," she said. "This is deep in the recesses of our minds. Why do Japanese take their trees and force them into the shape of acacias? Why do the rock outcroppings with vegetation near Olduvai Gorge look like Japanese rock gardens?"

Cynthia Moss was from Connecticut but felt at home in East Africa. I was from Texas but felt at home in East Africa. Even Carl Jung (1875–1961), one of the founding fathers of psychology, felt at home in East Africa and he was from Switzerland. He wrote that when he visited Kenya in 1925, he had "the most intense sentiment of returning to the land of my youth." He was tugged by a "recognition of the immemorially known."

As if he had been there before.

We see the place where we came from, and we recognize it. We feel at home in East Africa—*we* being people from all over the world—because it was our home a million or so years ago. And there is still no place like home no matter how long we have been away from it.

Thinking back over our trip, I realized that I had felt *not* at all at home in the dense jungles of Rwanda where the mountain gorillas lived. My legs had been too long. My arms had been too short. I didn't belong. I somehow knew that apes could never have become humans as long as they remained imprisoned behind the tangled walls of those rain forests. The metamorphosis from monkey to man could only have occurred once our stooped ancestors emerged from those impenetrable jungles to stand tall on the open savannas. Once upright on the plain, their hands would have been free to invent the tools with which to build civilizations. Their brains couldn't grow bigger until their legs grew longer and their arms grew shorter. Our forefathers and foremothers must have made a trip much like the one we had made: from the shackles of the jungles in the interior to the freedom of the prairies of East Africa. We had been following million-year-old footprints—actually footprints *and* knuckle prints at the beginning of the trail, footprints alone by the end—footprints that had led us home.

CONVINCED THAT I had at last found the answer that I had stalked across the face of Africa—convinced that I had a million-year-old memory of the savannas of East Africa—I had to see those plains once more. I took the road to the airport, then turned right at the soccer stadium, drove past an army installation surrounded by barbed wire, and kept on going until I reached Nairobi National

Park. I drove through the elaborate entrance, skirted the parking lot, passed by the stucco building where Richard Leakey had an office, and kept going into the park itself. The first animal I saw was a warthog, one of the world's worst-designed creatures. Since its neck was too short—or its front legs too long—its mouth couldn't reach its food. So this pig was in a characteristic position, down on its knees happily eating a salad of new grasses. Moving on, I saw two lyre-horned impalas grazing on the bank of a pond. Next I rolled slowly past a marsh dotted with black buffalo. I slammed on the brakes when an ostrich ran across the dirt road right in front of me. Then I started up again and kept on going until I reached my goal: a plain crowded with zebras, wildebeests, kongoni, and gazelles. They all welcomed me by raising their heads and looking my way.

Applying the brakes again, I paused for a moment in the middle of the dirt road, a track really. I felt the peace of the plain entering me, permeating me, relaxing me. Landscapes. Exterior landscapes. Interior landscapes. Now they were the same. The sun shown warmly on the outside and on the inside. The golden grass waved gently inside and outside. Afraid that if I stayed too long, I would not be able to sustain this sense of well being, I drove on.

But I soon stopped again to admire a herd of eland as big as horses. I picked out a huge bull with mossy horns and stared at him. He stared back. We made eye contact. I expected to make the leap, magical or imagined, from my identity to his. But I didn't feel shaggy horns on my head. My feet weren't cloven. I couldn't make the jump, couldn't become that grand antelope, couldn't even pretend to be him. I was puzzled at first. Why had I fallen short? Then it occurred to me that perhaps it was because I was no longer desperately driven to escape from myself at all costs. The fires of self-hatred, which had forced me to flee from my own identity as if it were a burning house, seemed to be smoldering out. From now on, it seemed, I would have to be just me. Just a husband. Just a father. Just a slow, groping, guessing, trying writer. So be it.

Driving on, I passed into the shadow of a cloud and my mood began to deteriorate. I somehow seemed to be moving among ghosts. I thought of that man lying dead in the middle of the dark Nairobi street, the random victim of a traffic accident. I thought of Dian Fossey, slain in the lonely mountain night. I thought of Joy and George Adamson, both murdered. I thought of Robert John "Bob" Ouko, mutilated and burned. I had come out to these plains in order to savor one last time that sense of euphoria and well-being that is the "African experience," but instead I was filled with funereal gloom. Maybe just being me wasn't such a good idea after all. It started to rain.

But my dark mood did not last. Which was a pleasant surprise. Normally one unpleasant thought would set off a whole chain reaction of unhappiness that would last for days or weeks or even months. But no more. Not here. Not in Africa. Not on these plains that I seemed to remember so well. The drops continued outside, but the drizzle in my soul turned out to be just a passing shower. Now one happy thought led to a whole chain reaction of optimism.

I told myself:

Memory doesn't die. Not completely. Memory lives on in our genes. Chromosomes are long sentences written in code. One sentence says: I will have blue eyes. One says: I will be six feet, three and a half inches tall, no more, no less, no matter what. One says: I will be right-handed. One says: I will have auburn hair that will begin receding in my forties.

And one says: *I once lived on an African plain.*

Your genes not only look forward in time to what you

will become. Your chromosomes also look backward to what you have been. DNA's long, spiraling sentences are written not only in the present and future tenses, but they are also written in the past tense. My genes had been right here and remembered.

I felt a connection to the thick-browed almost-humans who first stood up and walked out onto these savannas. These ancestors were older than history, but not older than memory, not even older than *my* memory. And if we can remember what these first almost-humans beheld at the dawn of humanity, when apes rose up from the earth like the sun, then what else do we remember? Perhaps some of us remember building the pyramids of Egypt. Perhaps others recall the Golden Age of Greece. Perhaps even more of us still have memories of the Renaissance. Of course, we call these memories by other names, such as wisdom, such as intuition, such as hunch, such as inspiration. When some inexplicable idea occurs to us, we generally say it has boiled up out of our subconscious, but perhaps it is really Socrates, or what we remember of Socrates, whispering to us through our genes. Or when a writer scribbles a graceful line, which comes to him from who knows where, perhaps his muse is actually Shakespeare or Marlowe or Tolstoy or, more likely, some poor forgotten scribbler who lives on in the prose of our chromosomes. After having been perplexed for years about this whole business of inspiration, I liked this thought, this epiphany, this *inspiration,* and wondered who I had to thank for it.

I felt a connection to the dead. For the dead live on in me just as I will live on in others. The dead and the living are all a part of a human memory that endures. We are all cells in the mind of man which keeps growing down the generations. I was looking at a plain where this mind began, which was the foundation for all that followed. Dawning humans left no monuments, but they left a memory in all of us.

I felt a connection to all those "immortal" minds that light our history, from Socrates to Shakespeare to Walt Disney, but most of all I felt a connection to someone else. Above all, I felt a connection to my dead sister, to Von Sharon. She had not lived to pass on her genes, but many of my genes were identical to those that had perished with her. We had the same blue-eyed gene and the same tall gene and the same auburn-hair gene—and the same memory genes. Staring at this familiar landscape, I was remembering what she would have remembered if she had lived to see it. I was her and she was me. And in some small way I hoped to pass on my memories of her to future generations, in part by what I would write with my hands, but also by what I would write with my genes.

I remembered what that wizened *macumba* priestess had told me in what now seemed the distant past. She said, *sim*, I would get back the girl I had lost. I had paid no attention to her, had laughed at her, because I knew my sister could never come back. So far as I was concerned, she was not only gone but almost forgotten. I had lost even the memory of her because I found it too painful to think of her. I had tried to dull the ache of her death by deadening all nerves. But dead feelings inevitably led to dead writing and lifeless living. More and more, I found myself longing to follow where my sister had gone.

But now I knew the old seer had been right, after all, *sim*, for my sister *had* come back, not to life, but to *my* life. Now she was a part of me. Now she would color everything I did and all I wrote. For I had found her once again, found her in Africa where she had never been, but where all memory started, a place that lives on in all our memories, as Von Sharon lives on in me.

Like the drizzle in my soul, the drops on my windshield slowed and then ceased altogether. I looked up and saw a great colored arch, a dome, sheltering all the animals of the Ark. I took this rainbow to be a promise: The flood had stopped and would not come again.